By

Jack Rabin
Professor of Public Administration and Public Policy
School of Public Affairs
The Pennsylvania State University–Harrisburg
Middletown, Pennsylvania

W. Bartley Hildreth
Regents Distinguished Professor of Public Finance
Hugo Wall School of Urban & Public Affairs
Wichita State University
Wichita, Kansas

Gerald J. Miller
Associate Professor of Public Administration
Graduate Department of Public Administration
Rutgers–The State University of New Jersey
Newark, New Jersey

CARL VINSON INSTITUTE OF GOVERNMENT
THE UNIVERSITY OF GEORGIA

Public Budgeting Laboratory Data Sourcebook
Second Edition, Revised

Editing: Inge Whittle

Design: Reid McCallister

Digital composition: Lisa Carson

Proofreading: Norma Pettigrew, Charlotte Eberhard

Publications editor: Emily Honigberg

Copyright © 1983, 1987, 1996 by the Carl Vinson Institute of Government, The University of Georgia. Printed in the United States of America. All rights reserved. No part of this publication may be used or reproduced in any manner whatsoever without written permission except in the case of brief quotations embodied in critical articles and reviews. For information, write Publications Program, Carl Vinson Institute of Government, 201 North Milledge Avenue, University of Georgia, Athens, Georgia 30602-5482. www.vinsoninstitute.org.

Third Printing 2003

ISBN (Set) 0-89854-180-8

ISBN (Data Sourcebook) 0-89854-182-4

Acknowledgments

The authors acknowledge the contribution of Rodger P. Hildreth, who helped in the initial development of the programmed learning design and methods.

We also want to thank Dr. Delmer D. Dunn for his help and encouragement in the gestation of this project.

Finally, we are grateful to all of the students who have participated in the pretests of the *Public Budgeting Laboratory* in their universities.

Foreword

The single most important policy document of any governmental jurisdiction is the annual operating budget. Traditionally, workshops and classrooms provided little opportunity for future "budgeteers" to experience budgeting successes and failures. The *Public Budgeting Laboratory* is designed to provide the knowledge and practical experience necessary for competency in budget preparation.

The *Public Budgeting Laboratory* allows participants to experience budgeting in a simulated environment. Participants learn how to analyze data relevant to budget decisions, including revenue forecasting, expenditure estimation, and budget balancing. The *Laboratory* requires both individual and collective work and fosters behavioral insights—crucial to those having to work with others on important tasks.

The *Laboratory* received extensive testing in graduate, undergraduate, and workshop applications. As a self-contained learning package, it provides step-by-step guides on developing a budget, a data supplement with five years of extensive revenue and expenditure records, and an anthology on budget formulation and execution. In addition, an instructor's manual provides suggestions on how to conduct the laboratory.

The *Public Budgeting Laboratory* results from a collaborative effort begun by the authors while they were associated with the Vinson Institute, and the first university application of the *Laboratory* occurred at the University of Georgia. Jack Rabin is professor of public administration and public policy, School of Public Affairs, The Pennsylvania State University–Harrisburg; W. Bartley Hildreth is Regents Distinguished Professor of Public Finance, Hugo Wall School of Urban & Public Affairs, Wichita State University; and Gerald J. Miller is associate professor of public administration, Graduate Department of Public Administration, Rutgers–The State University of New Jersey, at Newark.

Sam Mitchell
Interim Director
Carl Vinson Institute of Government

Contents

Introduction   1

1. Overview of the City   3

Physical Characteristics of the City   4
    Water   4
    Special Features   4
    Land Use   4
    Climate   5
Socioeconomic Characteristics   6
Impact of the State University on the Economy of the City and County   11
    The University and the Local Economy   11
Governmental Characteristics   13
    City Organization   13
    The County and Its Organization   13
City Fiscal Characteristics   15
    Revenue Sources of the City   15
    Alternate Revenue Source: Income Tax   20
    Earmarked Revenues   21
    Debt Limits   21
City Revenue and Expenditure Summaries   22

2. City Departments: (Account Titles)   29

A. General Fund   30

Animal Services   30
Building Inspection   33
City Clerk-Treasurer   36
City Hall   39
City Marshal   41
Civil Defense   43
Computer and Data Processing   46
Elective   48
Electrical Department   50
Fire Department   52

Fire Station, County   56
General Administrative   58
Human Resources   62
Parks and Recreation Department   64
Personnel Department   70
Planning Commission   73
Police Department   76
Police Planner   83
Public Works   84
Sanitation—Garbage Collection   86
Sanitation—Incinerator   90
Sanitation—Street Cleaning   91
Service Garage   93
Stockade   95
Streets Department   98

B. Water-Sewer Enterprise Fund   104

General Administrative   104
Water Filter Plant   110
Water Meters   113
Water Pollution Control Plant   115
Water-Sewer Distribution   121
Waterworks Commercial   128

3. City Personnel Data   131

City Employee Information, FY V   132
40-Hour Personnel Pay Schedule, Effective FY V   146
Alphabetical Classification Index by Title   150
Classification Index by Job Code   162
Classification Index by Pay   174

Exhibits

1. University-Related Cash Flow in the City/County Economy   12
2. Organization Chart of the City Government   14
3. Summary of Outstanding Bond Maturities and Interest Payments, General Obligation Bonds   59
4. Summary of Outstanding Water and Sewer Revenue Bonds and Interest Payments   105
5. The Indenture of Mortgage, Water and Sewer Utility System   106
6. Water and Sewer Utility—General Utility Operating Fund Statement of Operations FY VI   108

Introduction

This volume of the *Public Budgeting Laboratory* contains detailed City data, revised, in this new edition, to reflect the continuing increase of the price level since the *Laboratory's* original appearance in 1983. The data are organized in three sections: (1) general information about the City; (2) department-by-department line-item expenditures for the City government's past four and current fiscal years; and (3) a list of personnel classifications and pay scales currently in effect.

Part 1 provides both general and specific data on the City's physical, socioeconomic, and fiscal characteristics. Subsections report trends in population growth, social indicators, and economic development; describe the City's governmental structure and relationship among political and administrative units; and portray budget revenue and expenditure summaries for the past four fiscal years and the present fiscal year (which is about to end). The current year is FY V. A subsequent unit lists and explains each revenue source as used in the City. Details include the amount budgeted and the actual collections for the past four years and the estimated collections for the fiscal year which will end within weeks. This unit summarizes data on expenditures for the same period.

Part 2 provides expenditure information for each City department. These data include the amount budgeted and the amount actually expended for the five-year period. Furthermore, some general information, including each department's activities and needs, is presented.

Part 3 lists the personnel classifications and salary ranges currently in effect. These lists may be referred to in computing personnel wage and salary expenditures.

These data provide the essentials for the laboratory. However, some additional work will promote understanding. Independent research on departments and the activities they traditionally encompass will help one gain some degree of familiarity with appropriate terms, planning standards, and state-of-the-art technologies.

PART 1
OVERVIEW of the CITY

Physical Characteristics of the City

The City encompasses 34 square miles and the county 125 square miles. The City lies within the county's southeast and southwest quadrants. Both City and county are located in the upper reaches of a large river basin. Two rivers traverse the county, providing perhaps the most outstanding natural features of the landscape.

The urban settlement pattern of the City is typical of towns in the area, since the state's most rapid growth has occurred here.

Crystalline rock underlies the City area. However, the soil cover is not thick or capable of absorbing all runoff from rainfall. In fact, where steep slopes occur in combination with urban asphalt and concrete, runoff rates become extremely high. Because of the underlying crystalline rock, the confluence of the two major waterways, and conditions favoring an abundant year-round supply of surface water, the City uses the river as its public water supply.

WATER

The county's two rivers and the system of smaller streams that flow into them provide a dendritic drainage pattern for the entire county. The rivers seldom flood adjoining areas and the flood plain poses no major constraints on land use. The rivers provide power for the community through a power company's generator plant which has three 750 kilowatt generators for a combined capacity of 2,250 kilowatts. Planners consider this capacity sufficient for future growth.

The county also has many private recreational lakes for fishing and boating. The Rock Creek watershed, located in the northern portion of the county, is a 257-acre area with a recreational lake.

SPECIAL FEATURES

In FY V, the population of the City was 45,734 and population of the county was 87,594. The City is the site of a major state-supported university which has grown from a traditional small college to a major educational institution with 23,963 students. The university's educational programs and its athletic and cultural events draw thousands to the area annually.

The City also serves as a commercial and industrial center. Service industries—including printing and publishing firms, construction suppliers, and health care—constitute one major subsection of the economy. Manufacturing industries comprise still another. Local plants of major national companies produce clocks and watches; clothing, textiles, synthetic yarns and industrial cordage; electrical machinery and controls; poultry products; and metal fabrications.

The City has an architectural treasury of buildings from the Victorian period. Recent efforts have resulted in the designation of several parts of the city as historic preservation districts.

LAND USE

Land use in the county has been analyzed for two geographical areas. One area represents only the City and selected surrounding lands, all of which constitute the "built-up" portion of the county. The other area is the whole of the county, including the built-up area.

Table 1 reflects the number and percent of acres in each of the two land-use categories. Approximately 6,966 acres of land in the county are presently being used for residential purposes: 8.19 percent for single-family residences, 0.18 percent for duplexes, and 0.37 percent for multifamily units.

Commercial land usage totaling 649 acres represents 0.81 percent of the total land area of the county. Omitting open land from the total, commercial land represents 4.11 percent of the county's total acreage, close to the average for a community of this size. However, analysis of the built-up area, omitting open land, reflects an above-average figure of 6.06 percent. This higher figure no doubt relates to the City's university-based population, which supports a greater number of

TABLE 1
Number and Percent of Acres in Land-Use Categories

County	Amount (Acres)	Percent	Developed Land Total
Single-family	6,518.94	8.19	41.37
Duplex	149.41	0.18	0.94
Multifamily	298.09	0.37	1.89
Commercial	649.31	0.81	4.11
Industrial	1,290.35	1.62	8.18
Public and semipublic	4,921.20	6.18	31.23
Open and vacant land	63,870.40	80.22	
Streets and highways	1,936.00	2.43	12.28
TOTAL	79,633.70	100.00	100.00

Built-Up Area	Amount (Acres)	Percent	Developed Land Total
Single-family	3,586.90	23.87	44.56
Duplex	89.50	0.59	1.11
Multifamily	182.86	1.21	2.27
Commercial	488.55	3.24	6.06
Industrial	297.77	1.98	3.69
Public and semipublic	2,355.96	15.66	29.27
Open and vacant land	6,985.97	46.47	
Streets and highways	1,050.00	6.98	13.04
TOTAL	15,037.51	100.00	100.00

small eating establishments and entertainment facilities than would cities of comparable size without a large number of students.

Industrial land, totaling 1,290.35 acres, represents 1.62 percent of the land area of the county and 8.18 percent of the land area with open land omitted. The latter figure is approximately average for communities the size of the City. However, the figure does not include university property, which serves, in effect, as an industry in the county's economy. University property is included in the "Public and Semipublic" category of land use.

The category, "Public and Semipublic," with 4,921.20 acres, or 6.18 percent of the total and 31.23 percent of all acreage with open land omitted, is almost three times larger than that of similar sized cities. The reason for this distortion is that university property is included in this category. Deducting 3,900 acres of university property would reduce the percentage to 1.28 percent, approximately average for most other cities.

Open land in the county totals 63,870.40 acres, or 80.22 percent of the total land area. Much of this land consists of large acreage tracts in the outlying portions of the county.

Streets and highways, covering 1,936 acres, comprise 12.28 percent of the county's developed land area. This percentage is somewhat below that of similar sized cities, probably because many streets in the community are narrow and university dormitories and apartments concentrate a large portion of the population on a few streets.

The City considers the open land and vacant areas to have prime development potential. However, new development will probably occur outside the built-up area (primarily in the county) twice as rapidly as inside the area.

CLIMATE

The City is located in the climatic zone which is classified as "humid subtropical." Rainfall, which averages about 48 inches annually, is fairly evenly distributed through the year. A slight maximum of rainfall occurs in the late spring and early summer, and the minimum in the fall. The following data are averages recorded over a 25-year period by the U.S. Department of Commerce at the local weather station:

Mean temperature	December	45.5
	January	46.5
	June	80.8
	July	79.5
	August	78.6
Average minimum and maximum temperature	January	35 to 56
	July	60 to 90

Socioeconomic Characteristics

Planning and managing local finances require the use of demographic, social, and economic data about the City. This section contains tables of statistical data on the City to aid in forecasting costs and revenues for future years. All tables contain county data unless otherwise stated.

TABLE 2
Population Trends and Projections

Year	City	County
50 years before FY V	18,172	20,650
40 years before FY V	25,617	28,150
30 years before FY V	28,847	31,355
20 years before FY V	40,342	44,316
10 years before FY V	42,549	74,498
FY I	43,137	77,052
FY II	43,625	79,355
FY III	43,982	81,448
FY IV	44,433	83,930
FY V	45,734	87,594
10 years after FY V	48,900	98,156
20 years after FY V	53,802	112,087

TABLE 3
University Enrollment Trends: Cumulative Resident and Nonresident

Year	In-State Students	Out-of-State Residents	Foreign Students	Total Students
15 years ago	8,181	1,503	125	9,809
10 years ago	13,636	3,389	183	16,208
5 years ago	17,228	3,430	443	21,101
4 years ago	19,290	3,595	478	23,363
3 years ago	19,205	3,389	492	23,086
2 years ago	20,247	3,398	502	24,147
1 year ago	20,674	3,286	510	24,470
Current	20,416	3,071	475	23,963
Projected FY VI	20,300	2,900	450	23,650

TABLE 4
Percentage of City Population by Race

Year	Nonwhite	White
30 years before FY V	35.4	64.6
20 years before FY V	27.2	72.8
10 years before FY V	25.6	74.4
FY V	33.6	66.4

TABLE 5
Percentage of City Population by Age

Age	20 years before FY V	10 years before FY V	FY V
65 and over	6.5	7.2	10.2
25-64	44.7	40.8	34.6
16-24	23.8	23.5	41.0
5-15	14.2	17.5	9.1
Under 5	10.8	11.0	5.1

TABLE 6
City Population Education Status, FY V

	City	State	U.S.
Persons 3 years and over enrolled in school			
Preprimary school	547		
Public elementary or high school	4,231		
Private elementary or high school	353		
College	18,396		
Persons 16 to 19 years	6,333		
Employed but not in school or graduated from school	122		
Unemployed but not in school or graduated from school	50		
Not in labor force	57		
Persons 25 years or older	20,488		
Percent high school graduate or higher	72.2	57.2	63.5
Percent with bachelor's degree or higher	36.1	17.4	23.2

TABLE 7
Place of Work, FY V

Persons 16 years and over	39,245
Percent in labor force	53.7
In labor force and worked in county of residence	18,380

TABLE 8
Disposable Income of City Households, FY I-V*

	Percent of Total				FY V		
Income	FY I	FY II	FY III	FY IV	City	Metro Area	State
Under $10,000	32.7	32.0	32.9	30.6	28.7	18.2	10.7
$10,000–$19,999	29.9	29.4	28.9	28.7	28.3	23.1	15.1
$20,000–$34,999	19.2	19.5	19.3	20.0	20.6	27.0	24.3
$35,000–$49,999	9.3	9.2	9.2	9.5	9.8	16.4	20.7
$50,000 and over	8.9	9.9	9.7	11.2	12.6	15.3	29.2
TOTAL	100.0	100.0	100.0	100.0	100.0		
Total ($000)	398,549	418,851	426,852	455,760	493,198		
Median ($)	12,154	12,604	13,007	13,462	14,286	24,130	34,929

*Total income minus taxes, commonly thought of as that available for consumption.

TABLE 9
Income: City, County, and State

	Number of Households		
Income	City	County	State
Household income			
All households	16,915	33,113	
Less than $5,000	3,421	4,626	
$5,000-$9,999	3,056	4,324	
$10,000-$14,999	2,234	3,976	
$15,000-$24,999	3,095	6,131	
$25,000-$34,999	1,652	4,356	
$35,000-$49,999	1,682	4,127	
$50,000-$74,999	925	3,234	
$75,000-$99,999	449	1,220	
$100,000 or more	401	1,119	
Household median income	$14,286	$20,806	$29,021
Family median income	$23,348	$30,919	$33,529
Nonfamily median income	$ 9,225	$11,633	$16,782
Per capita income			
10 years before FY V	$ 5,613		
FY I	$ 8,586		
Percent of state average	84.3		
FY V	$ 9,252	$11,604	$13,631
Percent of state average	67.9	85.1	

	City	
Percent below poverty level	Persons	Families
10 years before FY V	26.6	17.7
FY I	28.1	19.6
FY V	30.8	22.8

TABLE 10
City Population Employment Status, FY V

Persons 16 years and over	39,245
Civilian labor force	
TOTAL	21,069
Percent of total persons 16 years and over	54.2
Percent unemployed	8.2

TABLE 11
City Retail and Wholesale Trade Trends

	Retail Firms		Wholesale Firms	
Fiscal Year	Number	Sales ($ millions)	Number	Sales ($ millions)
I	701	374.57	139	372.23
II	724	410.25	121	398.89
III	673	445.92	119	452.58
IV	702	511.36	121	526.41
V	721	555.64	125	583.47

TABLE 12
City Local Manufacturers: Ten Largest Manufacturers by Employment

Firm	Product(s)	Employment
Westinghouse Electric Corp. Trans. Division	transformers	1,215
General Time Corporation Westclox Division	electric clocks	1,117
Reliance Electric Company	medium sized electric motors	900
Central Soya, Inc.	poultry processing	800
Gold Kist, Inc.	poultry processing	530
Chicopee Mfg. Corp.	woven fabrics	528
Wilkins Industries, Inc.	women's jeans	500
The DuPont Company	winding beams, synthetic yarns	412
Thomas Textile Company, Inc.	infant clothing	363
Wellington Puritan Mills, Inc.	cordage and twine products	142

TABLE 13
Employment and Payrolls, County and United States, FY I and FY V

SIC	Employment Category Description	U.S. FY II Employ-ment	Percent of Total	Payrolls ($000s)	Percent of Total	U.S. FY V Employ-ment	Percent of Total	Payrolls ($000s)	Percent of Total	County FY II Employ-ment	Percent of Total	Payrolls ($000s)	Percent of Total	County FY V Employ-ment	Percent of Total	Payrolls ($000s)	Percent of Total
	Agriculture																
07	Agricultural services	384,284	0.46	5,310,391	0.33	460,060	0.50	7,214,260	0.36	136	0.38		0.00	204	0.53	2,499	0.40
	Construction																
15	General contractors	1,224,577	1.47	26,590,615	1.65	1,292,279	1.41	32,371,188	1.63	386	1.08	5,847	1.15	448	1.17	8,634	1.38
16	Heavy construction	693,078	0.83	18,486,848	1.15	687,858	0.75	21,796,093	1.10	357	1.00	6,932	1.36	292	0.76	6,654	1.07
17	Special trade contractors	2,721,543	3.26	58,654,398	3.65	3,003,459	3.28	72,132,178	3.62	556	1.56	10,992	2.16	748	1.95	13,292	2.13
	Manufacturing																
22	Textile products	667,969	0.80	10,780,363	0.67	676,161	0.74	12,296,586	0.62		0.00		0.00	1,751	4.57	36,153	5.80
23	Apparel	1,082,437	1.30	13,383,126	0.83	1,069,137	1.17	14,956,201	0.75	1,413	3.96	13,333	2.62	1,187	3.10	11,619	1.86
24	Lumber and wood	657,853	0.79	11,855,005	0.74	713,546	0.78	13,863,150	0.70	99	0.28	1,296	0.25	160	0.42	2,928	0.47
27	Printing and publishing	1,451,383	1.74	31,608,371	1.96	1,543,632	1.68	38,097,664	1.91	486	1.36	6,145	1.21	532	1.39	7,549	1.21
34	Fabricated metal	1,476,672	1.77	34,168,222	2.12	9,603,075	10.48	39,073,340	1.96	433	1.21	6,887	1.35	404	1.05	7,237	1.16
35	Industrial machinery	1,980,031	2.37	51,985,085	3.23	1,975,565	2.16	58,694,694	2.95	193	0.54	4,933	0.97	671	1.75	15,789	2.53
	Transportation and public utilities																
42	Trucking and warehousing	1,308,879	1.57	28,331,709	1.76	1,538,359	1.68	35,137,493	1.77	203	0.57	4,214	0.83	282	0.74	5,622	0.90
48	Communication	1,265,531	1.52	35,893,647	2.23	1,255,213	1.37	38,864,123	1.95	437	1.22	10,024	1.97	353	0.92	10,532	1.69
	Wholesale trade																
50	Durable goods	3,217,781	3.86	79,373,961	4.93	3,487,976	3.81	99,100,029	4.98	932	2.61	17,232	3.39	1,061	2.77	19,871	3.19
51	Nondurable goods	2,216,759	2.66	48,097,579	2.99	2,342,906	2.56	58,842,023	2.96	1,364	3.82	26,141	5.14	1,650	4.31	30,721	4.93
	Retail trade																
52	Building materials/garden supplies	626,477	0.75	9,276,185	0.58	698,107	0.76	11,440,544	0.57	371	1.04	5,425	1.07	347	0.91	5,309	0.85
53	General merchandise	1,954,204	2.34	18,767,711	1.17	2,082,173	2.27	21,885,198	1.10	1,316	3.69	11,566	2.27	1,379	3.60	13,156	2.11
54	Food stores	2,722,802	3.27	29,437,539	1.83	3,011,686	3.29	33,639,687	1.69	1,183	3.32	10,851	2.13	1,315	3.43	12,599	2.02
55	Auto dealers and service stations	1,930,359	2.32	34,196,919	2.13	2,129,072	2.32	39,394,163	1.98	842	2.36	14,265	2.81	1,077	2.81	20,124	3.23
56	Apparel	1,081,362	1.30	9,670,225	0.60	1,168,416	1.28	11,524,923	0.58	489	1.37	3,491	0.69	525	1.37	4,026	0.65
57	Furniture and homefurnishings	668,194	0.80	9,601,967	0.60	734,169	0.80	11,753,558	0.59	473	1.33	5,715	1.12	336	0.88	7,208	1.16
58	Eating and drinking	5,577,135	6.69	37,637,933	2.34	6,287,892	6.86	46,090,919	2.32	3,505	9.82	20,252	3.98	3,742	9.77	21,493	3.45
59	Miscellaneous retail	2,204,710	2.64	25,776,655	1.60	2,385,784	2.60	30,690,797	1.54	1,311	3.67	12,239	2.41	1,612	4.21	16,083	2.58
	Finance, insurance and real estate																
60	Banking	1,639,912	1.97	32,917,298	2.05	2,029,899	2.22	46,222,974	2.32	355	0.99	4,927	0.97	620	1.62	10,482	1.68
61	Credit agencies other than banks	813,318	0.98	17,914,303	1.11	484,878	0.53	13,129,721	0.66	299	0.84	5,780	1.14	182	0.47	4,101	0.66
62	Security and commodity brokers	377,278	0.45	21,490,870	1.34	406,129	0.44	25,296,765	1.27	79	0.22	3,618	0.71	75	0.20	3,032	0.49
63	Insurance carriers	1,313,076	1.57	31,669,298	1.97	1,389,966	1.52	37,818,085	1.90	286	0.80	6,164	1.21	277	0.72	6,932	1.11
64	Insurance agents, brokers, and service	597,436	0.72	13,563,765	0.84	694,387	0.76	18,821,387	0.95	150	0.42	2,401	0.47	220	0.57	4,449	0.71
65	Real estate	1,220,293	1.46	21,828,327	1.36	1,326,558	1.45	27,423,999	1.38	178	0.50	2,224	0.44	222	0.58	3,054	0.49
	Services																
70	Hotels and lodging places	1,331,620	1.60	13,938,358	0.87	1,467,566	1.60	17,417,085	0.88	471	1.32	3,836	0.75	564	1.47	4,903	0.79
72	Personal services	1,117,133	1.34	10,878,020	0.68	1,142,074	1.25	12,469,944	0.63	480	1.35	3,909	0.77	515	1.34	4,556	0.73
73	Business services	4,612,797	5.53	80,636,642	5.01	4,749,349	5.18	87,138,940	4.38	957	2.68	10,635	2.09	1,506	3.93	17,617	2.83
75	Auto repair, services, and parking	726,858	0.87	10,848,385	0.67	842,792	0.92	14,040,928	0.71	374	1.05	5,692	1.12	392	1.02	4,704	0.75
76	Miscellaneous repair services	338,723	0.41	6,162,074	0.38	372,580	0.41	7,848,857	0.39	91	0.26	1,104	0.22	102	0.27	1,516	0.24
79	Amusement and recreation	796,839	0.96	10,262,790	0.64	955,592	1.04	14,066,843	0.71	122	0.34	864	0.17	188	0.49	851	0.14
80	Health services	6,614,276	7.93	125,452,763	7.80	8,429,654	9.20	195,565,537	9.83	2,204	6.18	48,445	9.53	2,967	7.74	77,433	12.42
81	Legal services	745,566	0.89	22,065,712	1.37	892,143	0.97	32,908,775	1.65	242	0.68	4,438	0.87	302	0.79	7,457	1.20
82	Educational services	1,581,782	1.90	21,665,005	1.35	1,703,729	1.86	27,241,697	1.37	255	0.71	2,607	0.51	298	0.78	4,275	0.69
83	Social services	1,367,622	1.64	13,129,552	0.82	1,630,119	1.78	18,423,056	0.93	801	2.24	6,513	1.28	783	2.04	7,503	1.20
86	Membership organizations	1,696,145	2.03	16,835,779	1.05	1,837,318	2.01	20,897,521	1.05	673	1.89	4,359	0.86	770	2.01	5,732	0.92
87	Miscellaneous services	269,774	0.32	7,268,779	0.45	2,384,483	2.60	72,687,293	3.65	278	0.78	3,675	0.72	271	0.71	5,665	0.91
	Other not specifically disclosed	19,105,997	22.91	501,398,715	31.17	10,745,462	11.73	551,859,657	27.73	10,903	30.56	189,557	37.28	7988	20.85	170,035	27.28
	Total excluding undisclosed SIC codes	64,274,468	1	1,107,412,174	1	80,885,741	1	1,438,278,218	1	24,780	1	318,971	1				
	GRAND TOTAL	83,380,465		1,608,810,889		91,631,203		1,990,137,875		35,683		508,528					

Source: U.S. Bureau of Census, County Business Patterns, FY I and FY V.

TABLE 14
City and County Housing Units

Housing Status	Ten Years Ago City	Ten Years Ago County	FY V City	FY V County
Owner-occupied	5,549	12,423	5,446	14,663
Renter-occupied	9,506	14,164	11,289	18,507
Total occupied	15,055	26,587	16,735	33,170
Vacant for sale	123	178	168	772
Vacant for rent	331	811	1,305	2,029
Total vacant	454	989	1,473	2,801
Total units	15,509	27,576	18,208	35,971
Average annual percent change in total			1.74%	3.04%
Owner-occupied			−0.19%	1.80%
Renter-occupied			1.88%	3.07%
Average annual actual change in total			270	840
Owner-occupied			−10	224
Renter-occupied			178	434

TABLE 15
Alternative Price Indices*

Year	Implicit Price Deflator Base Yr=V	Implicit Price Deflator Base Yr=I	Consumer Price Index Base Yr=V	Consumer Price Index Base Yr=I
Seven years before FY V	76.1	87.4	71.2	82.0
Six years before FY V	79.4	91.2	73.5	84.6
Five years before FY V	81.9	94.1	76.8	88.4
FY I	87.0	100.0	86.9	100.0
FY II	91.7	105.4	91.1	104.9
FY III	94.2	108.2	93.8	108.0
FY IV	97.1	111.6	96.3	110.8
FY V	100.0	114.9	100.0	115.1
FY VI**	**103.0**	118.3	**103.5**	119.1

*Compute the inflation rate by finding the rate of change between the index numbers in any two years.

**Estimate.

Impact of the State University on the Economy of the City and County

The university, the City, and the county have grown from infancy to maturity almost as one. In FY V, the university's enrollment reached 23,963 students. Its campus covers 4,000 acres and includes more than 200 buildings comprising an investment of nearly $200 million. Its operating budget exceeds $150 million. Through 175 years of parallel growth, the university and the local community have benefited mutually by their many efforts of cooperation and reciprocity.

THE UNIVERSITY AND THE LOCAL ECONOMY

One set of relationships between the campus and the surrounding community lends itself to quantitative measurement. It is the impact of the university on the local economy, the subject of this summary study.

In FY V, the total direct and indirect expenditures in the local economy by the university and related activities amounted to $206 million. (See Exhibit 1.)

Nearly three-fifths of this total ($118 million) was in the form of direct payments by the university, its employees, students, and visitors to local business. The remainder ($88 million) accrued from the subsequent spending and respending of this money in the local economy in an incrementally decreasing recycling process.

Direct expenditures in the local economy from the university community equaled 35 percent of total sales. Adding in the amount of local business volume generated by university-related expenditures raises the proportion to 60 percent. Viewed another way, these data suggest that sales in the county would be less than half the present amount if university influences were excluded.

The university is the single largest employer in the county (6,700 jobs), ranking in size larger than all but two of the state's manufacturing employers. An additional 8,300 jobs in the local economy are supported by university-related business.

In all, one of every three persons employed in the county works for the university, while secondary employment generated by these jobs supports another 25 percent of the county's workforce.

These estimates of impact are generally conservative, portraying the university's influence to be less than it would be if all influences were known exactly. Although individual assumptions or cost derivations may be questioned, the overall economic impact of the university on the City and county would not likely vary greatly in any assessment.

Moreover, no consideration was given to many features of the university that enhance the quality of life in the City and county. For example, because the university is a research center of considerable importance, more than a dozen state and federal research facilities have located in the county over the years. Collectively, these installations employ more than 500 scientists and support personnel locally. No account was taken of the direct or indirect spending effects these facilities and their personnel have on the local economy.

Finally, no account was taken in this study of the cultural and recreational opportunities available to the citizens of the area merely because the university is located here rather than in another town.

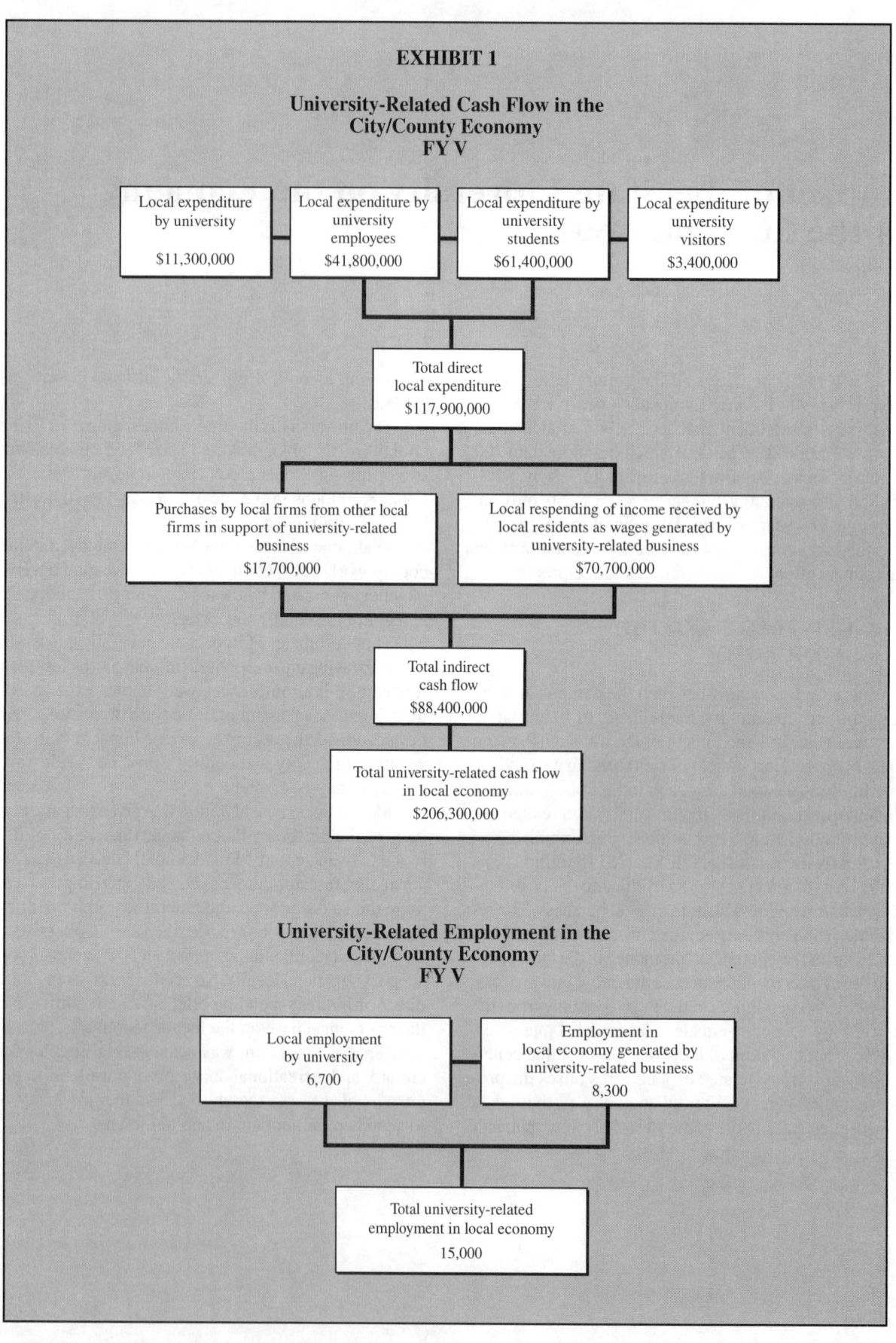

Governmental Characteristics

CITY ORGANIZATION

The City's government is the mayor-council type, with both the mayor and council being elected directly by the voters of the City for two-year terms. The mayor is the City's chief executive officer and can veto actions taken by vote in the council.

The mayor presides at all meetings of the City council. He or she is responsible for preparing the annual budget for submission to and approval by the council. It is also his or her duty to nominate the heads of specific City departments and agencies, subject to the council's approval.

The 10-member council is the City's chief legislative and policymaking body. Each of the City's five wards has two representatives on the council. Council members are elected for staggered two-year terms, so that one-half of the council faces election each year. It is the responsibility of the council to pass city ordinances and approve the annual budget. It confirms, upon nomination of the mayor, officials not elected by the voters. The council organizes itself into four committees: (1) public safety, (2) streets, parks, and recreation, (3) finance, and (4) public works. In these committees, the groundwork is laid for new regulations or ordinances.

An assistant to the mayor is appointed to aid the mayor in the day-to-day operations and management of the City. The assistant participates in all functions of City management and helps the mayor with the preparation of the budget; arrangements for regular meetings; and with decisions about interdepartmental matters, departmental organization and operation, and appointments to top departmental positions. The assistant gives particular attention to personnel matters. No union organizations have yet attempted to become bargaining agents for employees.

The mayor and council have organized a new City budget office, with staff members reporting to the assistant to the mayor.

A chart, Exhibit 2, depicting the organizational structure of the City is on page 14.

Although each department unit gets treated separately for accounting purposes, many linkages exist between departments. For instance, the "City Clerk's" office—one department—is physically located within the "City Hall," which is another budget unit. An "Elective" subdivision of the City allows direct expenditures of elected officials—the mayor and council—to be combined. Another example is provided by the large public works department which includes many separate budget units. Thus, the "Inspection" unit has to be viewed in terms of the tutelage by "Public Works Administration." The point is that each department must be viewed in its relationship to other unit(s). And, of course, there are several departments that generate revenues through a department's program. Thus, the linkage of certain revenues and expenditures must be taken into consideration. Earmarked revenues are listed on page 21.

THE COUNTY AND ITS ORGANIZATION

The county of which the City is county seat encompasses 125 square miles. It is the smallest county in the state, and the City is the lone incorporated area. Four cities with a population of 50,000 or greater lie within 100 miles, one of which is a major regional center of more than 1,000,000.

A board of five elected commissioners, acting as the chief executive body, governs the county. The board elects its chairperson and employs a county manager.

Other elected county officers are the coroner, sheriff, tax commissioner, and all judicial officials. In addition to the sheriff, there is a county police department.

The county, with state and federal financial aid, provides all health, library, and airport services. An independent board of education manages all elementary and secondary schools. An independent hospital board runs a hospital located within the City.

The county's board of commissioners is also responsible in budget matters for all courts.

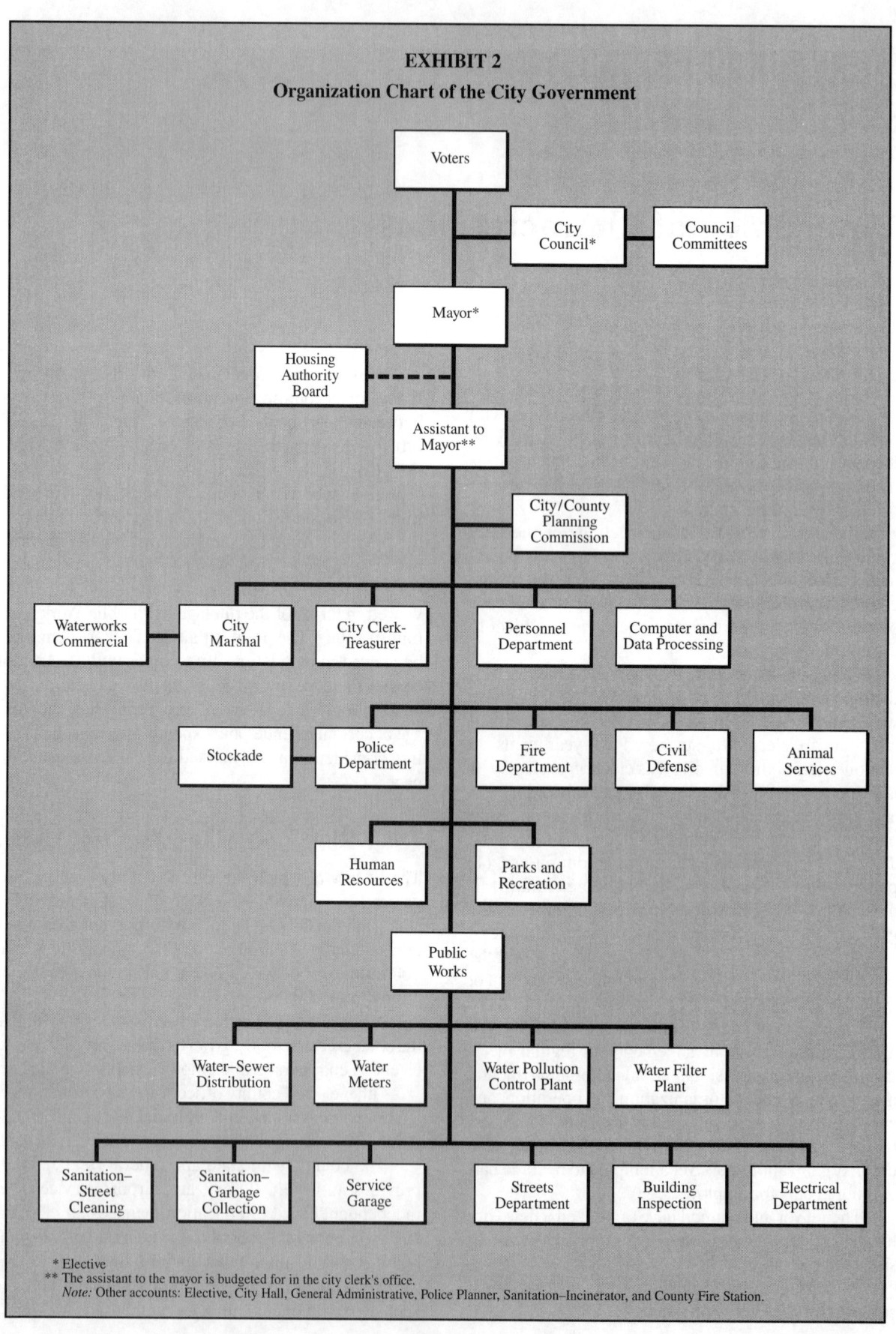

EXHIBIT 2
Organization Chart of the City Government

* Elective
** The assistant to the mayor is budgeted for in the city clerk's office.
Note: Other accounts: Elective, City Hall, General Administrative, Police Planner, Sanitation–Incinerator, and County Fire Station.

City Fiscal Characteristics

REVENUE SOURCES OF THE CITY

This section provides a detailed discussion of the individual revenue sources available for use by the City.

Ad Valorem (Property) Tax

This account provides for collections of the ad valorem tax (excluding motor vehicles). Under state law, the county provides the assessment of real and personal property to the City, without charge. State law stipulates that "all property must be assessed at 40 percent of its 'fair market [true] value.'" Required to use the county's assessment, the City council sets the millage rate sufficient to cover expenditure needs in excess of other revenues. No law limits the rate. The yearly assessments and rates are summarized below:

FY I	$239,453,708	FY IV	379,034,166
FY II	301,851,052	FY V	396,365,897
FY III	406,191,220		

The large increase in FY III assessments reflects an agreement negotiated between the City and a large clock manufacturer involving a one-time assessment of manufacturing inventory.

The collection rate has averaged approximately 96 percent over the period. A 95 percent collection rate is considered average in the profession.

The total millage rates for the City, county, and school district follow:

Millage Rates, FY I-V

Year	City Rate	Net City Rate (after rollback for sales taxes)	Total Rate**	Average Rate for Proximate Cities
FY I	14.0*	8.3	33.93	10.1
FY II	12.5	7.8	31.43	10.4
FY III	13.0	9.2	27.88	10.3
FY IV	13.0	8.5	28.87	10.4
FY V	12.0	7.1	28.70	10.6

*Also expressed as $14.00/$1,000 assessed value.
**City, county, and school district total.

Ad Valorem (Property) Tax for Motor Vehicles

This account provides for collections of ad valorem taxes on motor vehicles. The millage rate is the same for motor vehicles as it is for general property taxes. The county collects the amount based on last year's millage rate; for example, in FY V the county collected motor vehicle ad valorem taxes using FY IV's rate of 8.5 mills. In the two years prior to FY I, the rate was 9.9 mills.

Animal Services

Service fees are charged by the animal services department for impoundment ($10 a day) and board ($3 a day). A fee ($4) is also charged for rabies immunization. These rates have not changed in the last five years.

Beer and Wine Excise Tax

This tax is levied upon the wholesaler. The beer rate has been constant at $.05 per 12 oz. bottle. Wine is taxed at $.05 per pint. The wholesaler pays the appropriate amount without being billed.

Building Inspection Fees

Upon completion of required inspections for new or rehabilitated construction, the department assesses the owner 0.5 percent of the value of the project.

Burglar Alarm System

A burglar alarm system with direct connections to the police department may be obtained by local businesses and others. A new hookup costs $100. There is a $50 annual fee.

Cash Bonds on Fines

This includes the bonds for traffic offenses cited by the City police. (Citations by the county police department and state patrol within the City limits are not paid to the City.) In late FY IV, the cash bond amount increased by 30 percent. If a person does not appear before the magistrate's court to contest the traffic citation (and fine), he/she surrenders the cash bond. Other citations, such as failure to comply with building codes, are rarely enforced.

Cash Bonds on Parking Tickets

This includes the fines for those persons who receive a citation for not paying the parking meter. The basic charge (or cash bond) has not changed in the last five years. It is set at $4 per ticket, if paid the same day of the ticket. A $2 fee is charged for payment within 2 to 10 days. After 10 days, a charge of $3 is assessed. These rates are extremely low in comparison with statewide averages.

Civil Defense–County Share

The county reimburses the City for one-half of the nonfederal cost of the civil defense office.

Civil Defense–Federal Share

The U.S. government pays one-half of the cost of maintaining a civil defense program in the City up to a $100,000 ceiling. The federal share increases in times of disaster, upon presidential proclamation.

Container Rental

A charge is made to garbage collections of certain size garbage containers.

County Fire Protection

The county pays a fee for on-call City fire protection. The current fee is set at a rate per year negotiated every three years. The current contract expires at the end of FY V.

County Fire Station

The county constructed and equipped a fire station in the most developed section of the unincorporated part of the county. The City operates the fire station as just another unit of the City fire department. The county pays the City for the total annual cost of the station plus $2,000 in City overhead.

County Planning Commission

The county pays the City one-half of the yearly budgeted operating expenses of the City/county planning commission.

County Supplement
(Water-Sewer Enterprise Fund)

The county contracts with the City to install new water laterals (not transmission lines) in areas of the county outside the City limits. The county then provides financial assistance, according to a fixed contract, in repaying the cost of construction. The county currently pays the City an amount per year based on existing long-term contracts. Frequently, the county reimburses the City for short-term work for which the county, in turn, is reimbursed by property owners.

Court Fines

This account includes the fines established by the recorder's court (through FY III) and, since then, by the magistrate's court. There are state statutory limits on the fines that may be adjudged. The City has reached the limit of the state law.

Equipment Rental

This charge is made to contractors for use of city-owned equipment.

Fi. Fas. and Interest

A penalty is levied for nonpayment of taxes at the appropriate time. The charge is $1.50 per bill plus interest on the unpaid balance. "Fi. fa." stands for writs of "fieri facius," a mandatory order. It is a court order authorizing the sale of the delinquent taxpayer's property to satisfy unpaid taxes. This account includes fi. fas. and interest for property tax.

Fire Alarm System

A fire alarm system with direct connections to the fire department may be obtained by local businesses and others. A new hookup costs $100. There is a $50 per year fee.

Gross Earnings–Cable Television

This item is based upon a percentage of the gross earnings of the local TV cable franchise. The percentage, set at 3 percent, has been constant. TV cable is available to all sections of the City. Fifty-four percent of the households have cable TV.

Gross Earnings–Gas Company

This item is based upon a percentage of the gross earnings of the gas company in its service to City customers. The percentage, set at 3 percent, has been constant for five years.

Gross Earnings–Power Company

This item is based upon a percentage of the gross earnings of the statewide power company in its service to City customers. The percentage, set at 4 percent of gross earnings, has been constant for five years.

Hotel and Motel Tax

This tax was initiated in FY III. It is based upon 3 percent of the total gross sales of hotel and motel businesses in the City, less 3 percent compensation for collection by the hotel/motel. The amount due the City is remitted monthly.

Housing Authority

This is a payment in lieu of taxes. Simply stated, even though the housing authority does not have to pay local property taxes, a contribution is provided to the City government to help offset the loss of property taxes.

Intangible Taxes

This is an ad valorem (property) tax on intangibles. The same millage rate applies here as is used in setting general and motor vehicle ad valorem amounts. The county collects this tax for the City.

Interest Earned

This item depends upon the ability of the City treasurer to place funds in temporary interest-bearing accounts. Yearly collections mainly depend upon allowable interest rates and sound cash-flow management techniques.

State law limits the type of investments the City may purchase. The City is not authorized to "become a stockholder in any company, corporation, or association, or to appropriate money for, or to loan its credit to any corporation, company, association, institution, or individual except for purely charitable purposes."

The City may, however, invest excess funds in (1) U.S. obligations, agencies, and instruments; (2) in bonds of indebtedness of the state and its jurisdictions (cities, counties, and school districts); and (3) in collateralized (by any security in either group above) certificates of deposit in banks insured by the Federal Deposit Insurance Corporation when the amounts invested exceed the FDIC's limits.

Leaf and Limb Pickup

The sanitation department will pick up one load of leaves and limbs per household each season without charge. A $10 service charge is assessed for additional loads. The enforcement of this service charge is lax.

Lodal Sales

Charges for the sale of large refuse containers, to garbage collection customers.

Madison Avenue and Thomas Street Construction

These revenues are received from state government for specific street projects.

Miscellaneous Sales

This account provides for a way to handle revenue items that are infrequent and small in amount.

Other Reimbursements

This account is for the reimbursement property owners pay the City for work improvements made in and around their property, usually curb, gutter, and paving work.

Parking Meters

The City police department supervises meter readers. The rate for each half-hour of parking has not changed in the last five years. The City has a two-hour parking limit, however. Parking meters are located only in the central business district.

Paving and Paving Cuts

In developing their land, property owners who need access to City streets must pay for cuts and repairs to the curb and gutter. The fee has been constant for the last five years.

Planning Commission Miscellaneous Revenues

These are small revenues received from the sale and distribution of literature.

Recreation Department–County

The county pays the City to allow non-City residents to utilize City parks and recreation facilities. The fee is based upon a per capita amount (based on the number of residents living in the unincorporated part of the county). The amount for FY VI is set at 2 percent above the FY V amount.

Recreation Department–Pools

This account has the revenues generated by use of the City pools. The charge for use of the pool has not changed during the last five years. Children pay $.35; adults, $.50. The account is maintained separately from other recreation program revenues to allow an assessment of pool usage.

Recreation Department–Program Revenues

This account is for the revenues (FY I-III) from the various services and activities sponsored by the recreation department and the charges for use of City facilities (except the pools).

Recreation Department

This account contains miscellaneous revenues and contributions made to the recreation department.

Sales and Use Tax

Permitted by state law, the City levies a general sales tax of 1 percent on all goods and services bought and sold or used. State law requires that cities adopting the tax reduce or roll back ad valorem (property) taxes by an amount equal to the sales tax collections. In practice, the City must reduce property tax millage rates by an amount equal to the previous fiscal year's sales tax collections.

The calculation of the rollback is as follows:

Sales tax collections, FY II	$ 3,897,341
Assessed value, FY III	$ 406,191,220
Total value of property (assessed value divided by 40%), FY III	$1,015,478,050
Sales taxes divided by total value and expressed in mills (amount to be rolled back)	0.0038 ($3.80 per $1,000 assessed value)
Millage rate before rollback	0.0130 ($13.00 per $1,000 assessed value)
Property tax rate in mills after rollback	0.0092 ($9.20 per $1,000 assessed value)

The state collects this revenue on behalf of the city (along with the state's own 5 percent general sales tax). The brackets used by vendors are as follows:

Sales/Use Tax Collected	Bracket
0	0-19¢
1¢	20¢
2¢	21-40¢
3¢	41-60¢
4¢	61-80¢
5¢	81¢ – $1.00; then 5¢ on each $1.00 plus 1¢ for each 20¢ or fraction thereof above $1.00

The state treasury department computes the tax liability by multiplying a retail firm's total sales by the combined 5 percent state rate and the 1 percent City rate. The state concedes, as breakage, any difference between the amount collected by the vendor due to the brackets and the amount computed as tax liability.

The state has not, as yet, charged the city for collecting the tax, although law allows a charge of up to 1 percent of the tax liability. Amounts due the City are remitted by the state quarterly, beginning April 20.

Sanitation Department–Container Rental

During FY V, the City decided to discontinue renting large, metal garbage containers. In the past, the monthly rental fee that business and industry paid to use a "dumpster" was set at $10 for less than six-cubic-yard containers; $12 for a six-cubic-yard container; and $15 for an eight-cubic-yard container. These amounts are far lower than other municipalities' rates when considering statewide averages.

Sanitation Department–Lodal Sales

The City sells large, metal garbage containers that can be emptied by front-loading garbage trucks. Normally, only the six-cubic-yard size may be purchased for use in the City. The cost is $425, and the City has a monopoly in providing these containers.

Sanitation Service

The university pays the City $70,000 per year to dispose of university-collected solid wastes under a contract which lapses, and must be negotiated, at the end of FY V. Federal research facilities after FY V will pay the City to collect their solid wastes. There have been recent increases in the number of these federal facility contracts.

Special Taxes and Licenses

This account includes the yearly license fee each professional service and business unit must pay. The amount for a professional service is a flat fee of $90 that has been the same for the last five years.

For business concerns, the amount paid is based upon (1) gross receipts and (2) the number of employees.

The City rate is based partly upon each $1,000 of gross receipts. The first $3,000 of gross receipts are *not* taxed. See the following:

Gross Receipts Levels

$8,000*		$100,000		$1,000,000	
Tax	Rate Per $1,000	Tax	Rate Per $1,000	Tax	Rate Per $1,000
$14	$2.80	$77	$.77	$511	$.51

*After the first $3,000 has been exempted ($8,000 – $3,000 = $5,000 × $2.80 per $1,000 = $14 tax).

In addition, each business also pays a tax based upon the number of employees. The first employee (usually the owner) is *not* taxed. See the following:

Number of Employees

2-9	10-99	100-499	500 or More
$20	$59.25	$441.50	$1,840.50

Insurance companies are taxed based upon the premiums paid in the city according to the following schedule:

1 percent of life insurance premiums

2$^1/_2$ percent of casualty insurance premiums

1 percent of fire insurance premiums

Each business completes a form mailed by the City treasurer. If the form is not returned by February 15, a 5 percent penalty of the fee is levied. Bills are sent out based upon the information provided. Nonpayment by April 1 results in a penalty of 10 percent of the fee plus 7 percent interest per year. Arrangements can be made to pay the amount in two installments (due April 1 and August 1).

Sprinkler and Hydrant Rent
(Water-Sewer Enterprise Fund)

A stand-by fee is charged for customers who have special fire protection mechanisms. Sprinkler rent is set at $75 per year for City locations and $150 per year for non-City locations. Hydrant rent is set at $10 per year for City locations and $80 per year for non-City locations. The rates have been constant for five years. In FY IV, 48 percent of the sprinklers and hydrant rentals were located in the City.

State Contracts

This is an account for grants from the state for specific, named street project improvements. The individual grants terminate with completion of the specific project.

State Transportation Department Contract: Maintenance

This is paid by the state for City maintenance of state roads and rights of way. The amount is based on the number of miles of U.S. and state highways located within the City. The state pays $5,280 per mile. Within the next two years, a bypass will be completed around the City. This 45-mile state highway will increase the number of miles the City will be paid to maintain.

Streets Department–Equipment Rental

All major road and street work is done by contracts. The City rents special equipment to contractors.

Tap and Meter Charges–Water and Wastewater
(Water-Sewer Enterprise Fund)

Water and sewer mains are located under the street pavement. It is often necessary for new residents and businesses to make a new connection (a lateral) off the main. Charges appear in the schedule of rates under "Water Revenue."

Transportation Bond Program

The state Department of Transportation provided the City with a one-time grant under its Urban Bond Program for use in making major street improvements.

Wastewater Charges
(Water-Sewer Enterprise Fund)

For residential and most commercial customers, monthly charges are a function of the volume of wastewater as measured by water consumption. In order to avoid counting water used in lawn sprinkling, wastewater volume is calculated as 80 percent of water volume for these customers. For industrial consumers, however, strength of the contaminants in the wastewater is the important variable. Under current federal water pollution control laws, industrial customers must pretreat their sewerage before discharging it into the public system, or pay a strength surcharge sufficient to cover the added costs. As a result, wastewater meters are required for industrial customers. The strength surcharge increases with higher concentrations of contaminants. An industrial cost recovery charge on processed wastewater is computed by the City's Waterworks Commercial Department for each affected customer.

The City charges both for the initial connection to the wastewater system and for month-to-month service. These charges are shown in "Water Revenue" below.

The City sells wastewater service to customers in the developed part of the county, the same area receiving water service. These customers pay a rate $2^1/_2$ times that of customers inside the City limits. See "Water Revenue" for information on the number of customers and their residential location.

The table of rates appears under "Water Revenue" also. As with water revenues, customers outside the City limits pay rates $2^1/_2$ times City rates.

Water and Wastewater Connection Fees
(Water-Sewer Enterprise Fund)

The City installs all water meters connected to the water distribution system. Charges appear in the schedule of rates under "Water Revenue" below.

There is no charge if a water meter is already located on the property.

Water Revenue
(Water-Sewer Enterprise Fund)

The most recent study (in FY V) indicates City residents comprise approximately 62 percent of the total number of metered customers, and non-City residents amounted to approximately 38 percent of the total number.

The City charges all customers outside its limits a rate higher than City residents ($2^1/_2$ times the City rate). The City uses a rate schedule based upon consumption. The FY V study indicated that 47 percent of the revenue collections came from City residents, while 53 percent came from non-City residents. It also indicated that, out of a total of 3,987.5 million gallons, 49 percent were consumed by City customers and 51 percent by non-City customers.

This account also includes penalties and cut-off fees.

The higher cost for non-City use of the water system is to pay for amortization of the debt on the central facilities—water supply and purification—along with administrative costs and costs of distribution facilities.

FEE SCHEDULE FOR WATER AND WASTEWATER SERVICES

Charges for using the system are as follows:

Water

Charge by Consumption			Basic Charge by Meter Size	
Consumption	Residential	Non-residential	Size	Charge
Per 100 cu. ft.	$1.57	$1.35	⅝" or ¾"	$ 5.06
			1"	5.71
			1½"	7.31
			2"	22.30
			3"	29.70
			4"	39.21
			6"	89.34
			8"	116.64

Wastewater

The wastewater charge is computed as the sum of the base charge and the unit charged based on consumption.

Consumption	Residential	Nonresidential
Per 100 cu. ft.	$1.20	$1.20
Base charge	$4.71	$4.71

Residential wastewater volume is equal to eighty (80) percent of the water volume unless approved differently by the Waterworks Commercial Department.

WASTEWATER SURCHARGE RATES

Concentration of Contaminant (mg./l.)	Charge ($/1000 lb.)
101–150	80.00
151–200	160.00
201–500	320.00
501–750	480.00
751–1000	640.00

An industrial cost recovery charge on processed wastewater is computed by the Waterworks Commercial Department.

CHARGES TO ESTABLISH SERVICE
Connection Fees

Meter Size	Water Connection Fee	Wastewater Connection Fee
¾"	$270.00	$380.00
1"	450.00	630.00
1½"	900.00	1,270.00
2"	2,700.00	3,800.00
3"	4,725.00	6,650.00
4"	9,450.00	13,300.00
6"	18,900.00	26,600.00

Tap and Meter Charges

¾" water meter	$166.00	2"water meter	$2,900.00
¾" water stub	210.00	2"water stub	350.00
1" water meter	310.00	4"water stub	240.00*
1" water stub	225.00	6"water stub	250.00*
1½" water meter	450.00	8"water stub	285.00*
1½" water stub	300.00	Paving cuts–minimum	275.00**
		Bullheads–minimum	100.00**

Note: Sizes larger than those listed are calculated by the Waterworks Commercial Department; installations requiring state Department of Transportation right-of-way encroachment permit = +$100.00.
  *Plus casing manhole.
**Plus additional amounts as determined by the Waterworks Commercial Department based on actual labor, material, and equipment charges.

Whiskey Excise Tax

Since mixed drinks cannot be taxed according to state law, the tax is fixed at $.05 per pint of liquor. This tax is levied upon the wholesaler. The wholesaler pays the appropriate amount without being billed.

ALTERNATIVE REVENUE SOURCE: INCOME TAX

This tax applies to an individual's income from rents, dividends, interest, and other returns from investments, as well as from salaries, wages, and profits from proprietorships, partnerships, and corporations.

The state allows the City to levy an income tax. However, it can be implemented only after a local referendum results in majority vote for approval and with the requirement that 50 percent of the registered voters participate in the election. The City has not chosen thus far to levy an income tax.

If approved, the tax would be 1 percent of net taxable income of both persons and corporations residing within the local taxing jurisdiction. (There is a $7,500 exemption of gross income for any individual.) It would be collected by the state, and the funds sent to the local jurisdiction.

Data on the estimated taxable income base of the City is as follows:

Net Taxable Income

Year	Income
FY I	$474,082,006
FY II	502,179,880
FY III	512,871,215
FY IV	546,694,435
FY V	593,080,459

EARMARKED REVENUES BY CITY DEPARTMENT/FUNCTION AND BY REVENUE ACCOUNT

Police Department
    Parking meters
    Court fines
    Cash bonds on fines
    Cash bonds on parking tickets
    Police planner
    Burglar alarm system

Streets Department
    State contracts
    Paving and paving cuts
    Equipment rental
    Thomas Street and Madison Avenue construction projects
    Transportation bond
    State transportation department contract–maintenance

Water and Sewer (Filter, Water, Sewer, Pollution Control, and Meters)
    Water meter installation
    Sprinkler and hydrant rental
    Tap and meter charges
    Wasterwater charges
    Water and wastewater connection fees
    Water revenue
    County supplement
    Construction funds (federal)

Sanitation (Garbage Collection, Street Cleaning, and Incinerator)
    University rent
    Miscellaneous sales
    Lodal sales
    Sanitation service
    Container rental
    Leaf and limb pickup

Recreation Department
    Pools
    Program revenue
    County recreation

Fire Department
    Fire alarm system
    County fire protection
    County fire station

Civil Defense
    County
    Federal

Animal Services
    Animal services

City/County Planning
    County planning commission
    Planning commission miscellaneous revenues

Building Inspection
    Building inspection fee

DEBT LIMITS

The state places limits on the amount and characteristics of city debt obligations.

General obligation bonds. A majority vote of the citizens is required to impose the property tax as security; the debt limit is equal to 7 percent of assessed valuation; maturity of bonds must not exceed the life of the asset financed, but no less than two years or more than 30 years.

Special assessment bonds. Majority of benefited property owners must give signed approval for special assessment (property tax) to be levied on them, with maturity of bonds not to exceed the life of the asset financed (but no more than 20 years); does not count against general obligation debt limit.

Revenue bonds. Maturity of bonds must not exceed the life of the asset financed, but no more than 40 years.

Short-term notes. The aggregate amount cannot exceed 75 percent of the total general fund revenues for the preceding fiscal year or 75 percent of the anticipated revenue of the year in which they are issued; notes must be repaid within the fiscal year in which they are issued.

Leases. When the contract includes a "non-appropriation" clause, a lease may be entered into without it counting as part of the outstanding debt of the city (therefore excluding leases from the general obligation debt limit).

City Revenue and Expenditure Summaries

The following tables portray the revenues and expenditures of the City. Anticipated revenues, the first table, refer to revenue forecasts before the fiscal year indicated. Collected revenues, the second table, are those amounts actually collected, as recorded in the City's accounts at the end of the fiscal year.

Budgeted expenditures, the next table, are those recorded in the various accounts at the beginning of the fiscal year indicated. The numbers refer to planned spending or those amounts set by city council action, followed by allotment to department accounts. Spent expenditures indicate funds actually spent through the fiscal year.

Notice that, generally, the sources of revenue named in the tables follow closely the sources of revenue already described. The expenditures are itemized by department name; descriptions of these departments and greater detail on spending are presented in Part 2, "City Departments."

ANTICIPATED REVENUES

Sources of Revenue	Year I Anticipated	Year II Anticipated	Year III Anticipated	Year IV Anticipated	Year V Anticipated
GENERAL FUND					
Ad valorem taxes–Property	$2,100,000	$2,200,000	$2,500,000	$2,800,000	$3,050,000
Ad valorem taxes–Motor vehicles	150,000	164,000	170,000	170,000	170,000
Animal services	0	200	2,000	10,000	12,000
Beer and wine excise tax	780,000	700,000	860,000	1,120,000	1,280,000
Building inspection fees	200,000	210,000	240,000	280,000	325,000
Burglar alarm system	0	0	0	4,500	11,000
Cash bonds on fines	112,000	130,000	130,000	170,000	140,000
Cash bonds on parking tickets	72,000	112,000	100,000	80,000	90,000
Civil defense–County share	7,002	9,342	27,212	80,204	12,560
Container rental	0	0	0	116,000	124,000
County fire protection	80,000	80,000	80,000	80,000	80,000
County fire station	0	0	346,204	358,986	399,230
County planning commission	86,962	86,512	105,440	109,516	110,534
Court fines	36,000	42,000	120,000	136,000	180,000
Equipment rental	0	0	0	4,000	10,000
Fi. fas. and interest	16,000	16,000	24,000	38,000	46,000
Fire alarm system	0	0	0	4,500	4,000
Gross earnings–Cable television	23,000	22,000	22,000	24,000	30,000
Gross earnings–Gas co.	120,000	120,600	120,600	163,878	170,000
Gross earnings–Power co.	495,000	581,200	601,200	973,200	1,051,300
Hotel and motel tax	0	0	100,000	120,000	160,000
Housing authority	56,000	60,000	80,000	100,000	67,600
Intangible taxes	36,000	30,000	30,000	40,000	40,000
Interest earned	100,000	140,000	180,000	200,000	210,000
Leaf and limb pickup	1,200	1,500	1,800	2,000	2,200
Lodal sales	0	0	0	30,000	14,000
Madison Avenue construction	100,000	0	0	0	0
Miscellaneous sales	36,000	20,000	6,000	10,000	30,000
Other reimbursements	0	0	0	104,600	150,600
Parking meters	170,000	180,000	180,000	180,000	160,000
Paving and paving cuts	32,000	30,000	30,000	20,000	20,000
Planning commission miscellaneous revenues	1,200	1,800	2,000	2,400	3,000
Recreation dept.–County	0	0	237,000	450,000	450,000
Recreation dept.–Pools		10,000	19,000	21,000	24,000
Recreation dept.–Program revenues	0	0	0	28,000	5,000
Recreation department	18,800	14,000	10,000	0	0
Sales and use tax	3,460,000	3,900,000	4,200,000	4,800,000	5,300,000
Sanitation department–Container rental	73,000	80,000	135,000	0	0
Sanitation department–Lodal sales	20,000	20,000	30,000	0	0
Sanitation service	124,000	130,000	140,000	130,000	140,000
Special taxes and licenses	1,900,000	2,000,000	2,200,000	2,500,000	2,800,000
State contracts	461,070	461,070	461,070	461,070	460,600
State transportation dept. contract–Maintenance	84,100	84,100	84,100	84,100	84,100
Streets dept. equipment rental	24,400	60,000	0	0	0
Thomas Street construction	200,000	0	0	0	0
Transportation bond program	0	0	0	0	303,046
Whiskey excise tax	250,000	200,000	190,000	190,000	190,000
Carryover previous fiscal year	0	0	0	0	600,000
Subtotal (General Fund)	$11,425,734	$11,896,324	$13,764,626	$16,195,954	$18,509,770

ANTICIPATED REVENUES (continued)

Sources of Revenue	Year I Anticipated	Year II Anticipated	Year III Anticipated	Year IV Anticipated	Year V Anticipated
WATER-SEWER ENTERPRISE FUND					
County supplement	36,000	86,000	96,000	80,000	90,000
Wastewater charges	824,000	862,400	1,663,696	1,803,960	1,860,000
Sprinkler and hydrant rent	30,000	30,000	30,000	32,000	50,000
Tap and meter charges–Water and wastewater	170,000	130,000	100,000	56,000	110,000
Water and wastewater connection fees	126,000	100,000	70,000	60,000	90,000
Water revenue	4,000,000	4,400,000	4,400,000	4,928,000	5,150,000
Subtotal (Water-Sewer Enterprise Fund)	$ 5,186,000	$ 5,608,400	$ 6,359,696	$ 6,959,960	$ 7,350,000
FEDERAL FUNDS					
Civil defense–Federal share	14,000	19,000	49,000	160,000	25,000
Total (Federal Funds)	$ 14,000	$ 19,000	$ 49,000	$ 160,000	$ 25,000
TOTAL (All Funds)	$16,625,735	$17,534,724	$20,173,322	$23,315,914	$25,884,770

COLLECTED REVENUES

Sources of Revenue	Year I Collected	Year II Collected	Year III Collected	Year IV Collected	Year V Collected
GENERAL FUND					
Ad valorem taxes–Property	$1,884,063	$2,267,520	$3,591,295	$3,097,164	$2,717,573
Ad valorem taxes–Motor vehicles	356,697	359,936	365,789	372,494	377,400
Animal services	0	2,772	11,904	13,830	15,974
Beer and wine excise tax	753,734	892,864	1,163,368	1,297,038	1,368,798
Building inspection fees	262,641	161,292	245,843	287,814	377,121
Burglar alarm system	0	0	20,412	11,324	8,466
Cash bonds on fines	175,136	152,754	183,888	137,690	372,178
Cash bonds on parking tickets	115,680	95,028	91,304	86,586	90,230
Civil defense–County share	6,796	8,244	11,120	54,498	38,104
Container rental	0	0	0	123,228	132,632
County fire protection	73,334	79,992	79,992	79,992	80,000
County fire station	0	0	223,274	289,082	392,914
County planning commission	76,808	87,604	99,754	103,382	111,038
Court fines	45,034	126,838	148,680	142,930	159,716
Equipment rental	0	0	0	9,324	19,080
Fi. fas. and interest	14,618	24,874	25,442	249,718	26,464
Fire alarm system	0	0	5,900	3,444	3,724
Gross earnings–Cable television	23,634	20,600	26,680	30,576	32,318
Gross earnings–Gas co.	129,294	124,130	257,010	370,458	521,470
Gross earnings–Power co.	522,204	596,962	717,846	975,498	980,014
Hotel and motel tax	0	0	135,006	155,516	189,242
Housing authority	80,450	49,738	70,510	81,132	66,864
Intangible taxes	828,244	820,822	852,888	845,966	855,160
Interest earned	149,005	222,356	536,889	314,764	119,344
Leaf and limb pickup	890	950	1,210	1,580	1,820
Lodal sales	0	0	0	12,054	16,018
Madison Avenue construction	12,030	79,604	0	0	0
Miscellaneous sales	152,022	58,666	45,624	56,482	124,272
Other reimbursements	0	280,000	400,000	60,480	70,594
Parking meters	202,330	186,226	159,370	167,294	173,616

COLLECTED REVENUES (continued)

Sources of Revenue	Year I Collected	Year II Collected	Year III Collected	Year IV Collected	Year V Collected
Paving and paving cuts	29,340	51,358	39,438	21,374	15,960
Planning commission miscellaneous revenues	1,214	1,850	2,060	2,410	3,270
Recreation dept.–County	0	0	225,000	412,296	450,000
Recreation dept.–Pools	14,194	16,424	20,572	23,248	21,358
Recreation dept.–Program revenues	0	90,258	43,306	34,090	30,850
Recreation department	9,068	16,362	21,334	0	0
Sales and use tax	3,558,442	3,897,341	4,236,240	4,857,920	5,278,580
Sanitation dept.–Container rental	79,270	81,934	122,928	0	0
Sanitation dept.–Lodal sales	18,196	32,360	33,540	0	0
Sanitation service	126,452	131,300	131,250	132,318	137,956
State contracts	466,482	461,014	345,910	460,598	460,516
State transportation dept. contract–Maintenance	91,108	84,098	84,100	84,100	84,100
Streets dept. equipment rental	4,620	1,808	0	0	0
Thomas Street construction	220,224	0	0	0	0
Transportation bond program	0	0	0	0	292,550
Whiskey excise tax	397,502	390,150	388,262	395,588	406,708
Carryover from previous FY	0	350,443	72,468	694,879	1,248,086
Subtotal (General Fund)	$10,880,755	$12,306,472	$15,237,406	$16,550,159	$17,872,078
WATER-SEWER ENTERPRISE FUND					
Water revenue	4,300,428	4,478,902	4,426,000	5,019,690	5,283,850
Sprinkler and hydrant rent	30,622	30,804	31,880	42,126	54,724
Wastewater charges	1,176,490	1,222,028	1,624,942	1,858,916	1,940,874
County supplement	35,826	68,648	99,028	77,176	101,780
Tap and meter charges– Water and wastewater	150,980	120,296	62,730	155,668	120,874
Water and wastewater connection fees	101,114	91,134	59,798	84,802	102,752
Subtotal (Water-Sewer Enterprise Fund)	$ 5,795,460	$ 6,011,812	$ 6,304,378	$ 7,238,378	$ 7,604,854
FEDERAL FUNDS					
Water-sewer improvements	41,456	40,328	319,200	3,975,272	0
Water filter plant expansion	0	0	99,674	0	4,972,602
Civil defense-federal share	13,594	16,490	22,240	108,996	40,000
Total (Federal Funds)	$ 55,050	$ 56,818	$ 441,114	$ 4,084,268	$ 5,012,602
TOTAL (All funds)	$16,731,265	$18,375,102	$21,982,898	$27,872,805	$30,489,534

EXPENDITURE SUMMARY

Department	Year I Budgeted	Year II Budgeted	Year III Budgeted	Year IV Budgeted	Year V Budgeted
GENERAL FUND					
Animal services	$ 0	$ 80,000	$ 102,266	$ 112,176	$ 91,564
Building inspection	114,646	118,708	130,604	135,686	210,488
City clerk-Treasurer	216,982	274,996	296,666	308,476	309,566
City hall	57,194	98,850	89,600	81,890	100,840
City marshal	53,846	56,850	66,494	68,930	77,232
Civil defense	28,010	37,376	102,270	320,822	50,240
Computer and data processing	0	76,304	129,404	147,338	154,184
Elective	102,020	124,000	133,100	136,650	146,650
Electrical department	0	40,000	371,036	361,980	403,100
Electrical dept.–Streetlights	354,000	262,000	0	0	0
Fire department	1,435,816	1,455,720	2,026,764	1,946,356	2,188,384
Fire station, County	0	0	342,202	364,986	395,230
General administrative	2,874,152	2,518,682	2,995,506	3,467,232	3,706,376
Human resources	0	0	189,246	206,304	209,356
Parks and recreation dept.	555,094	1,012,656	1,762,872	1,495,140	1,457,396
Cardinal Park	0	400,000	0	0	0
Personnel department	45,290	106,600	118,406	127,918	144,622
Planning commission	173,926	173,026	210,880	219,032	221,068
Police department	1,623,506	1,808,278	2,023,548	2,608,288	2,696,712
Police planner	27,860	415,504	449,624	0	0
Public works	125,868	116,980	126,086	163,050	176,066
Sanitation–Garbage collection	943,728	1,223,146	874,056	1,546,406	1,726,582
Sanitation–Incinerator	253,780	234,586	184,982	0	0
Sanitation–Street cleaning	335,474	256,194	438,298	308,254	218,926
Service garage	228,960	252,262	633,186	492,398	555,766
Stockade	48,060	50,668	51,396	120,800	122,536
Streets department	1,164,454	1,251,460	1,209,954	1,372,160	1,360,760
Downtown beautification	0	0	200,000	0	0
Subtotal (General Fund)	$10,726,666	$12,444,846	$15,258,446	$16,112,272	$16,723,644
WATER–SEWER ENTERPRISE FUND					
General administrative	$ 3,090,000	$ 3,231,600	$ 3,307,200	$ 3,396,600	$ 3,358,400
Water filter plant	460,820	587,344	741,354	878,766	775,326
Water meters	210,300	223,200	246,316	174,300	183,192
Water pollution control plant	335,320	578,312	831,042	1,126,442	0
South plant	0	0	0	0	228,426
North plant	0	0	0	0	570,078
Oxidation pond operations	0	0	0	0	65,032
Water-sewer distribution	0	172,088	424,766	466,100	507,082
Sewer distribution	13,100	0	0	0	0
Water distribution	124,750	0	0	0	0
Waterworks commercial	158,322	187,260	185,608	163,354	156,864
Subtotal (Water-sewer enterprise fund)	$ 4,392,612	$ 4,979,804	$ 5,736,286	$ 6,205,562	$ 5,844,400
FEDERAL FUNDS					
Police-community relations	$159,560	0	0	0	0
Water-sewer improvements	51,000	49,614	160,426	4,000,000	0
Water filter plant expansion	0	0	1,000,000	0	5,000,000
Subtotal (Federal Funds)	$ 210,560	$ 49,614	$ 1,160,426	$ 4,000,000	$ 5,000,000
TOTAL (All Funds)	$15,365,838	$17,474,264	$22,155,158	$26,317,834	$27,568,044

EXPENDITURE SUMMARY

Department	Year I Spent	Year II Spent	Year III Spent	Year IV Spent	Year V Spent
GENERAL FUND					
Animal services	0	$ 56,444	$ 97,688	$ 84,828	$ 75,764
Building inspection	104,598	119,472	131,682	177,398	224,232
City clerk-Treasurer	217,028	259,058	275,322	275,689	334,010
City hall	109,876	111,442	80,292	92,696	127,092
City marshal	56,766	56,666	65,630	70,138	76,368
Civil defense	27,192	32,978	44,486	217,996	152,426
Computer and data processing	0	82,524	127,464	141,246	157,010
Elective	98,344	107,046	124,046	153,458	149,538
Electrical dept./Inspection	0	22,118	355,230	324,926	568,818
Electrical dept.–Streetlights	337,014	310,044	0	0	0
Fire department	1,335,496	1,455,946	1,992,876	1,927,694	2,147,226
Fire station, County	0	0	219,266	285,078	388,910
General administrative	2,435,968	2,304,031	2,982,633	3,162,583	3,651,250
Human resources	0	0	180,558	195,999	237,369
Parks and recreation dept.	539,728	805,150	1,528,410	1,472,332	1,626,840
Cardinal Park	714	400,000	236,122	0	0
Personnel department	42,434	82,152	93,906	129,398	146,304
Planning commission	153,520	175,208	219,702	206,766	222,084
Police department	1,685,402	1,871,948	2,224,696	2,582,316	2,869,722
Police planner	7,268	167,638	145,472	0	0
Public works	98,870	94,538	135,356	162,108	174,126
Sanitation–Garbage collection	949,064	1,354,466	909,750	1,578,930	1,786,666
Sanitation–Incinerator	254,416	231,666	67,476	0	0
Sanitation–Street cleaning	325,260	239,656	378,722	289,466	251,834
Service garage	258,980	292,958	479,278	494,494	565,681
Stockade	42,322	46,714	38,262	104,200	114,630
Streets department	1,120,662	1,447,424	1,344,174	1,172,334	1,408,884
Thomas Street widening	162,854	0	0	0	0
General project	150,296	0	0	0	0
Madison Avenue, 1st leg	16,240	0	0	0	0
Madison Avenue, 2d leg	0	106,716	0	0	0
Downtown beautification	0	0	64,028	0	0
Subtotal (General Fund)	$10,530,312	$12,234,003	$14,542,527	$15,302,073	$17,456,784
WATER-SEWER ENTERPRISE FUND					
General administrative	$ 3,117,194	$ 3,219,116	$ 3,300,058	$ 3,306,850	$ 3,310,912
Water filter plant	506,484	676,884	829,176	808,210	964,872
Water meters	289,101	245,790	138,536	176,040	229,734
Water pollution control plant	346,208	643,736	665,218	852,623	
South plant	0	0	0	0	192,184
North plant	0	0	0	0	601,678
Oxidation pond operations	0	0	0	0	59,706
Water-sewer distribution		92,144	332,072	424,608	599,960
Sewer distribution	12,864	0	0	0	0
Water distribution	129,544	0	0	0	0
Waterworks commercial	158,178	188,370	149,112	167,270	147,714
Subtotal (Water-Sewer Enterprise Fund)	$ 4,559,573	$ 5,066,040	$ 5,414,172	$ 5,735,601	$ 6,106,760
FEDERAL FUNDS					
Police–Community relations	$ 39,282	0	0	0	0
Water-sewer improvements	$ 41,456	$ 40,328	$ 319,200	$ 3,975,272	0
Water filter plant expansion	0	0	99,674	0	4,972,602
Subtotal (Federal Funds)	$ 80,738	$ 40,328	$ 418,874	$ 3,975,272	$ 4,972,602
TOTAL (All Funds)	$15,170,623	$17,340,371	$20,375,573	$25,012,946	$28,536,146

PART 2
CITY DEPARTMENTS
A. General Fund
B. Water-Sewer Enterprise Fund

A. General Fund

ACCOUNT TITLE: Animal Services

This department, established in FY II, has the responsibility of providing temporary shelter and care for stray animals and trying to place them in permanent homes.

The animal services director supervises day-to-day work, manages the budget, and shares the field work. Three full-time animal services officers patrol and answer complaints. A clerk and volunteers (from the local chapter of an animal rights group) handle duties on the premises.

Dogs are kept for about 10 days before they are destroyed. Disposal takes place by arrangement with the county, which has landfill facilities dedicated to this purpose. A study in FY V showed that about 30 complaints were responded to weekly and that approximately 75 to 100 animals were handled monthly. An impoundment fee of $10 and a daily board fee of $3 are charged when an animal is picked up. A fee of $4 is charged for rabies immunization which is handled as follows: the animal's owner pays the animal services unit; the animal services unit issues a purchase order to the owner; the owner gives the purchase order to a veterinarian; the veterinarian immunizes the animal, issues a rabies tag, and bills the City.

The animal services unit has two three-year-old Dodge vans in operation. Within two years, both vans will have to be replaced.

Activity Indicators	FY V	FY V % Achieved	FY VI Estimate
Complaints responded to per week	30	100%	40
Animals handled monthly	75	100%	100

EXPENDITURE DATA

Animal Services

Object of Expenditure	Year II Budgeted	Year III Budgeted	Year IV Budgeted	Year V Budgeted
Salaries	$80,000	$ 79,006	$ 81,376	$71,624
Office supplies	0	0	12,000	8,000
Heat and power	0	0	0	0
Telephone	0	0	0	0
Gas and oil	0	0	0	0
Equipment repairs	0	1,300	600	400
Janitorial supplies	0	0	0	0
Laboratory supplies	0	0	0	0
Tools and supplies	0	9,000	0	0
Paint	0	0	0	0
Joint materials	0	0	0	0
Building materials and bedding	0	0	0	0
Groceries	0	0	0	0
Medical	0	0	0	0
Capital improvements	0	0	11,000	3,640
Other	0	0	0	0
Utilities	0	1,680	3,600	3,600
Communications	0	780	1,300	1,200
Printing	0	400	400	600
Travel	0	500	0	1,200
Freight and express	0	200	100	100
Professional services	0	1,600	1,400	1,200
Real property repairs	0	4,600	400	0
Dues and subscriptions	0	200	0	0
Equipment purchase	0	3,000	0	0
Training	0	0	0	0
TOTAL	$80,000	$102,266	$112,176	$91,564

Animal Services

Object of Expenditure	Year II Spent	Year III Spent	Year IV Spent	Year V Spent
Salaries	$21,136	$76,496	$63,694	$55,294
Office supplies	538	0	8,582	7,810
Heat and power	366	0	0	0
Telephone	324	0	0	0
Gas and oil	872	0	0	0
Equipment repairs	442	954	66	352
Janitorial supplies	154	0	0	0
Laboratory supplies	88	0	0	0
Tools and supplies	4,984	12,124	0	0
Paint	30	0	0	0
Joint materials	1,752	0	0	0
Building materials and bedding	30	0	0	0
Groceries	828	0	0	0
Medical	378	0	0	0
Capital improvements	24,390	0	5,440	5,558
Other	132	0	0	0
Utilities	0	3,372	3,412	2,778
Communications	0	1,286	844	1,244
Printing	0	100	340	622
Travel	0	36	496	854
Freight and express	0	34	40	44
Professional services	0	1,524	1,208	1,204
Real property repairs	0	472	706	0
Dues and subscriptions	0	0	0	0
Equipment purchase	0	1,290	0	0
Training	0	0	0	4
TOTAL	$56,444	$97,688	$84,828	$75,764

ACCOUNT TITLE: Building Inspection

The building inspection department enforces zoning ordinances and administers the building, housing, electrical, heating and air conditioning, and plumbing codes. The department is known to the public mostly for its issuance of building permits and for building inspections. During FY III, separate county inspection activities were merged with the City inspection office so that the area now served includes all of the City and county.

The chief building officer and department head also manages the budget of the Electrical Department, page 50.

Of inspection department activities, the housing code compliance program involves the following activities:

- Sending out letters of intent to inspect
- Conducting initial inspections
- Placarding houses unsafe for habitation
- Sending out notices to units not in compliance with the housing code
- Reinspecting and sending subsequent notices
- Sending notices of pretrial hearings for noncompliance
- Preparing agenda and conducting pretrial hearings
- Preparing court cases
- Assisting city attorney at trial of noncompliance cases
- Making follow-up inspections to see if court decisions have been carried out
- Sending out notices to units not in compliance with housing code
- Informing relocation agency about houses to be condemned
- Responding to complaints on housing and related activities
- Inspecting fireplaces and chimneys for citizens for a fee

Other programs and attendant activities conducted by the department include the following:

- Enforcement of Building and Related Construction Codes
  - Reviewing plans and issuing permits
  - Making on-site inspections
  - Issuing notices and stop-work orders
  - Spot-checking areas to see that work is being done with a permit
- Permits for Demolition and for Moving Houses
  - Processing building demolition permits
  - Making on-site demolition inspections
  - Processing permits for moving houses

The expenses of the board of zoning appeals are included in the inspection department budget. The board has the responsibility of hearing and deciding appeals for zoning variances to the City zoning ordinance. It has five members and a secretary, all of whom are appointed by the mayor and council for five-year terms of office. The members are paid $10 and the secretary $15 per meeting. The City-county planning commission coordinates the meetings and researches the background material.

Activity Indicators	FY V	FY V % Achieved	FY VI Estimate
Inspections with subsequent notices of noncompliance with code	22	N/A	25
Permits for demolition	46	N/A	70
Meetings of board	11	100%	23

Operating needs: One additional inspector to increase demolition program.

Capital budget needs: One automobile for inspector, to begin reversing past practice of using private automobiles.

The following vehicles are assigned to the inspection department:

Manufacturer	Age (years)	Type
Chevrolet	10	Pickup truck
Plymouth	3	Auto
Ford-350 Custom	3	Bucket truck

Inspectors use their own cars and are given a travel allowance.

Number of Permits and Cost of Building Activity

Type of Building	FY I	FY II	FY III	FY IV	FY V
Single Family Residences					
Number of permits	338	244	581	626	756
Work costs	$16,229,878	$14,652,870	$25,022,000	$27,856,000	$35,334,000
Average cost	$ 48,017	$ 60,053	$ 43,067	$ 44,498	$ 46,738
Multifamily Complexes and Duplexes					
Number of permits	17	13	38	27	51
Number of units	295	179	677	508	734
Work costs	$ 6,374,309	$ 4,837,249	$13,120,400	$10,172,335	$15,437,593
Average cost	$ 374,959	$ 372,096	$ 345,274	$ 376,753	$ 302,698
Residential Housing					
Total permits	355	257	619	653	807
Average work costs	$ 63,674	$ 75,837	$ 61,619	$ 58,236	$ 62,914
Total units	633	423	1258	1134	1490
Nonresidential Units					
Number of permits	128	73	45	109	93
Work costs	$26,021,548	$ 8,964,008	$ 7,589,656	$12,824,196	$17,757,528
Additions and Alterations					
Number of permits	152	270	306	375	349
Work costs	$ 3,902,496	$ 3,804,194	$ 3,436,458	$ 6,710,296	$ 6,895,166
TOTAL COST	$52,528,231	$32,258,321	$49,168,514	$57,562,827	$75,424,287

EXPENDITURE DATA

Building Inspection

Object of Expenditure	Year I Budgeted	Year II Budgeted	Year III Budgeted	Year IV Budgeted	Year V Budgeted
Salaries	$ 93,368	$ 97,826	$111,106	$117,348	$179,228
Office supplies	5,546	1,600	1,800	3,400	3,570
Telephone and telegraph	850	750	800	0	0
Tools and supplies	950	1,340	1,300	0	0
Car allowance	4,800	4,800	6,000	0	0
Travel	0	0	0	9,600	19,200
Dues and subscriptions	220	340	400	798	1,048
Communications	0	0	0	1,720	2,142
Printing	0	0	0	1,200	1,700
Repairs to equipment	0	0	0	300	400
Capital improvements	4,600	6,500	5,688	0	800
Training	2,100	2,300	1,600	1,320	2,400
Utilities	0	1,800	1,800	0	0
Professional services	0	0	0	0	0
Truck and car expense	1,920	1,180	110	0	0
Tires, tubes, and batteries	292	272	0	0	0
Other labor	0	0	0	0	0
Advertising	0	0	0	0	0
TOTAL	$114,646	$118,708	$130,604	$135,686	$210,488

Building Inspection

Object of Expenditure	Year I Spent	Year II Spent	Year III Spent	Year IV Spent	Year V Spent
Salaries	$ 90,340	$ 99,830	$110,980	$148,154	$182,360
Office supplies	4,286	1,732	1,782	5,012	3,918
Telephone and telegraph	546	612	1,392	0	0
Tools and supplies	1,092	1,242	854	0	0
Car allowance	3,400	5,500	7,500	0	0
Travel	208	0	0	15,200	19,896
Dues and subscriptions	146	330	500	748	816
Communications	0	0	0	2,470	2,348
Printing	0	0	0	1,156	1,752
Repairs to equipment	0	0	0	536	610
Capital improvements	944	6,662	5,198	2,400	11,254
Training	1,170	840	722	1,606	1,072
Utilities	224	1,190	2,644	0	206
Professional services	0	0	0	100	0
Truck and car expense	1,736	1,400	110	0	0
Tires, tubes, and batteries	236	134	0	0	0
Other labor	270	0	0	0	0
Advertising	0	0	0	16	0
TOTAL	$104,598	$119,472	$131,682	$177,398	$224,232

ACCOUNT TITLE: City Clerk–Treasurer

The City charter provides that the clerk of the City council also be the ex officio tax collector, treasurer, and finance director. This budget unit also covers the City attorney, administrative assistant to the mayor, mayor's secretary, and federal aid coordinator. Members of the council have questioned the need for a federal aid coordinator in a period of diminished federal aid.

The clerk's office is a focal point for all business conducted by the various departments of the City government. The books of the City, including a general ledger, accounts receivable, and accounts payable, are maintained by this office for all financial transactions. The clerk's office receives and disburses all revenues collected by the City. Ad valorem taxes, street taxes, sewer rentals, and beer and wine taxes are collected directly from the taxpayers. All other City departments, such as City marshal and police department, turn over their revenues to this office.

A list of the various activities performed by this department follows:

Revenue Collections
    Receiving and recording revenues
    Depositing revenues

Disbursement of Money
    Receiving and processing invoices
    Authorizing payments

Tax Administration
    Preparing and mailing tax notices
    Verifying tax digest
    Informing City marshal of delinquent tax cases

Money Management
    Making short-term investments
    Conducting long-term debt administration

Contracts
    Managing financial contracts

Administration of Employee Benefits
    Administering employee pensions

Payroll Administration
    Posting payroll changes for data processing
    Making payroll deductions and associated payments
    Distributing paychecks

Official Records Administration
    Keeping official minutes of City council and finance committee meetings
    Maintaining official City documents

General Accounting
    Posting all financial transactions in official records
    Preparing financial statements

The salary and expenses of the City attorney, the expenses of the mayor's secretary, and the expenses of the administrative assistant to the mayor are items on the City clerk's budget. The position of City attorney is a part-time appointment made by the mayor and council for a one-year term; the attorney provides his or her own clerical support. The administrative assistant to the mayor is also appointed; this official is responsible for assisting the mayor in the day-to-day operations and management of the City. He or she participates in all functions of City management and helps the mayor with the preparation of the budget, preparation for regular meetings, decisions of an interdepartmental nature, departmental organization and operation, and appointments to vital departmental positions.

Another expense included within this office is the salary of the grant coordinator. The coordinator prepares and coordinates federal and state grants (combined with some local funds) that are used to conduct community development activities such as human services programs and capital improvement projects. The clerk's office provides funds directly to City departments for the implementation of planned projects.

Activity Indicators	FY V	FY V % Achieved	FY VI Estimate
Special studies	0	0	3
Departments exceeding annual appropriation	65%	35%	40%
Percentage of staff participating in seminars, workshops, or other job-related training	100%	100%	100%

Operating needs: Cash management plan (consultant, $8,000); study of implementation of risk management plan, and conversion of accounting system to meet generally accepted accounting principles.

Capital budget needs: More office space ($100,000 for purchase of modular office cubicles and for remodeling the already existing space these new offices would take) and a computer-driven management information system to encompass cash management, risk management, and accounting system ($125,000).

EXPENDITURE DATA

City Clerk-Treasurer

Object of Expenditure	Year I Budgeted	Year II Budgeted	Year III Budgeted	Year IV Budgeted	Year V Budgeted
Salaries	$174,032	$209,546	$240,916	$249,576	$242,230
Training	0	0	0	0	0
Professional services	0	0	0	5,600	3,600
Travel	750	750	500	700	1,100
Dues and subscriptions	200	250	400	400	500
Telephone/Communications	1,000	800	600	600	600
Office supplies	19,000	15,000	10,000	10,000	9,400
Equipment repairs	3,000	3,000	3,000	3,200	400
Bank fees and interest	4,000	4,700	5,000	0	0
Advertising	1,000	2,400	1,600	2,400	600
Equipment	0	0	0	0	0
Capital improvements	2,000	2,550	0	0	0
Payroll services	12,000	4,000	0	0	0
Federal aid coordinator	0	32,000	34,000	36,000	38,000
Capital items	0	0	650	0	12,536
Printing	0	0	0	0	600
TOTAL	$216,982	$274,996	$296,666	$308,476	$309,566

City Clerk-Treasurer

Object of Expenditure	Year I Spent	Year II Spent	Year III Spent	Year IV Spent	Year V Spent
Salaries	$183,366	$204,996	$220,350	$224,398	$270,144
Training	0	0	0	260	0
Professional services	0	0	0	5,442	3,884
Travel	286	204	230	258	1,714
Dues and subscriptions	294	470	402	576	604
Telephone/Communications	674	656	364	421	534
Office supplies	8,876	7,566	9,938	7,732	4,960
Equipment repairs	2,880	2,950	4,160	422	1,256
Bank fees and interest	4,754	5,926	3,606	0	0
Advertising	3,012	1,352	2,292	666	1,084
Equipment	164	0	0	0	0
Capital improvements	12,722	1,784	0	0	0
Payroll services	0	1,414	0	0	0
Federal aid coordinator	0	31,740	33,330	34,998	36,750
Capital items	0	0	650	516	12,806
Printing	0	0	0	0	274
TOTAL	$217,028	$259,058	$275,322	$275,689	$334,010

ACCOUNT TITLE: City Hall

This portion of the budget is allocated for maintenance and upkeep of City Hall. It is an old building, built in 1904, and occasionally requires major renovations. A recent study indicated that within the next three to five years the following improvements would be needed.

Revovation Item	Cost
Paint interior	$ 5,400
Paint exterior	9,000
Restore clock tower	20,000
Repair roof gutters and eaves	40,000
Upgrade exterior entrance doors and windows	80,000
Air-condition top floor	30,000
Replace wiring and selected light fixtures	20,000
Repair floor in council chambers	6,000
Carry out exterior beautification	42,000

The following departments are located in the three-story City Hall structure:

First floor: City marshal, City clerk, computer services, custodian, and waterworks commercial.

Second floor: Council chambers (118-seat capacity), grant coordinator, and license offices (beer and wine, liquor, business).

Third floor: Building inspector, City engineer (public works administration), inspection department, mayor's office, and committee room.

The police department moved out of the ground floor level of City Hall in FY II, and the space was renovated for other office use.

EXPENDITURE DATA

City Hall

Object of Expenditure	Year I Budgeted	Year II Budgeted	Year III Budgeted	Year IV Budgeted	Year V Budgeted
Salaries	$20,450	$21,650	$23,400	$24,890	$ 26,140
Heat and power	15,000	16,000	24,000	0	0
Utilities	0	0	0	30,000	31,000
Equipment repairs	5,000	5,000	4,000	4,600	3,000
Photocopying	8,000	9,000	15,000	15,000	17,000
Janitorial supplies	2,344	3,200	0	0	0
Tools and supplies	2,400	2,000	0	0	0
Office supplies	0	0	0	5,100	8,100
Supplies	0	0	5,000	0	0
Real property repairs	4,000	5,000	16,000	2,000	0
Capital improvements	0	37,000	2,200	0	15,500
Freight and express	0	0	0	300	100
Communications	0	0	0	0	0
TOTAL	$57,194	$98,850	$89,600	$81,890	$100,840

City Hall

Object of Expenditure	Year I Spent	Year II Spent	Year III Spent	Year IV Spent	Year V Spent
Salaries	$ 20,450	$ 21,650	$23,400	$24,890	$ 26,132
Heat and power	15,344	20,026	27,352	0	0
Utilities	0	0	0	30,922	31,008
Equipment repairs	7,810	3,404	5,544	3,190	4,796
Photocopying	11,916	19,010	14,268	16,866	16,814
Janitorial supplies	3,726	2,946	0	0	0
Tools and supplies	1,416	2,128	0	0	0
Office supplies	0	0	0	8,692	7,422
Supplies	0	0	6,254	0	0
Real property repairs	7,656	298	1,048	6,352	17,646
Capital improvements	41,558	41,980	2,426	1,784	20,496
Freight and express	0	0	0	0	0
Communications	0	0	0	0	2,778
TOTAL	$109,876	$111,442	$80,292	$92,696	$127,092

ACCOUNT TITLE: City Marshal

This department is one of the few multipurpose offices in the City's government. The individual responsible for the operation of the office must give attention to three jobs: those of City marshal, water bill collector, and business license and other nonproperty tax administrator.

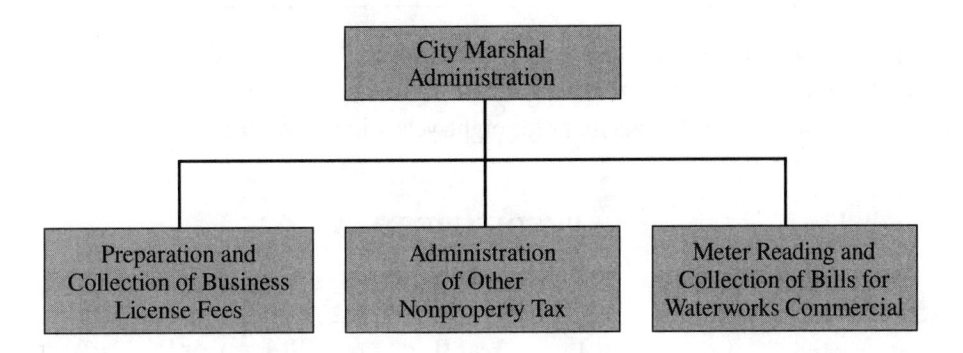

```
                    City Marshal
                   Administration
                          |
        ┌─────────────────┼─────────────────┐
  Preparation and    Administration    Meter Reading and
  Collection of Business   of Other     Collection of Bills for
    License Fees      Nonproperty Tax  Waterworks Commercial
```

Activities of the City marshal's department, except for those pertaining to water/sewer bill collection (see Waterworks Commercial Department, p. 128), follow:

Revenue Collections
    Receiving and recording business license fees
    Receiving and recording liquor taxes
    Receiving and recording paving assessment and first-year sewer rental
    Receiving and recording water/sewer bills (see "Account Title: Waterworks Commercial")
    Depositing revenues

Delinquent Tax Administration
    Mailing notices for delinquent property taxes
    Making field investigations of delinquent tax cases
    Issuing warrants and selling property

Administration and Enforcement of Business License Ordinance
    Processing business license applications
    Preparing and mailing licenses for each business located within the City
    Computing the fee for each business in the City
    Collecting business license fees and issuing business licenses
    Enforcing the City's business license code

General Administrative Activities
    Reporting to the clerk on receipts and deposits
    Helping to prepare revenue section of annual budget

Miscellaneous Activities
    Monitoring sales/use tax compliance activities by the state (for impact on amounts remitted to City).
    Exchanging data with state to ensure that new businesses collect the sales and use tax
    Processing paving assessments

The City marshal's office has a four-year-old mid-sized sedan and an eight-year-old full-sized sedan assigned to it for use in business license and delinquent tax administration.

Activity Indicators	FY V	FY V % Achieved	FY VI Estimate
Business licenses prepared	2,320	98%	2,560
Taxes and assessments processed	12,312	86%	14,500
Field investigations of delinquent taxes	120	95%	135

Operating needs: One additional clerk to help process licenses and assessments; field investigator for delinquent tax cases.

Capital budget needs: Replacement for eight-year-old automobile.

EXPENDITURE DATA

City Marshal

Object of Expenditure	Year I Budgeted	Year II Budgeted	Year III Budgeted	Year IV Budgeted	Year V Budgeted
Salaries	$50,766	$52,110	$60,594	$63,130	$70,432
Professional services	0	0	0	200	200
Telephone/Communications	440	440	3,200	2,800	2,800
Office supplies	1,600	2,400	1,800	1,200	1,200
Equipment repairs	200	200	200	100	200
Advertising	200	200	200	400	400
Capital improvements	0	800	0	0	0
Printing	0	0	0	1,100	2,000
Legal	160	200	200	0	0
Tires, tubes, and batteries	80	100	0	0	0
Gas and oil	200	200	300	0	0
Truck and car repairs	200	200	0	0	0
TOTAL	$53,846	$56,850	$66,494	$68,930	$77,232

City Marshal

Object of Expenditure	Year I Spent	Year II Spent	Year III Spent	Year IV Spent	Year V Spent
Salaries	$53,052	$52,578	$60,318	$64,124	$71,346
Professional services	0	0	0	88	92
Telephone/Communications	422	1,722	2,602	2,728	2,848
Office supplies	2,786	1,026	1,488	1,912	1,354
Equipment repairs	158	46	36	66	222
Advertising	0	0	772	28	50
Capital improvements	0	200	0	0	0
Printing	0	0	0	1,192	456
Legal	178	180	108	0	0
Tires, tubes, and batteries	44	90	0	0	0
Gas and oil	78	176	306	0	0
Truck and car repairs	48	648	0	0	0
TOTAL	$56,766	$56,666	$65,630	$70,138	$76,368

ACCOUNT TITLE: Civil Defense

The function of this agency is to coordinate all local governmental departments in developing emergency operational plans and assisting industry, business, and community leaders in planning for emergency help in time of natural disaster, military hostilities, or civil disturbances. The agency's funding is from local, state, and federal services. The director of this joint City-county agency is appointed by the governor upon the recommendation of the mayor, the City council, and the board of county commissioners.

The civil defense office is located in the basement of the City police department building. The director is a county employee, but a portion of his/her salary (of $48,000 per year) is carried in the Civil Defense budget.

Activity Indicators	FY V	FY V % Achieved	FY VI Estimate
Plans developed	40	100%	45
Plans	29	79%	50

Operating needs: Join interstate system for severe weather watch coordination and forewarning ($8,000 per year).

Capital budget needs: Bring all shelters up to minimum standards provided by state regulations (100 shelters @ $2,000 each = $200,000).

EXPENDITURE DATA

Civil Defense

Object of Expenditure	Year I Budgeted	Year II Budgeted	Year III Budgeted	Year IV Budgeted	Year V Budgeted
Salaries	$24,426	$30,752	$ 38,164	$ 39,540	$42,858
Office supplies	340	400	400	400	500
Heat and power	0	0	0	0	0
Utilities	0	0	0	0	2,292
Communications	0	0	1,000	1,000	1,450
Telephone and telegraph	520	560	0	0	0
Gas and oil	0	0	0	0	0
Truck and car repair	0	0	0	0	0
Photocopying	100	100	0	0	0
Travel	1,000	1,000	1,400	1,200	1,200
Postage	224	264	0	0	0
Equipment repairs	0	800	400	400	200
Real property repairs	0	0	0	2,100	0
Recurring charges	0	300	300	0	0
Social security	0	1,800	0	0	0
Other aggregate	0	1,000	0	0	0
Publications fund	0	400	0	0	0
Printing	0	0	320	240	240
Contingency fund	0	0	1,000	0	0
Training	0	0	2,000	1,000	1,000
Dues and subscriptions	0	0	200	100	400
Surplus property	0	0	200	0	0
Capital improvements	1,400	0	56,886	273,542	0
Freight and express	0	0	0	100	100
Advertising	0	0	0	0	0
Equipment leasing	0	0	0	1,200	0
TOTAL	$28,010	$37,376	$102,270	$320,822	$50,240

Civil Defense

Object of Expenditure	Year I Spent	Year II Spent	Year III Spent	Year IV Spent	Year V Spent
Salaries	$25,076	$28,436	$38,234	$ 39,856	$ 46,758
Office supplies	236	468	254	520	864
Heat and power	188	0	0	0	0
Utilities	0	0	0	0	2,848
Communications	0	0	860	1,106	1,684
Telephone and telegraph	372	692	0	0	0
Gas and oil	78	0	0	0	0
Truck and car repair	528	0	0	0	0
Photocopying	100	50	0	0	0
Travel	452	1,100	824	2,216	2,162
Postage	64	100	0	0	0
Equipment repairs	0	0	0	116	516
Real property repairs	0	0	0	1,422	182
Recurring charges	0	172	234	0	0
Social security	0	1,590	0	0	0
Other aggregate	0	160	0	0	0
Publications fund	0	210	0	0	0
Printing	0	0	76	42	242
Contingency fund	0	0	0	0	0
Training	0	0	0	142	386
Dues and subscriptions	0	0	20	232	212
Surplus property	0	0	30	0	0
Capital improvements	98	0	3,954	171,522	96,572
Freight and express	0	0	0	0	0
Advertising	0	0	0	22	0
Equipment leasing	0	0	0	800	0
TOTAL	$27,192	$32,978	$44,486	$217,996	$152,426

ACCOUNT TITLE: Computer and Data Processing

It is the responsibility of the computer and data processing department to provide computerized reports and dependable facilities for the storage, analysis, and reproduction of information and data as required by the various departments within the City. A single shift of the computer department personnel performs six basic functions for the City government:

1. Computing and printing all water and sewer bills, including reminder and cut-off notices, on a monthly basis
2. Computing and printing the City's property tax bills three times a year (April, August, and November)
3. Printing an annual list of local businesses for the purpose of computing business license fees
4. Computing and printing payroll checks on a biweekly, weekly, and monthly basis
5. Providing managerial-type printouts on a monthly basis, which summarize revenue by source and expenditures by type for the different departments
6. Providing special management-type reports requested by City government officials

The operating structure of the computer and data processing department, which became operational at the start of Fiscal Year II, is shown in the following diagram:

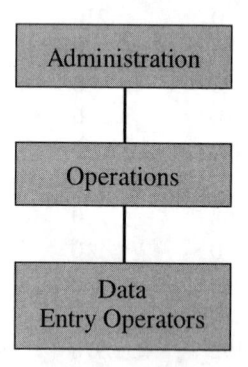

```
Administration
     |
 Operations
     |
    Data
Entry Operators
```

In addition, a review committee (i.e., a policy committee) composed of the City marshal, the clerk, the police chief, the director of the planning commission, the director of computer and data processing services, and the personnel director (chair) determines the sequencing of computer applications to City departments and the necessity of hiring new personnel, contracting with consultants, and adding new equipment.

Activity Indicators	FY V	FY V % Achieved	FY VI Estimate
Percentage delay in providing paperwork support for departments	0	100%	0
Number of special studies for City government officials	12	100%	25

Operating needs: Management analyst to meet demand for special reports.

Capital budget needs: Increased capacity of present computer in order to maintain pace with growth in City government, in the short run ($15,000); a consultant to study conversion to a decentralized network of personal computers, in the long run ($10,000); a data bank safe ($5,000).

EXPENDITURE DATA

Computer and Data Processing

Object of Expenditure	Year II Budgeted	Year III Budgeted	Year IV Budgeted	Year V Budgeted
Salaries	$40,000	$ 69,054	$ 73,812	$ 87,840
Office supplies	6,000	5,000	7,000	7,000
Telephone/Communications	0	400	960	960
Travel	700	500	500	0
Equipment rental	25,504	52,400	0	0
Capital improvements	2,700	750	240	1,050
Contingency	600	0	0	0
Freight	800	0	0	0
Training/Education	0	1,300	800	0
Dues and subscriptions	0	0	100	0
Rent	0	0	0	0
Repairs to equipment	0	0	0	1,000
Equipment leasing	0	0	63,926	56,334
TOTAL	$76,304	$129,404	$147,338	$154,184

Computer and Data Processing

Object of Expenditure	Year II Spent	Year III Spent	Year IV Spent	Year V Spent
Salaries	$43,396	$ 69,216	$ 78,688	$ 91,384
Office supplies	5,382	5,590	5,862	5,392
Telephone/Communications	512	902	936	1,142
Travel	0	0	0	0
Equipment rental	22,766	50,890	0	0
Capital improvements	9,164	710	240	1,046
Contingency	640	0	0	0
Freight	664	0	0	0
Training/Education	0	156	0	0
Dues and subscriptions	0	0	0	426
Rent	0	0	0	0
Repairs to equipment	0	0	170	454
Equipment leasing	0	0	55,350	57,166
TOTAL	$82,524	$127,464	$141,246	$157,010

ACCOUNT TITLE: Elective

The budget in this section covers the expenses of the elected officials: the mayor and the 10 City council members. Moneys are allocated for the mayor's salary of $28,650, for each council member's annual salary of $7,400, and for their office needs, travel expenses, and training allowance.

Activity Indicators	FY V	FY V % Achieved	FY VI Estimate
Prebudget discussion sessions and field reviews	N/A	N/A	8
Budget study sessions	8	125%	10
Ordinances adopted	190	93%	190
Day council meetings	40	100%	40
Night council meetings	12	100%	12
Public hearings	42	145%	70

Operating needs: Better graphics for budget analysis.

Capital budget needs: Redecoration of City council chambers.

EXPENDITURE DATA

Elective

Object of Expenditure	Year I Budgeted	Year II Budgeted	Year III Budgeted	Year IV Budgeted	Year V Budgeted
Salaries	$ 70,000	$ 92,000	$ 92,000	$ 98,650	$102,650
Office supplies	2,000	2,000	2,000	2,000	3,000
Telephone	500	500	1,800	1,800	2,000
Equipment repairs	400	400	400	400	200
Advertising	2,000	2,000	1,800	1,800	1,800
Legal	3,000	3,000	3,000	0	0
Travel, conferences, and goodwill	11,000	11,000	18,000	24,200	32,000
Expense allowance	11,600	11,600	12,600	0	0
Dues and subscriptions	1,520	1,500	1,500	4,800	2,000
Training	0	0	0	3,000	3,000
TOTAL	$102,020	$124,000	$133,100	$136,650	$146,650

Elective

Object of Expenditure	Year I Spent	Year II Spent	Year III Spent	Year IV Spent	Year V Spent
Salaries	$70,000	$ 92,000	$ 92,000	$ 98,650	$102,650
Office supplies	2,652	1,684	1,108	3,898	7,328
Telephone	1,522	1,900	1,886	2,430	3,052
Equipment repairs	0	276	402	0	308
Advertising	0	162	1,296	1,712	1,810
Legal	6,532	1,176	2,666	0	0
Travel, conferences, and goodwill	2,290	6,156	20,624	30,682	28,088
Expense allowance	12,832	0	0	0	0
Dues and subscriptions	2,516	2,988	4,064	13,086	3,302
Capital improvements	0	704	0	0	0
Training	0	0	0	3,000	3,000
TOTAL	$98,344	$107,046	$124,046	$153,458	$149,538

ACCOUNT TITLE: Electrical Department

This department inspects electrical facilities in the City. The City electricians also maintain City streetlights (in conjunction with the power company) and, at Christmas, handle downtown lighting decorations. They are under the supervision of the inspection department head.

In FY I, only a streetlights account was maintained. In FY II, and only then, two separate accounts were maintained: one for streetlights and one for electrical services in general. In other years, only the electrical account was maintained.

The following number of streetlights are now in the system:

Number	Illuminating Power
1,603	7,000 lumen
155	21,000
409	20,000
73	11,000
61	50,000

The electrical inspectors have only one pickup truck, purchased five years ago. A recent capital improvements study listed the following four-year equipment and project needs.

Item	Cost per Item
Aerial truck	$46,000
Pickup truck	14,400
Signal improvements (24 locations)	20,000 average
Traffic signal controls (4 locations)	2,500 average

Activity Indicators	FY V	FY V % Achieved	FY VI Estimate
Streetlights and standards repair	1,219	83%	1,300
Citations issued for code violations	86		90

EXPENDITURE DATA

Electrical Department–Streetlights

Object of Expenditure	Year I Budgeted	Spent	Year II Budgeted	Spent
Streetlights	$240,600	$207,096	$220,000	$232,176
Equipment repairs	20,000	28,714	20,000	56,688
Tools and supplies	400	1,776	0	0
Christmas lights	3,000	1,008	2,000	2,008
Underground wiring	90,000	0	0	0
Capital improvements	0	98,420	20,000	19,172
TOTAL	$354,000	$337,014	$262,000	$310,044

Electrical Department

Object of Expenditure	Year II Budgeted	Year III Budgeted	Year IV Budgeted	Year V Budgeted
Salaries	$40,000	$ 33,508	$ 41,230	$ 42,866
Truck and car repairs	0	0	0	0
Travel expense	0	0	0	0
Supplies	0	0	0	0
Office supplies	0	350	32,510	30,000
Street lighting	0	260,000	0	0
Telephone	0	488	0	0
Gas and oil	0	1,710	0	0
Equipment repairs	0	38,000	1,000	1,600
Tools and supplies	0	6,400	0	0
Christmas lights	0	2,000	0	0
Real property repairs	0	4,000	400	0
Education and training	0	700	800	0
Dues and subscriptions	0	180	160	160
Utilities	0	0	253,480	249,484
Printing	0	0	700	100
Capital improvements	0	23,700	31,000	78,390
Communications	0	0	700	500
TOTAL	$40,000	$371,036	$361,980	$403,100

Electrical Department

Object of Expenditure	Year II Spent	Year III Spent	Year IV Spent	Year V Spent
Salaries	$ 9,876	$ 33,784	$ 38,682	$ 45,922
Truck and car repairs	64	0	0	0
Travel expense	366	0	96	0
Supplies	4,508	0	0	0
Office supplies	0	280	28,744	34,802
Street lighting	0	239,192	0	0
Telephone	0	660	0	0
Gas and oil	0	0	0	0
Equipment repairs	0	51,778	0	1,068
Tools and supplies	0	16,872	0	0
Christmas lights	0	312	0	0
Real property repairs	0	1,734	92	858
Education and training	0	0	0	4
Dues and subscriptions	0	0	0	0
Utilities	0	0	229,040	282,766
Printing	0	0	0	0
Capital improvements	7,304	10,618	27,806	202,724
Communications	0	0	466	674
TOTAL	$22,118	$355,230	$324,926	$568,818

ACCOUNT TITLE: Fire Department

The City Fire Department is organized to protect life and property from fire hazards. It has three basic functions: response to calls for protection from fire, response to calls for help or rescue, and fire prevention in the community. (The county provides a 911 emergency telephone service as well as Emergency Medical Service.)

While the name implies a service restricted to City residents, in reality, the service is available to the entire county through a contractual agreement with the county board of commissioners. Thus, fire protection coverage is provided for the 125-square-mile countywide area for which the county pays a base fee of $80,000 (in FY VI) and the cost of the fire station located in the county (outside the City's boundaries) for the county's part of the services.

There are four fire stations within the City limits and one county station (see "Fire Station, County" on p. 56).

The Insurance Service Organization (ISO) rating for the City is Class 3. Areas outside the incorporated area have ratings ranging from 4 (near the county fire station) to 10. In addition to setting fire insurance rates, ISO determines the minimum requirements regarding the location of fire facilities, the adequacy and replacement schedule of firefighting equipment, the level of services, and the adequacy of the fire prevention and code compliance programs. The standards are not based upon a generalized index, such as the number of firefighters per thousand population, but rather upon a spatial arrangement of fire stations and equipment necessary to protect life and property within the urban area.

The City has installed an alarm system. Four circuit systems, out of a proposed 10, are in operation; they cover the central business district (CBD), the adjacent high-value districts, and the older sections of the City. The system is designed to register calls by box number and time of day on a permanent record and alert all stations to the emergency.

One full-time fire marshal is assigned duty as an inspector, with the goal of preventing fires through an active code compliance program.

A review of the facilities and equipment of the fire department follows:

Station Number 1

This facility, built in 1912, is the headquarters of the Fire Department and is located adjacent to the CBD. There are three truck parking bays, two offices, and living quarters for 31 people. Parking facilities at this site are limited to the ramp in front of the building, and no spaces are provided for employee or visitor parking. The tallest building downtown is eight stories; the aerial ladder will reach to the eighth floor.

Vehicular equipment located at this station includes the following:

Age (years)	Type
25	Aerial ladder truck
15	Ford pumper: 1,000 gallons per minute (GPM)
6	Ford water wagon (1,200 GPM)
4	Station wagon (fire marshal's vehicle)
3	Chrysler sedan (fire chief's car)

Station Number 2

This facility, situated in the historic section of the City in a structure built in 1901, serves a growing commercial area. Its company also answers calls in the CBD areas since it is only one mile from Station Number 1.

The building contains one bay and is in poor structural condition. Since the building completely covers this site, there is no space for off-street parking or for future building expansion. The station contains sleeping and kitchen facilities for 12 persons.

The only truck located at this station is a four-year-old Ford pumper that pumps 1,000 GPM.

Station Number 3

This facility, housed in a structure built in 1950, serves the south portion of the City, including the University, and answers calls from Station 1. The building contains two bays and living facilities for 12 persons. The site is small and cannot accommodate additional parking spaces or future bays.

Vehicular equipment located at this station includes the following:

Age (years)	Type
3	Ford Snorkel with elevating ladder
14	Ford pumper (1,000 GPM)
23	Peter Piersch pumper (750 GPM)

Station Number 4

This facility serves the northwest part of the City and will assume a more important role as the urban area continues to expand in this direction.

The building, constructed in 1965, contains two bays and living facilities for 12 persons. The site contains adequate space for future building additions and for off-street parking; this is the only local fire station with this potential.

Vehicular equipment includes the following:

Age (years)	Type
11	Peter Piersch pumper (1,000 GPM)
11	Peter Piersch pumper (1,000 GPM)
12	International panel truck (outfitted as a rescue truck)
	Outboard motor boat

Needed Improvements

Under review for a number of years has been a proposal to build a new fire station to replace both Stations 1 and 2, which are on opposite ends of the CBD.

Activity Indicators	FY V	FY V % Achieved	FY VI Estimate
Average time from receipt of alarm to station response	25 seconds	90%	21 seconds
Number of inspections of commercial property	100	50%	250
Dollar value of losses due to fire reported by insurance companies	$1,256,000	67%	$800,000

Operating needs: Begin retirement of vehicles according to standards required by ISO; install incentive pay for firefighters both for performance and for upgrading job skills.

Capital budget needs: Replacement of Stations 1 and 2.

EXPENDITURE DATA

Fire Department

Object of Expenditure	Year I Budgeted	Year II Budgeted	Year III Budgeted	Year IV Budgeted	Year V Budgeted
Salaries	$1,297,876	$1,353,450	$1,600,258	$1,687,920	$1,857,588
Office supplies	900	900	900	47,100	89,900
Heat and power	8,000	9,000	12,000	13,200	14,600
Telephone and telegraph	4,000	7,430	6,000	8,400	8,700
Gas and oil	2,800	5,000	10,000	0	0
Truck and car repairs	2,000	2,000	2,000	0	0
Equipment repairs	200	200	200	10,000	10,000
Tires, tubes, and batteries	1,400	1,400	414	0	0
Claims	200	0	0	0	0
Freight and express	100	100	100	0	0
Postage	40	40	40	0	0
Janitorial supplies	1,400	1,400	2,000	0	0
Tools and supplies	800	800	1,000	0	0
Real property repairs	3,000	3,000	3,000	3,000	0
Building furnishings/Bedding	600	600	600	0	0
Clothing	2,400	2,400	22,800	0	0
Medical	400	400	400	0	0
Fire alarm repairs	2,000	2,000	1,000	0	0
Fire equipment apparatus	600	600	1,600	0	0
Soda, acids, and chemicals	200	200	0	0	0
Hose and supplies	2,400	2,400	1,600	0	0
Education and training	3,000	3,000	3,000	3,000	4,000
Fire prevention safety	300	1,000	1,000	0	0
Hydrant	200	200	200	0	0
Dues and subscriptions	200	200	200	400	400
Capital improvements	100,800	58,000	356,452	170,936	201,196
Professional services	0	0	0	400	1,000
Rent	0	0	0	1,000	0
Printing	0	0	0	1,000	1,000
TOTAL	$1,435,816	$1,455,720	$2,026,764	$1,946,356	$2,188,384

Fire Department

Object of Expenditure	Year I Spent	Year II Spent	Year III Spent	Year IV Spent	Year V Spent
Salaries	$1,222,006	$1,360,630	$1,562,140	$1,661,466	$1,754,290
Office supplies	936	382	904	45,836	92,716
Heat and power	10,726	11,330	12,928	17,060	21,766
Telephone and telegraph	5,076	6,578	6,892	8,878	10,490
Gas and oil	6,178	10,630	14,608	0	0
Truck and car repairs	4,368	3,042	12,158	0	0
Equipment repairs	70	136	0	10,126	22,748
Tires, tubes, and batteries	1,908	2,720	414	0	0
Claims	200	0	0	0	0
Freight and express	30	40	14	0	0
Postage	0	0	0	0	0
Janitorial supplies	1,972	2,590	3,058	0	0
Tools and supplies	962	988	436	0	0
Real property repairs	26,618	3,462	2,650	4,260	9,972
Building furnishings/Bedding	492	1,292	988	0	0
Clothing	2,688	1,330	21,188	0	0
Medical	350	970	320	0	0
Fire alarm repairs	506	498	420	0	0
Fire equipment apparatus	2,322	2,540	3,862	0	0
Soda, acids, and chemicals	170	0	0	0	0
Hose and supplies	116	0	0	0	0
Education and training	1,854	2,748	1,926	5,872	5,262
Fire prevention safety	626	0	938	0	0
Hydrant	0	114	0	0	0
Dues and subscriptions	288	246	326	434	606
Capital improvements	45,034	43,680	346,706	171,658	227,912
Professional services	0	0	0	1,622	1,114
Rent	0	0	0	0	0
Printing	0	0	0	482	350
TOTAL	$1,335,496	$1,455,946	$1,992,876	$1,927,694	$2,147,226

ACCOUNT TITLE: Fire Station, County

The City operates a fire station in a highly developed area of the county (east of the City) built and equipped by the county. Through a contractual arrangement begun in Fiscal Year III, the county pays the City to staff the station. County officials have become increasingly vocal about the rate of increase in costs.

The equipment and firefighters are available to serve any area of the City, as directed by the fire chief.

The county is currently considering the feasibility of building another fire station beyond the western side of the City, which would operate under a similar arrangement with the City.

Activity Indicators	FY V	FY V % Achieved	FY VI Estimate
Average response time ("out the door")	28 seconds	90%	25 seconds
Dollar value of losses	$312,000	60%	$150,000

Operating needs: Retirement plan for vehicles.

Capital budget needs: New station on western side of City.

EXPENDITURE DATA

Fire Station, County

Object of Expenditure	Year III Budgeted	Year IV Budgeted	Year V Budgeted
Salaries	$299,766	$306,600	$343,030
Other labor	0	0	0
Supplies	0	0	0
Truck and car repairs	0	0	0
Insurance-general	4,000	0	0
Workers' compensation	2,000	0	0
Janitorial supplies	1,000	0	0
Supplies	17,636	0	0
Real property repairs	0	0	0
Bedding	1,000	0	0
Protective clothing	9,600	0	0
Pension	7,200	0	0
Medical	0	0	0
Fire equipment apparatus	0	0	0
Education and training	0	640	1,000
Office supplies	0	57,746	51,200
Repairs to equipment	0	0	0
Communications	0	0	0
TOTAL	$342,202	$364,986	$395,230

Fire Station, County

Object of Expenditure	Year III Spent	Year IV Spent	Year V Spent
Salaries	$208,312	$279,486	$373,500
Other labor	1,004	0	0
Supplies	56	0	0
Truck and car repairs	58	0	0
Insurance-general	0	0	0
Workers' compensation	0	0	0
Janitorial supplies	1,180	0	0
Supplies	380	0	0
Real property repairs	50	70	958
Bedding	808	0	0
Protective clothing	7,166	0	0
Pension	0	0	0
Medical	140	0	0
Fire equipment apparatus	36	0	0
Education and training	76	542	330
Office supplies	0	4,660	13,898
Repairs to equipment	0	320	144
Communications	0	0	80
TOTAL	$219,266	$285,078	$388,910

ACCOUNT TITLE: General Administrative

This section of the budget includes the nondepartmental costs. It covers expenses that benefit all departments (such as group insurance and pensions), those concerning no certain department (such as bond repayment), as well as appropriations by the City to non-City government agencies (such as the regional planning commission) and civic and charitable organizations. The costs of retired City personnel are carried by this account.

The City has a contractual agreement with an insurance company to provide pension benefits for City employees. A trust fund is maintained for the accumulation and payment of current City and employee contributions. The General Fund pays pension contribution (employer share) costs, at present 10 percent of total annual salaries. The retirement system is presently fully funded.

The General Obligation Bonded Debt accounts hold funds for owners and pays principal and interest as bonds mature. Until the payment date, idle funds earn interest through investment in certificates of deposit through local banks. For FY VI, there should be just one line item for "G.O. Bond-Total Debt Service" based upon Exhibit 3.

To compute Social Security, Medicare, workers' compensation, disability insurance, and unemployment insurance, a review of current federal and state law will be necessary.

Activity Indicators	FY V	FY V % Achieved	FY VI Estimate
Special studies	0	0	3

Operating needs: Studies of indirect costs for grants (consultant), of property and group health insurance coverage, and of alternatives such as self-insurance and inter-local pools. Analysis of additional contributions required by federal law for Social Security (FICA) and Medicare and current prescribed contributions to workers' compensation, disability and unemployment insurance.

EXHIBIT 3
Summary of Outstanding Bond Maturities and Interest Payments,
General Obligation Bonds

Payment Date	Principal	Interest Payment	Total Payment	Principal Balance
5 years prior to FY V	$90,000	$320,000	$410,000	$3,910,000
I	95,000	312,800	407,800	3,815,000
II	100,000	305,200	405,200	3,715,000
III	110,000	297,200	407,200	3,605,000
IV	120,000	288,400	408,400	3,485,000
V	130,000	278,800	408,800	3,355,000
VI	140,000	268,400	408,400	3,215,000
VII	150,000	257,200	407,200	3,065,000
VIII	160,000	245,200	405,200	2,905,000
IX	175,000	232,400	407,400	2,730,000
X	190,000	218,400	408,400	2,540,000
XI	205,000	203,200	408,200	2,335,000
XII	220,000	186,800	406,800	2,115,000
XIII	235,000	169,200	404,200	1,880,000
XIV	255,000	150,400	405,400	1,625,000
XV	275,000	130,000	405,000	1,350,000
XVI	300,000	108,000	408,000	1,050,000
XVII	325,000	84,000	409,000	725,000
XVIII	350,000	58,000	408,000	375,000
XIX	375,000	30,000	405,000	0
TOTAL	$4,000,000	$4,143,600	$8,143,600	

EXPENDITURE DATA

General Administrative

Object of Expenditure	Year I Budgeted	Year II Budgeted	Year III Budgeted	Year IV Budgeted	Year V Budgeted
Debt Service Fund					
G.O. bonded debt principal 1	$ 95,000	$ 100,000	$ 110,000	$ 120,000	$ 130,000
G.O. bonded debt interest 1	312,800	305,200	297,200	288,400	278,800
G.O. bonded debt principal 2	100,000	50,000	60,000	60,000	70,000
G.O. bonded debt interest 2	138,350	80,010	78,370	75,760	72,760
Purchase Jackson Street property (city hall parking)	4,200	0	0	0	0
Mayor/Council contingency fund	200,000	160,000	297,100	350,000	300,000
Elections, general and special	10,000	10,000	10,000	0	0
Professional services, audit	20,000	24,000	24,000	40,000	40,000
City code updating	8,000	8,000	1,800	0	0
Postage	60,000	40,000	44,000	60,000	66,000
Dues and subscriptions	10,000	10,000	10,000	12,400	12,400
City directory	0	0	6,364	0	0
Disaster expense Subcontracted cleanup for city hall	0	0	0	0	0
Area Planning and Development Commission	22,172	22,172	22,172	22,172	22,172
Rocky Creek Nature Center City match for federal grant	0	53,800	0	0	0
Convention and tourism bureau	0	0	0	120,000	108,690
Contract escrow	411,404	80,000	90,000	78,000	47,054
Trust fund					
Pension/Retirement system City share	500,000	575,000	725,000	800,000	925,000
Old City pensions	17,500	16,500	15,500	15,500	13,500
Social security City share	400,000	435,000	550,000	615,000	700,000
Insurance General, property, and workers compensation	264,726	224,000	254,000	360,000	420,000
Group health insurance	300,000	325,000	400,000	450,000	500,000
TOTAL	$2,874,152	$2,518,682	$2,995,506	$3,467,232	$3,706,376

General Administrative

Object of Expenditure	Year I Spent	Year II Spent	Year III Spent	Year IV Spent	Year V Spent
Debt Service Fund					
G.O. bonded debt principal 1	$ 95,000	$ 100,000	$ 110,000	$ 120,000	$ 130,000
G.O. bonded debt interest 1	312,800	305,200	297,200	288,400	278,800
G.O. bonded debt principal 2	100,000	50,000	60,000	60,000	70,000
G.O. bonded debt interest 2	138,350	80,010	78,370	75,760	72,760
Purchase Jackson Street property (city hall parking)	27,578	0	0	0	0
Mayor/Council contingency fund	166,704	115,318	413,644	152,722	240,312
Elections, general and special	72,228	2,362	7,128	0	0
Professional services, audit	26,054	23,500	23,960	46,672	40,226
City code updating	25,800	8,774	7,154	0	0
Postage	35,074	44,374	46,434	62,176	64,948
Dues and subscriptions	17,844	8,922	8,922	11,010	12,356
City directory	0	0	6,364	0	0
Disaster expense					
Subcontracted cleanup for city hall	1,168	0	0	0	0
Area Planning and Development Commission	22,172	22,172	22,172	22,172	50,710
Rocky Creek Nature Center					
City match for federal grant	0	42,388	0	0	33,754
Convention and tourism bureau	0	0	4,300	85,000	136,000
Contract escrow	60,000	0	2,000	30,946	10,238
Trust fund					
Pension/Retirement system					
City share	499,304	567,240	720,722	802,308	910,756
Old City pensions	17,500	16,500	15,500	15,500	13,500
Social security					
City share	381,967	433,938	551,352	613,765	696,728
Insurance					
General, property, and workers compensation	136,843	142,989	174,977	294,768	343,709
Group health insurance	299,582	340,344	432,433	481,385	546,453
TOTAL	$2,435,968	$2,304,031	$2,982,633	$3,162,583	$3,651,250

ACCOUNT TITLE: Human Resources

The Human Resources Department is intended to act as a link between the residents of the community and the services provided by the local governmental departments. Also, it provides child care and a 24-hour informational referral service for the community. This referral service is supported by follow-up visits from resource specialists who make sure that a person who needs and asks for help gets it. The Human Resources Department also has reference books, fact books, directories, newsletters, and encyclopedias to help people obtain information. This department, an outgrowth of federal grant programs, has attracted little federal funding recently. With little federal aid available, the department's activity indicators suggest that it will have local funding for only about one-third its FY V levels of activity next year.

The Human Resources Department rents space in office buildings near City Hall.

A list of the various activities provided by this department follows:

Child Care
    Contracting social service agencies to set up and operate child-care centers
    Providing administrative assistance to child-care centers
    Checking child-care centers and agencies to make sure they are following guidelines of the Department of Health and Human Services (contract compliance)
    Bookkeeping and helping prepare budgets for child-care centers
    Providing training to child-care staff
    Assisting boards of child-care centers

Direct Services
    Counseling (supportive listening)
    Providing field services (outreach)
    Providing transportation and escort service
    Helping fill out forms
    Acting as notary public

Information and Referral
    Providing information to callers and walk-ins
    Referring people to appropriate agencies
    Collecting and recording data on individuals requesting help or information
    Following up contacts with people referred to other agencies
    Updating information and referral resource file and director of community resources

General Administrative Activities
    Writing publicity for department programs
    Planning and evaluating programs
    Preparing monthly plan and report

The Human Resources Department has two vehicles: a three year-old station wagon and a two-year-old van. A recently completed capital improvements program indicated the need for the following vehicles within the next three years:

Item (number)	Cost per item
11-passenger van (2)	$17,250
Station wagon	16,300

Activity Indicators	FY V	FY V % Achieved	FY VI Estimate
Inspections of child-care centers	10	100%	10
No. hours of training for child-care staff	1,260	65%	400
No. hours counseling	2,040	100%	700
No. referrals or information bits provided	10,630	50%	500

Operating needs: Twelve additional telephone lines for information and referral service; management trainer to assist child-care centers in understanding management and budget.

EXPENDITURE DATA

Human Resources

Object of Expenditure	Year III Budgeted	Spent	Year IV Budgeted	Spent	Year V Budgeted	Spent
Salaries	$149,720	$152,712	$160,940	$162,276	$178,228	$206,178
Office supplies	4,560	4,068	9,660	7,482	7,860	7,966
Secretarial services	5,530	0	0	0	0	0
Telephone	2,880	3,120	0	0	0	0
Insurance	1,156	1,020	0	0	0	0
Equipment repairs	0	0	5,734	1,014	1,800	1,732
Gas and oil	5,000	2,580	0	0	0	0
Equipment rental	0	0	7,770	7,770	0	40
Miniature library	800	800	0	0	0	0
Publicity and advertising	3,600	3,546	4,000	2,028	3,600	3,674
Office rent	14,760	12,460	11,760	10,780	11,760	11,760
Travel	860	22	960	47	360	284
Postage	380	230	0	0	0	36
Dues and subscriptions	0	0	800	374	600	596
Communications	0	0	4,680	4,078	5,148	5,103
Printing	0	0	0	150	0	0
TOTAL	$189,246	$180,558	$206,304	$195,999	$209,356	$237,369

ACCOUNT TITLE: Parks and Recreation Department

Eight parks, two community centers, and a nature study center are under the jurisdiction of the Parks and Recreation Department. The director of this department manages the park system and administers a comprehensive, year-round recreation program. Additionally, three recreation centers and two community centers are located on housing authority property. The director appoints two assistants: one to manage the parks and the other to help with the recreation program.

The recreation program includes both structured and unstructured activities in sports, music, art, and hobbies. In contrast to other governmental departments, this department has many seasonal activities, team sports, tournaments, pet fairs, holiday affairs, and classes for teaching skills for personal leisure time. These classes include knitting, dog obedience, belly dancing, camping, and aquatics. Many of the programs and activities are conducted at the two new community centers. The Rocky Creek Nature Center is a unique, environmental resource center with many different natural areas for school children and the general public to enjoy. The countywide public school district serves as the center's fiscal agent and shares the cost of its operation with the City and county governments. (See the "General Administrative" section on page 58, for the City-match information.)

A current compilation of existing parks and recreation facilities follows:

Monument Park—a 72-acre site, wooded and hilly, located on the south side of the City
- Activities and office buildings
- Playgrounds
- One 6-acre lake
- A small, native-animal zoo
- Picnic facilities
- Multipurpose courts
- Swimming pool

Preston Park—a 7-acre site located on the east side of the City
- Activities building
- Play field and playground
- Multipurpose courts
- Picnic facilities
- River, creek, and wooded areas

Banks Park—a 7-acre park located on the northeast side of the City
- Activities building
- Play field and athletic field
- Playground
- Swimming pool
- Picnic facilities
- Multipurpose courts

Taylor Park—a heavily wooded park located on a 30-acre site north of the City
- Terrain variety
- Picnic facilities and restrooms
- Scenic vistas

Honor Park—a 10-acre site located on the west side of the City
- A large baseball field
- Wooded area
- Picnic facilities and restrooms

Trillium Park—a 6-acre site located on the northeast side of the City
- Athletic field
- Activities building
- Multipurpose court
- Playground
- Wooded areas

Cardinal Park—a 15-acre, complete physical activities complex
- Eight tennis courts
- Three athletic fields (combined softball and football)
- Five basketball courts
- Jogging track
- Senior citizen area
- Picnic pavilion
- Swimming pool
- Multipurpose recreation hall
- Two tot lots
- Bike and walking trails

From FY I to FY III, major capital improvements to Cardinal Park were undertaken.

North Cherokee River Park—a 7-acre site on a river with picnic facilities

Clearsprings Recreation Center—a 6-acre facility located adjacent to the public housing project on the southwest side of the City
- Athletic building
- Athletic field
- Swimming pool
- Two playgrounds
- Multipurpose courts
- Bathhouse

Johnson House Recreation Center—a 3-acre facility located north of the central business district
- Activities building
- Athletic field
- Playground
- Multipurpose court

Rocky Creek Nature Center—a 257-acre recreational area located in the northern portion of the county
- Two ponds
- A pine ridge
- A deciduous forest

Recreation centers on City Housing Authority property. These three sites, being only one-half acre in size, have very little property for open space. Each area includes playground equipment, basketball courts, and a small activities building.

In addition, two community centers have recently opened: one located in the eastern side of the City, the other north of the central business district (adjacent to the Johnson House Recreation Center). A variety of recreational services and activities are available at these facilities.

The Parks and Recreation Department also has use of several school sites, but this access could be restricted at any time. A review of the facilities available around the public schools follows:

Type of School	Facilities
Elementary	185 acres of 12 school sites. The size varies from 5 to 60 acres.
Middle	100 acres, divided almost equally, at 4 school sites. Each has its own gym and two multipurpose fields.
High	80 acres at 2 school sites. The site inside the City has 50 acres. The county-located school has 30 acres. There are separate football fields, baseball fields, and gyms.

In addition to these public facilities, there are facilities at the university and at nongovernmental operations such as the YMCA, YWCO, and Boy's Club.

The Parks and Recreation Department has the following vehicles:

Manufacturer (number)	Age (years)	Type
Dodge	6	Van
Dodge (2)	5	Van
Dodge	9	Van
Dodge	8	Pickup truck, ³/₄-ton
Dodge	7	Bus (carpenter body)
Dodge (2)	3	Pickup truck, ³/₄-ton
Dodge	3	Flatbed truck
Ford (2)	3	Economy pickup
Dodge (2)	2	Pickup truck, ³/₄-ton
Wenger	6	Snowmobile
Homemade (3)	2	Trailer
Ford	2	Sedan
Ford	2	Station wagon
Dodge	11	Pickup truck, ³/₄-ton
Dodge	1	Station wagon
Ford	1	Crew cab truck

Activity Indicators	FY V	FY V % Achieved	FY VI Estimate
Sports teams offered for competition	20	90%	25
Junior teams organized	102		110
Senior teams organized	80		86
Average per class learn-to-swim participation	10	100%	10
Recreation center participation	23,622		24,000
Plantings in parks	5,800	35%	15,000

Operating needs: Ten additional members for grounds maintenance; 12 additional summer recreation program staff members; repair of picnic areas in all parks ($20,000); additional arts and crafts teachers for senior citizens program.

Capital budget needs: Additional irrigation equipment ($35,000); replacement of all vehicles over six years; 12 additional tennis courts at Monument Park.

EXPENDITURE DATA

Parks and Recreation Department

Object of Expenditure	Year I Budgeted	Year II Budgeted	Year III Budgeted	Year IV Budgeted	Year V Budgeted
Salaries	$336,746	$456,042	$913,824	$1,004,680	$1,068,628
Office supplies	1,600	2,800	3,900	6,000	4,600
Utilities	0	0	0	155,300	145,300
Heat and power	26,000	48,980	150,670	0	0
Telephone	0	6,490	9,116	0	0
Gas and oil	10,000	10,000	19,000	0	0
Equipment repairs	0	6,000	3,774	7,000	12,000
Janitorial supplies	7,600	8,000	12,000	17,000	21,000
Laboratory supplies	0	0	0	0	0
Tools and supplies	19,000	20,000	26,520	5,000	5,000
Paint	0	0	0	0	0
Joint materials	0	0	0	0	0
Bldg. furnishings and bedding	0	0	0	0	0
Groceries	5,000	2,000	0	0	0
Medical	0	0	0	0	0
Capital improvements	22,000	309,236	337,318	94,982	5,200
Pool salaries	32,328	32,328	140,330	0	0
Communication	0	0	0	14,628	14,628
Repairs to equipment	3,600	0	0	0	0
Printing	0	0	0	3,500	2,000
Travel and conference	1,800	2,932	4,384	3,090	3,090
Freight and express	0	0	0	250	250
Pool maintenance	0	0	0	0	0
Professional services	0	0	0	2,200	2,200
Real property repairs	24,000	29,000	46,800	0	0
Dues and subscriptions	420	932	932	900	700
Equipment purchase	0	0	0	0	0
Real property maintenance	0	0	0	24,500	31,000
Training	0	0	0	1,490	800
Telephone and telegraph	5,000	0	0	0	0
Truck and car repairs	12,000	12,000	3,572	0	0
Tires, tubes, and batteries	2,800	3,000	564	0	0
Legal	2,000	0	0	0	0
Special contracts	1,200	1,200	1,200	0	0
Education and training	0	0	0	0	0
Supplies	26,000	0	0	0	0
Concession supplies	6,000	0	0	0	0
Recreational supplies	0	43,628	63,380	58,800	67,000
Concessions	0	1,500	0	0	0
Pool supplies and improvements	0	9,000	18,000	27,000	16,000
Zoo	0	7,588	7,588	6,600	6,600
Fuel and lubricants	0	0	0	21,000	17,400
Aggregate	0	0	0	41,220	34,000
Pools	10,000	0	0	0	0
TOTAL	$555,094	$1,012,656	$1,762,872	$1,495,140	$1,457,396

Parks and Recreation Department

Object of Expenditure	Year I Spent	Year II Spent	Year III Spent	Year IV Spent	Year V Spent
Salaries	$306,562	$434,194	$ 774,780	$ 989,450	$1,122,172
Office supplies	3,804	2,828	4,168	4,858	6,970
Utilities	0	0	0	137,834	155,610
Heat and power	32,056	47,036	109,008	0	0
Telephone	0	6,026	12,328	0	0
Gas and oil	5,854	11,898	18,340	0	0
Equipment repairs	7,456	5,986	9,424	0	16,750
Janitorial supplies	6,078	9,036	13,042	26,644	27,402
Laboratory supplies	0	0	0	0	0
Tools and supplies	29,962	20,614	27,506	4,622	5,170
Paint	0	0	0	0	0
Joint materials	0	0	0	0	0
Bldg. furnishings and bedding	0	0	0	0	0
Groceries	5,672	1,610	0	0	0
Medical	200	0	0	0	0
Capital improvements	8,984	93,042	349,584	89,028	61,238
Pool salaries	31,860	39,954	73,440	0	0
Communication	0	0	0	15,106	18,582
Repairs to equipment	0	0	0	15,740	0
Printing	0	0	0	1,498	5,078
Travel and conference	1,558	3,234	2,572	2,220	9,264
Freight and express	0	0	0	102	98
Pool maintenance	7,136	0	0	0	0
Professional services	0	0	0	1,482	1,768
Real property repairs	24,880	32,802	41,562	0	0
Dues and subscriptions	716	838	944	760	602
Equipment purchase	0	0	0	0	0
Real property maintenance	0	0	0	32,546	42,610
Training	0	0	0	434	670
Telephone and telegraph	5,184	0	0	0	0
Truck and car repairs	12,948	13,842	3,572	0	0
Tires, tubes, and batteries	3,350	3,106	564	0	0
Legal	1,500	0	0	0	0
Special contracts	1,200	1,200	1,200	0	0
Education and training	152	0	0	0	0
Supplies	34,630	0	0	0	0
Concession supplies	580	0	0	0	0
Recreational supplies	0	49,336	65,194	68,466	68,896
Concessions	0	186	0	0	0
Pool supplies and improvements	0	22,580	15,478	16,678	19,986
Zoo	0	5,802	5,704	8,444	8,374
Fuel and lubricants	0	0	0	17,908	19,868
Aggregate	0	0	0	38,512	35,732
Pools	7,406	0	0	0	0
TOTAL	$539,728	$805,150	$1,528,410	$1,472,332	$1,626,840

Cardinal Park						
Object of Expenditure	Year I Budgeted	Spent	Year II Budgeted	Spent	Year III Budgeted	Spent
Special contracts	$0	$242	$3,000	$3,000	$0	$0
Advertising	0	472	0	0	0	0
Capital improvements	0	0	397,000	397,000	0	236,122
TOTAL	$0	$714	$400,000	$400,000	$0	$236,122

ACCOUNT TITLE: Personnel Department

The Personnel Department performs six functions:

1. Recruitment of personnel
2. Administration of the employee safety program
3. Personnel record keeping
4. Job classification and wage comparison studies
5. Enforcement of mandated (federal) legislation
6. Provision of information to employees

Recruitment involves advertising vacant positions, interviewing prospective employees, and testing job applicants.

The safety program requires periodic training and the employment of a risk management specialist who evaluates City work processes that have an impact on employee health. Personnel records include information on individual wages and salaries, accumulated vacation and sick leave, pensions, and employee evaluation. The City now provides the following benefits for each employee:

Vacation
Two weeks per year with an additional day per year of employment above 20 years, not accumulated over a period greater than five years.

Sick leave
Seven days per year, not accumulated over a period greater than a year.

Holiday pay
Eight paid holidays per year, for which the individual is paid double time for holidays worked ($2^1/_2$ times if overtime).

Pension plan
The employee pays 5 percent of salary and the City 10 percent of total salaries per year (including basic salaries and overtime). The plan is a defined contribution plan vested after 20 years of employment with the City.

Group health insurance
The employee is responsible for 75 percent of the insurance premium and the City 25 percent; the insurance plan covers only the employee.

Enforcing mandated legislation refers primarily to the City's affirmative action programs and disability (federal mandates regarding people with disabilities) programs.

The personnel board, consisting of five citizens, appointed by the mayor and City council and confirmed by the county grand jury, reviews proposed changes in the City's merit system prior to their being submitted to the mayor and City council. The mayor and City council may either accept or reject the proposals, but they may not amend them. Each board member is paid $50 per meeting and has a maximum salary of $1,000 per year.

The department received hiring authority during October of FY V to implement several community development programs.

The City has pursued a policy of hiring temporary workers, at minimum wage levels, in many departments to reduce health and pension costs. Moreover, the personnel director has advised the mayor and council of the rapidly rising overtime costs (paid in accordance with state wage and hour laws) in most, if not all, departments. Specifically, the director has explained the need for personnel procedures regarding recruitment of temporary workers and the grant of overtime pay. No policy now exists in either area.

Activity Indicators	FY V	FY V % Achieved	FY VI Estimate
Number of job applications evaluated	122	100%	275
Number of individuals tested	85	90%	235
Number of individuals trained for five hours or more	325	100%	440
Number of board meetings	5	100%	10

Operating needs: One personnel information system specialist.

Capital budget needs: Program for management information system satisfactory for both job and equal employment opportunity goals (software, $5,000); complete analysis of selection and promotion system to prevent unintentional, equal employment opportunity violations (consultant, $20,000).

EXPENDITURE DATA

Personnel Department

Object of Expenditure	Year I Budgeted	Year II Budgeted	Year III Budgeted	Year IV Budgeted	Year V Budgeted
Salaries	$28,000	$ 81,900	$ 85,306	$112,818	$126,662
Personnel board	0	0	10,000	0	0
Professional services	0	0	0	0	0
Office supplies	2,600	6,000	8,000	6,000	2,640
Postage	400	0	0	0	0
Printing and duplication	1,000	2,400	8,400	4,400	7,440
Telephone/Communications	1,500	3,200	2,400	3,000	3,600
Advertising	1,200	1,200	1,000	400	2,080
Travel	2,000	1,000	600	600	440
Equipment repairs	400	400	400	500	380
Education and training	2,590	2,468	2,000	0	500
Dues and subscriptions	400	300	300	200	880
Rent	0	1,980	0	0	0
Capital improvements	5,200	5,752	0	0	0
TOTAL	$45,290	$106,600	$118,406	$127,918	$144,622

Personnel Department

Object of Expenditure	Year I Spent	Year II Spent	Year III Spent	Year IV Spent	Year V Spent
Salaries	$34,708	$62,560	$71,112	$113,226	$124,648
Personnel board	0	0	10,000	0	0
Professional services	0	0	0	0	658
Office supplies	4,900	9,622	4,044	2,700	2,996
Postage	0	0	0	0	0
Printing and duplication	800	1,848	2,672	7,030	6,988
Telephone/Communications	1,396	2,206	2,632	3,692	3,792
Advertising	370	614	356	1,236	1,712
Travel	190	68	1,504	764	784
Equipment repairs	0	216	760	298	202
Education and training	46	1,062	826	0	2,758
Dues and subscriptions	0	150	0	452	1,766
Rent	0	1,320	0	0	0
Capital improvements	24	2,486	0	0	0
TOTAL	$42,434	$82,152	$93,906	$129,398	$146,304

ACCOUNT TITLE: Planning Commission

The duties of this department include all planning functions vital to the operations of the City and county: e.g., revision of the comprehensive plan, administration and supervision of plan implementation, stimulation of planning as a process in the administrative departments, and the coordination of planning between the City and county governments.

The staff also works with the zoning commission on agenda material. The functions of the department are defined by state enabling legislation, the City and county governments, and by the planning commission. This joint department was established 10 years ago when state legislation made it possible for cities, counties, and regions to have planning agencies.

A four-year-old compact car is assigned to the department.

The department has recently been criticized for the perceived lack of effort in attracting federal grants.

Activity Indicators	FY V	FY V % Achieved	FY VI Estimate
Number of comprehensive citywide planning elements maintained	8	100%	8
Number of sector and district plans analyzed	3	80%	5
Number of subdivision plats and zoning cases reviewed	203	N/A	250
Number of board of adjustment cases reviewed	22	N/A	22
Number of urban design concept studies prepared	5	100%	5
Number of projects monitored for urban design	25	85%	30
Number of updates to computerized database	6	60%	10
Number of customers provided data and planning information	153	N/A	200

Operating needs: Additional travel funds; study to determine method and cost of converting base maps from paper to image (digitizing form) appropriate to a geographical information system.

Capital budget needs: One copier for subdivision plans and other requirements of customers ($52,000) (this blueprint-like copier will pay for itself out of expected customer sales); a complete geographical information systems hardware/software system ($200,000).

EXPENDITURE DATA

Planning Commission

Object of Expenditure	Year I Budgeted	Year II Budgeted	Year III Budgeted	Year IV Budgeted	Year V Budgeted
Salaries	$132,450	$140,210	$161,376	$171,404	$173,994
Office supplies	4,000	4,240	5,088	6,270	4,516
Heat and power	0	0	0	0	0
Telephone	1,000	1,400	1,680	0	0
Gas and oil	0	0	350	0	0
Equipment repairs	800	800	676	760	760
Janitorial supplies	0	0	0	0	0
Laboratory supplies	0	0	0	0	0
Tools and supplies	0	0	0	0	0
Paint	0	0	0	0	0
Joint materials	0	0	0	0	0
Building materials and bedding	0	0	0	0	0
Groceries	0	0	0	0	0
Medical	0	0	0	0	0
Capital improvements	8,650	360	108	200	200
Insurance	0	0	720	0	0
Miscellaneous	600	600	600	0	0
Utilities	0	0	0	0	0
Communications	0	0	0	3,734	4,368
Printing, copying, and publishing	3,000	2,000	4,500	5,900	5,160
Travel	0	0	0	1,668	1,866
Freight and express	0	0	0	0	0
Professional services	0	0	0	758	758
Real property repairs	0	0	0	0	0
Dues and subscriptions	824	824	924	2,416	2,384
Equipment rental	4,850	5,090	5,462	4,680	5,410
Training	2,200	2,200	2,464	890	1,300
Advertising	250	0	0	0	0
Postage	902	902	1,380	0	0
Community planning	0	0	6,000	0	0
Fire equipment	0	0	0	0	0
Rent	14,400	14,400	19,552	20,352	20,352
TOTAL	$173,926	$173,026	$210,880	$219,032	$221,068

Planning Commission

Object of Expenditure	Year I Spent	Year II Spent	Year III Spent	Year IV Spent	Year V Spent
Salaries	$121,698	$146,086	$171,404	$163,172	$176,002
Office supplies	5,182	6,644	6,270	6,600	4,710
Heat and power	0	0	0	0	0
Telephone	1,674	1,558	0	0	0
Gas and oil	56	320	0	0	0
Equipment repairs	1,290	716	760	180	190
Janitorial supplies	0	0	0	0	0
Laboratory supplies	0	0	0	0	0
Tools and supplies	0	0	0	0	0
Paint	0	0	0	0	0
Joint materials	0	0	0	0	0
Building materials and bedding	0	0	0	0	0
Groceries	0	0	0	0	0
Medical	0	0	0	0	0
Capital improvements	7,790	22	200	26	200
Insurance	0	0	0	0	0
Miscellaneous	476	0	670	0	0
Utilities	0	0	0	0	0
Communications	0	0	3,734	3,884	4,322
Printing, copying, and publishing	1,234	3,308	5,900	4,644	5,202
Travel	276	0	1,668	1,628	2,418
Freight and express	0	0	0	0	0
Professional services	0	0	758	0	0
Real property repairs	0	0	0	0	0
Dues and subscriptions	912	974	2,416	2,486	2,406
Equipment rental	4,586	5,392	4,680	4,680	5,378
Training	1,878	1,772	890	810	904
Advertising	0	0	0	0	0
Postage	1,134	1,288	0	0	0
Community planning	32	0	0	0	0
Fire equipment	118	0	0	0	0
Rent	5,184	7,128	20,352	18,656	20,352
TOTAL	$153,520	$175,208	$219,702	$206,766	$222,084

ACCOUNT TITLE: Police Department

The services of this department center on enforcing laws, keeping the peace, and creating better community relations. They are accomplished through enforcing City ordinances and state penal laws and providing community relations programs, traffic control, and general public services. The latter include employment of crosswalk guards for school-bound children and use of police officers for security during local sports events. Police officers also serve summonses, subpoenas, and orders. Officers also back up personnel in the stockade as stockade personnel scheduling requires. Ordinarily, the services of this department are available only to City residents, but at special times they are available to other areas as part of mutual assistance and cooperation with other law enforcement agencies.

A chief of police, appointed by the mayor and serving at the mayor's pleasure, serves as the head of the Police Department. The incumbent chief of police, who took office at the start of FY IV, reorganized the department. There are now three divisions: uniformed operations, criminal investigation, and administrative services. In addition, there are five units that report to the chief of police in a staff capacity. The organizational arrangement of the police department is presented on the next page. The head of each of the three divisions is a division commander with a rank of major. Two related accounts are "Stockade" and "Police Planner."

In FY II, the police moved from City Hall to a renovated structure next door.

Police Department Vehicles

Manufacturer (number)	Age (years)	Type of Vehicle
Plymouth	1	4-door large sedan
Plymouth	2	4-door medium-size sedan
Plymouth	4	4-door medium-size sedan
Mercury	3	4-door medium-size sedan
Dodge	3	Van
Dodge	6	Station wagon
Dodge	6	Van
Pontiac	6	2-door large sedan
Plymouth	2	Station wagon
Dodge	2	Van
Plymouth (15)	2	4-door medium-size sedan
Plymouth (7)	1	4-door medium-size sedan
Harley-Davidson (2)	1	2-wheel motorcycle
Harley-Davidson (2)	3	2-wheel motorcycle
Harley-Davidson (4)	5	2-wheel motorcycle
Harley-Davidson	4	2-wheel motorcycle

ORGANIZATION OF POLICE DEPARTMENT

COMMAND SECTION

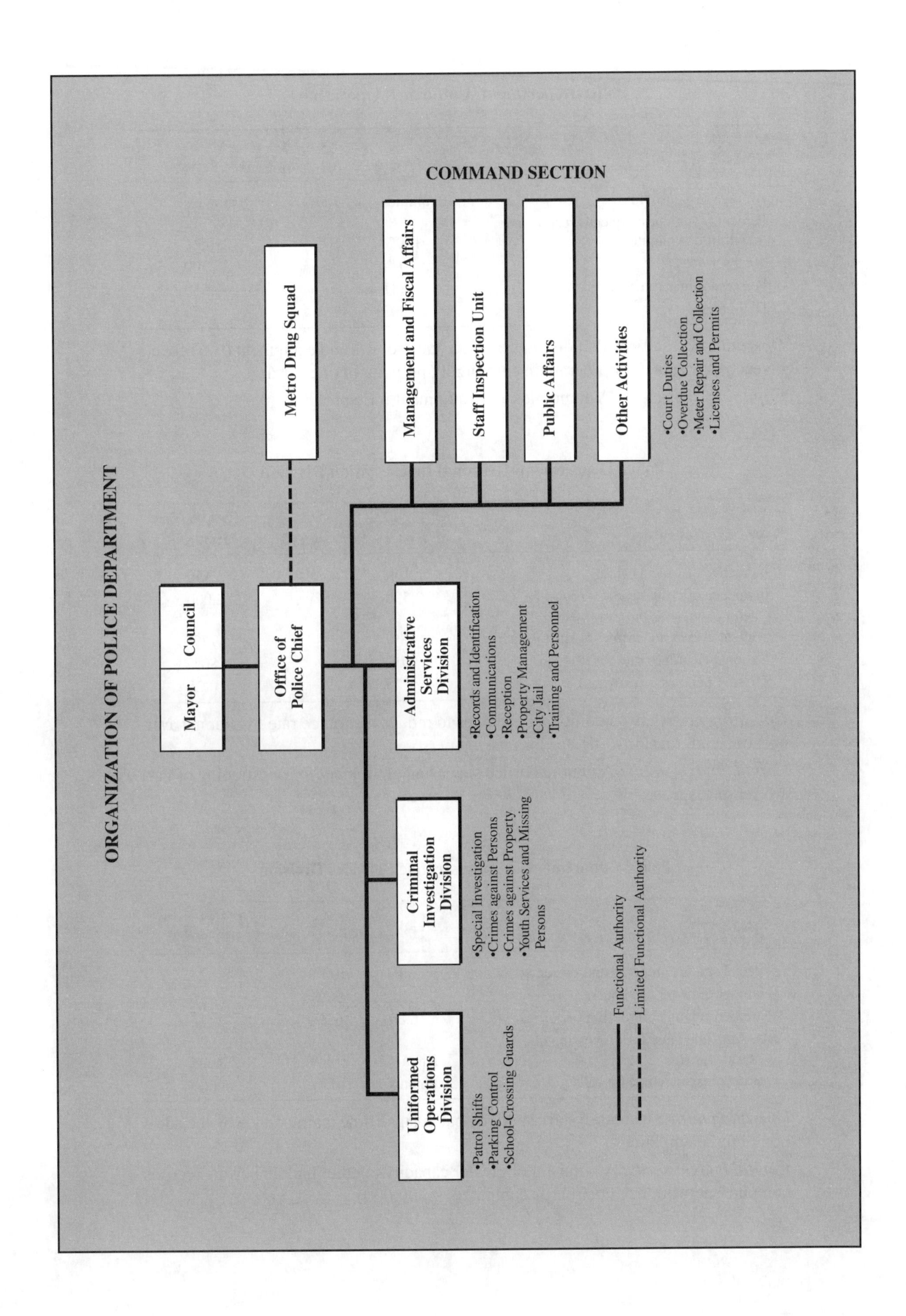

- Mayor
- Council
- Office of Police Chief
- Metro Drug Squad
- Management and Fiscal Affairs
- Staff Inspection Unit
- Public Affairs
- Other Activities
  - Court Duties
  - Overdue Collection
  - Meter Repair and Collection
  - Licenses and Permits

Uniformed Operations Division
- Patrol Shifts
- Parking Control
- School-Crossing Guards

Criminal Investigation Division
- Special Investigation
- Crimes against Persons
- Crimes against Property
- Youth Services and Missing Persons

Administrative Services Division
- Records and Identification
- Communications
- Reception
- Property Management
- City Jail
- Training and Personnel

――― Functional Authority
- - - Limited Functional Authority

Police Department–Uniformed Operations

Activity Indicators	FY V	FY V % Achieved	FY VI Estimate
Average response time	10 minutes	100%	8 minutes
Percent of high priority calls responded to within five minutes	100%	100%	100%
Total service calls	36,044		37,500
Personal injury traffic accidents	831		950
DUI arrests	203		250

Operating needs: Two additional patrols with automobiles and equipment (two officers on each) to begin pilot program in community policing in one ward.

Capital budget needs: Automobiles and equipment for patrols.

Police Department–Criminal Investigation Division

Activity Indicators	FY V	FY V % Achieved	FY VI Estimate
Incidence of violent crimes	169		150
Incidence of crimes against property	2,598		2,000
Clearance rate for Part 1 offenses (violent crimes and crimes against property)	88%		77%
National clearance rate for Part 1 offenses	77%		80%
Missing persons investigated	25		25

Operating needs: Two additional detectives to reduce clearance rate to national average; one additional investigator for missing persons.

Capital budget needs: Additional office space and equipment for questioning of Part 1 offense suspects.

Police Department–Administrative Services Division

Activity Indicators	FY V	FY V % Achieved	FY VI Estimate
Special studies prepared and presented	10	100%	15
Number of in-service courses	6	90%	10
Number of hours of training per officer	6.89	65%	15
Average time lapse for processing of offense reports	2 hours	100%	2 hours
Average dispatch time on calls	2.5 minutes	100%	2 minutes

Operating needs: Increased staffing for dispatch lapse time maintenance by the addition of three employees.

Capital budget needs: Attainment of greater capacity to enter national crime records computer network from patrol car computers ($300,000).

Police Department–Command Section

Activity Indicators	FY V	FY V % Achieved	FY VI Estimate
Number of chargeable accidents involving department vehicles	6	N/A	5
Divisions exceeding annual appropriations	0	100%	0
Number of Standard Operating Procedure changes reviewed	30	90%	35
Number of complaints against police personnel	4	N/A	0
Number of public affairs appearances at local meetings	154	83%	200

Operating needs: Management/fiscal analyst.

Capital budget needs: Evaluation program for community policing, including computer systems for support, with training by outside consultant ($100,000).

In addition to new patrol cars, the department needs the following items within the next three years:

Item	Cost
Mobile radios/telephones recording system	$38,500
Office phone system	45,000
Mobile evidence collection van	60,000
Videotape unit	15,000
Computer terminals in patrol cars and supporting office software/hardware	3,000 per vehicle
Transmitter and signal booster	5,500

EXPENDITURE DATA

Police Department

Object of Expenditure	Year I Budgeted	Year II Budgeted	Year III Budgeted	Year IV Budgeted	Year V Budgeted
Salaries	$1,423,360	$1,598,868	$1,713,562	$2,087,416	$2,221,308
Other labor	0	0	0	0	0
Groceries	0	0	0	0	0
Office supplies	10,000	10,000	14,000	14,000	20,000
Heat and power	600	600	16,000	0	0
Utilities	0	0	0	26,000	23,200
Communications	0	0	0	15,500	23,000
Telephone and telegraph	3,600	3,600	12,000	0	0
Gas and oil	25,000	25,000	50,000	0	0
Car repairs	28,000	28,000	0	0	0
Motorcycle repairs	10,000	10,000	0	0	0
Equipment repairs	7,000	7,000	28,120	43,400	24,000
Tires, tubes, batteries	8,000	10,000	0	0	0
Claims	600	600	400	0	0
Printing	0	0	0	0	10,000
Advertising	100	100	8,000	9,000	200
Legal	100	100	0	0	0
Travel expense	800	800	2,000	5,400	7,200
Freight and express	0	0	0	0	0
Postage	0	0	0	0	0
Janitorial supplies	200	200	600	600	600
Fuel and lubricants	0	0	0	72,000	110,000
Alkalizer and intoximeter	0	0	1,000	1,000	1,000
Tools and supplies	3,200	3,200	4,000	0	0
Professional services	0	0	0	1,500	4,000
Special contracts	0	0	0	0	0
Consulting fee	0	0	1,300	0	0
Investigation fee	0	0	0	1,400	1,900
Real property repairs	0	0	400	14,400	7,000
Riot agents	0	0	0	2,000	3,000
Ammunition	0	0	0	5,000	4,000
Protective equipment	0	0	0	9,000	9,000
Clothing, badges, guns	0	30,816	58,000	0	0
Badges, guns	3,714	0	0	0	0
Uniform allowance	25,300	0	0	60,000	60,000
Medical	1,600	1,600	1,000	0	0
Training	0	0	0	3,000	24,000
Education and training	8,000	8,000	10,000	0	0
Recreation supplies	0	0	0	0	0
Dues and subscriptions	100	100	150	600	800
Car allowance	2,400	2,400	2,400	0	0
Burglary car rental	0	0	5,600	0	0
Equipment leasing	0	0	0	7,158	5,672
Photocopier rental	0	0	3,240	4,360	11,000
Capital improvements	61,832	67,294	91,776	225,554	125,832
TOTAL	$1,623,506	$1,808,278	$2,023,548	$2,608,288	$2,696,712

Police Department

Object of Expenditure	Year I Spent	Year II Spent	Year III Spent	Year IV Spent	Year V Spent
Salaries	$1,404,230	$1,522,844	$1,829,968	$2,007,280	$2,373,734
Other labor	12	0	0	0	0
Groceries	0	0	0	10	20
Office supplies	11,204	18,130	15,476	22,684	20,592
Heat and power	0	9,276	33,476	0	0
Utilities	0	0	0	25,324	28,764
Communications	0	0	0	26,312	32,780
Telephone and telegraph	5,360	11,410	16,096	0	0
Gas and oil	15,968	52,700	99,798	0	0
Car repairs	38,964	45,896	0	0	0
Motorcycle repairs	8,738	13,218	0	0	0
Equipment repairs	8,658	13,584	38,370	26,158	26,050
Tires, tubes, batteries	16,212	12,338	0	0	0
Claims	130	300	100	0	0
Printing	0	0	0	14,506	12,888
Advertising	0	58	9,360	36	196
Legal	0	10	0	0	0
Travel expense	892	678	80	6,600	7,544
Freight and express	46	0	0	0	0
Postage	34	0	0	0	0
Janitorial supplies	322	1,544	1,222	580	796
Fuel and lubricants	0	0	0	115,266	106,114
Alkalizer and intoximeter	0	0	426	1,000	1,554
Tools and supplies	1,108	6,952	6,996	0	0
Professional services	0	0	0	5,908	3,342
Special contracts	0	380	0	0	0
Consulting fee	0	0	0	0	0
Investigation fee	0	0	0	1,578	1,762
Real property repairs	0	736	624	6,818	6,826
Riot agents	0	0	0	3,094	2,814
Ammunition	0	0	0	4,900	3,898
Protective equipment	0	0	0	8,858	8,674
Clothing, badges, guns	0	31,970	59,268	0	0
Badges, guns	0	0	0	0	0
Uniform allowance	27,046	0	0	60,662	72,258
Medical	890	660	810	0	0
Training	0	0	0	5,816	25,258
Education and training	15,102	15,296	8,708	0	0
Recreation supplies	0	1,296	0	0	0
Dues and subscriptions	80	116	304	796	900
Car allowance	2,200	2,400	4,000	0	0
Burglary car rental	0	0	4,422	0	0
Equipment leasing	0	0	0	7,158	4,262
Photocopier rental	0	0	4,884	9,470	9,660
Capital improvements	128,206	110,156	90,308	221,502	119,036
TOTAL	$1,685,402	$1,871,948	$2,224,696	$2,582,316	$2,869,722

Police Community Relations (Federal Funds)		
Object of Expenditure	**Year I Budgeted**	**Spent**
Salaries	$159,560	$38,136
Office supplies	0	44
Heat and power	0	184
Gas and oil	0	8
Car repairs	0	42
Tires, tubes, and batteries	0	304
Paint	0	14
Furnishings and bedding	0	28
Capital improvements	0	522
TOTAL	$159,560	$39,282

ACCOUNT TITLE: Police Planner

It was the responsibility of the police planner to develop federal and state funding requests dealing with law enforcement and to keep the records and make the reports required by the grants. Formerly, the budget of the police planner was separated from the regular police department budget to facilitate the administration of federal and state grants-in-aid. It was merged into the regular police department budget at the beginning of FY IV. Thus, to get a true understanding of police department finances in earlier years, the expenditures for the office of the police planner must be added to those of the regular police department.

Each of the grants under the police planner's budget is concerned with the utilization of law enforcement personnel and equipment and uses the same distribution of money for salaries (50%), for capital items (35%), and for operating expenses (15%).

EXPENDITURE DATA

Police Planner Budget

Object of Expenditure	Year I Budgeted	Spent	Year II Budgeted	Spent	Year III Budgeted	Spent
Salaries	$25,320	$4,740	$0	$0	$0	$0
Office supplies	220	0	0	0	0	0
Telephone and telegraph	120	360	0	0	0	0
Rent	1,200	600	0	0	0	0
Capital improvements	1,000	24	0	0	0	0
Training grant	0	0	0	994	0	0
Management analysis	0	0	70,800	2,656	0	0
Reduction of burglary and larceny	0	0	111,840	26,908	111,840	30,236
Police management	0	0	22,560	10,166	12,554	28,182
Continuation of existing community relations	0	0	37,440	22,686	25,094	51,656
Police planning unit	0	0	27,660	7,642	0	0
Juvenile law investigators	0	0	16,308	3,836	0	0
Completion and improvement of existing records system	0	0	0	3,888	0	592
Improved manual records-keeping system	0	1,544	33,896	7,210	0	0
Computer terminals	0	0	0	632	2,436	1,758
Statewide strategic intelligence units	0	0	24,000	10,738	24,000	6,078
Youth service bureau	0	0	0	25,178	178,400	20,730
Youth service bureau #2	0	0	0	33,092	0	0
Reduction of property crimes	0	0	71,000	12,012	61,152	3,580
Metropolitan enforcement group	0	0	0	0	29,276	460
Continuation of computer terminals	0	0	0	0	4,872	2,200
TOTAL	$27,860	$7,268	$415,504	$167,638	$449,624	$145,472

ACCOUNT TITLE: Public Works

The Public Works Department is the largest and most complex of all departments in the City government. The operations of this department, which are essential to the functioning of the community, cover a wide variety of duties. These duties include the supervision of streets (their planning, construction, and maintenance); the planning, construction, and maintenance of sewer lines; the planning, installation, and maintenance of streetlights; the planning, construction, and maintenance of water lines; and the operation of City Hall, including the upkeep of the grounds.

The City engineer, as director of the Public Works Department, is appointed on a yearly basis by the mayor and council. He or she serves as director of waterworks and appoints the superintendent of the street department and the superintendent of the water and sewer distribution system. The offices of the City engineer, an administrative assistant, and another staff member are located in City Hall. A retired City engineer has a consulting contract with the department.

An assistant City engineer, appointed by the mayor to help the City engineer, is responsible for appointing superintendents of the water filter and the water pollution control activities. The assistant City engineer maintains an office at one of the water pollution control plants.

The City does not have a central traffic engineering department; instead, responsibilities are divided among the director of permits and inspections, the City engineer, and the county traffic engineer. Signal installation and maintenance are administered by the director of permits and inspections. Sign construction, installation, and pavement marking are directed by the City engineer. Upon the request of the City council and at no direct cost to the City, the county traffic engineer analyzes and makes recommendations about problem intersections and handles other traffic research questions. The traffic engineer has no supervisory duties over City personnel.

The City engineer has a four-year-old compact car available for official use; the assistant City engineer has the use of a five-year-old compact car.

Recently, the department has been trying to obtain a blueprint machine ($8,500) and a mid-size automobile.

Activity Indicators	FY V	FY V % Achieved	FY VI Estimate
Problem areas studied	2	100%	5

Operating needs: One additional clerk-typist I.

Capital budget needs: One personal computer ($3,200); blueprint machine ($8,500); and an automobile ($24,000).

EXPENDITURE DATA

Public Works

Object of Expenditure	Year I Budgeted	Year II Budgeted	Year III Budgeted	Year IV Budgeted	Year V Budgeted
Salaries	$111,068	$102,180	$105,886	$133,000	$150,566
Office supplies	400	400	1,600	1,700	2,000
Telephone and telegraph	0	0	1,800	0	0
Tools and supplies	0	0	0	0	0
Consulting engineering services	14,400	14,400	14,400	0	0
Car allowance	0	0	2,400	0	0
Professional services	0	0	0	14,400	14,400
Travel	0	0	0	7,900	4,800
Dues and subscriptions	0	0	0	450	400
Communications	0	0	0	1,600	3,000
Freight and express	0	0	0	200	100
Printing	0	0	0	600	400
Advertising	0	0	0	0	0
Repairs to equipment	0	0	0	400	400
Capital improvements	0	0	0	2,800	0
Training	0	0	0	0	0
TOTAL	$125,868	$116,980	$126,086	$163,050	$176,066

Public Works

Object of Expenditure	Year I Spent	Year II Spent	Year III Spent	Year IV Spent	Year V Spent
Salaries	$80,206	$79,074	$113,632	$135,274	$151,206
Office supplies	400	1,064	1,894	2,148	1,766
Telephone and telegraph	174	0	2,030	0	0
Tools and supplies	14	0	0	0	0
Consulting engineering services	18,076	14,400	14,400	0	0
Car allowance	0	0	3,400	0	0
Professional services	0	0	0	14,400	10,800
Travel	0	0	0	5,102	4,870
Dues and subscriptions	0	0	0	152	0
Communications	0	0	0	2,676	3,278
Freight and express	0	0	0	6	0
Printing	0	0	0	194	716
Advertising	0	0	0	104	0
Repairs to equipment	0	0	0	108	424
Capital improvements	0	0	0	1,944	0
Training	0	0	0	0	1,066
TOTAL	$98,870	$94,538	$135,356	$162,108	$174,126

ACCOUNT TITLE: Sanitation–Garbage Collection

The activities of this department include collecting, hauling, and disposing of all refuse (garbage) at the landfill operation. The City pays the county $28 per ton for use of the landfill.

The City provides "behind-the-home" garbage collection service. The collection service is twice weekly to residences, three times per week to businesses, and daily to businesses in the central business district (CBD). One route covers the CBD and a few nearby areas; nine routes cover the remaining pickups. Residential collection is based upon a crew of workers assigned to a rear-loading garbage truck. One-person scooters are used in some residential sections to allow satellite collection. In the industrial and heavily commercial sections of the City, front-loading equipment is utilized.

The old incinerator is now used as a transfer loading facility. The garbage trucks dump their individual loads into a large garbage trailer.

The university operates its own garbage collection service and pays the City for letting university garbage trucks deposit garbage from the university at the landfill. Each week, approximately 90 tons are collected at the university. (This is about 22 percent of the total weekly amount deposited by the City at the landfill.) Also, approximately 10 additional tons of garbage are collected by the university after home football games (averaging five per year).

A list of the department's current equipment follows:

Manufacturer (number)	Age (years)	Type of Vehicle
White	4	Front loader
White	2	Front loader
Dodge	2	Front loader
Kenworth	3	Front loader
Dodge	2	Front loader
Dodge	2	Front loader
Dodge	6	Front loader
Diamond T	13	Tractor
Dodge	10	Pickup
Dodge	6	Pickup
Dodge	5	Pickup
Cushman (7)	3	Scooter
Cushman	7	Scooter
Plymouth	3	Sedan
Heil (2)	4	Garbage trailer
Dodge	3	Rear loader
Dodge	1	Rear loader
Dodge (3)	5	Rear loader
Dodge (4)	3	Rear loader
Dodge	6	Rear loader
Dodge	2	Rear loader

Activity Indicators	FY V	FY V % Achieved	FY VI Estimate
Tons of refuse collected, residential	5,700	N/A	6,100
Tons of refuse collected, CBD	4,900	N/A	5,500
Tons of refuse collected, other	6,500	N/A	7,100
Total pickups	889,620	N/A	1,050,000
Residential customers served as a percentage of all possible residential customers	85%	N/A	95%

The Chamber of Commerce recently recommended that the City conduct a feasibility study on the use of private contractors to collect refuse. In other cities, the chamber noted, cost efficiencies were achieved by contracting for sanitation-garbage collection. The last city administration rejected the need for a study.

Operating needs: Expanded residential service to meet new demand (3 new staff positions); expanded central business district service to meet demand (3 new positions). The new goal is to serve 95 percent of all possible residential customers. The landfill contract with the county calls for a fee increase in FY VI to $30 per ton.

Capital budget needs: In order for service expansion to meet demand, one rear loader ($180,000), one scooter ($9,200), and one front loader ($175,000).

EXPENDITURE DATA

Sanitation–Garbage Collection

Object of Expenditure	Year I Budgeted	Year II Budgeted	Year III Budgeted	Year IV Budgeted	Year V Budgeted
Salaries	$565,928	$ 638,646	$656,578	$ 772,806	$ 828,482
Telephone	1,100	1,000	0	0	0
Gas and oil	40,000	44,000	56,000	0	0
Equipment repairs	130,000	136,000	48,988	0	0
Tires, tubes, batteries	32,000	32,000	5,890	0	0
Claims	4,000	4,400	0	0	0
Travel expense	500	500	0	1,000	600
Freight and express	200	200	4,200	200	200
Janitorial supplies	7,000	7,000	4,000	0	0
Tools and supplies	8,000	10,000	20,000	0	0
Paint	1,000	0	0	0	0
Diesel fuel and oil	5,000	8,000	16,000	0	0
Real property repairs	200	400	1,000	31,000	0
Clothing	800	4,000	4,000	0	0
Medical	100	100	0	0	0
Education and training	400	400	0	500	500
Recreation supplies	300	500	0	0	0
Dues and subscriptions	200	200	0	200	200
Lodal container repairs	3,000	10,000	16,000	0	0
Capital improvements	144,000	325,800	41,400	146,800	151,200
Professional services	0	0	0	5,100	2,000
Communication	0	0	0	800	1,000
Utilities	0	0	0	10,000	8,400
Office supplies	0	0	0	118,000	30,000
Fuel and lubricants	0	0	0	0	104,000
Landfill fees	0	0	0	460,000	600,000
TOTAL	$943,728	$1,223,146	$874,056	$1,546,406	$1,726,582

Sanitation–Garbage Collection

Object of Expenditure	Year I Spent	Year II Spent	Year III Spent	Year IV Spent	Year V Spent
Salaries	$579,106	$ 614,964	$673,352	$ 779,200	$ 849,248
Telephone	1,032	910	0	0	0
Gas and oil	45,200	59,730	57,148	0	0
Equipment repairs	167,034	170,354	48,988	284	0
Tires, tubes, batteries	34,864	24,730	5,890	0	0
Claims	3,650	2,462	0	0	0
Travel expense	12	38	0	290	322
Freight and express	76	92	2,568	16	134
Janitorial supplies	4,264	2,820	3,118	0	0
Tools and supplies	18,322	23,768	34,352	0	0
Paint	0	0	0	0	0
Diesel fuel and oil	8,984	9,050	22,124	0	0
Real property repairs	416	898	0	22,874	0
Clothing	0	0	1,580	0	0
Medical	0	0	0	0	0
Education and training	0	46	0	0	126
Recreation supplies	444	0	0	0	0
Dues and subscriptions	102	44	0	70	70
Lodal container repairs	7,560	37,646	21,018	0	0
Capital improvements	77,998	406,914	39,612	165,898	180,294
Professional services	0	0	0	1,364	1,478
Communication	0	0	0	782	756
Utilities	0	0	0	9,264	8,530
Office supplies	0	0	0	142,168	40,536
Fuel and lubricants	0	0	0	0	114,372
Landfill fees	0	0	0	456,720	590,800
TOTAL	$949,064	$1,354,466	$909,750	$1,578,930	$1,786,666

ACCOUNT TITLE: Sanitation–Incinerator

For 22 years prior to FY III, the City operated an incinerator to dispose of garbage collected by the sanitation department. The Sanitation-Incinerator Office, within the Sanitation Department, was responsible for the operation of the incinerator; it is now merged with the department of sanitation-garbage collection. At the end of FY III, the City discontinued use of the incinerator because of federal and state laws and began using a sanitary landfill operated by the county. That landfill will reach its capacity in FY VII.

However, the City will study the costs and benefits of repairing the incinerator, building a new one, constructing another landfill alone or with the county, or privatizing landfill operations alone or along with garbage collection. The study must be finished with the completion of the budget draft from FY VI.

EXPENDITURE DATA

Sanitation–Incinerator

Object of Expenditure	Year I Budgeted	Spent	Year II Budgeted	Spent	Year III Budgeted	Spent
Salaries	$100,178	$82,770	$34,786	$44,230	$125,782	$47,416
Office supplies	1,100	786	1,100	896	1,100	1,766
Heat and power	8,000	5,600	8,000	4,816	8,000	8,796
Telephone	400	216	0	0	1,000	826
Gas and oil	0	5,332	0	0	0	0
Equipment repairs	6,000	8,520	6,000	3,944	58	58
Tires, tubes, and batteries	0	312	0	0	0	0
Freight and express	0	6	0	0	0	0
Janitorial supplies	1,000	28	1,000	244	1,000	814
Tools and supplies	400	662	900	714	900	788
Diesel fuel	2,600	6,156	6,000	4,102	0	0
Real property repairs	1,000	7,634	2,000	36,254	4,900	6,148
Clothing	300	0	400	0	400	0
Disposal site lease	3,600	0	2,900	0	0	0
Rental and landfill	54,376	65,360	0	0	0	0
Capital improvements	72,376	71,034	171,500	136,466	0	0
Gravel per trench	2,450	0	0	0	0	0
Travel expense	0	0	0	0	1,000	234
Medical	0	0	0	0	100	0
Training	0	0	0	0	500	0
Recreation	0	0	0	0	500	524
Dues and subscriptions	0	0	0	0	200	106
Scraper	0	0	0	0	39,542	0
TOTAL	$253,780	$254,416	$234,586	$231,666	$184,982	$67,476

ACCOUNT TITLE: Sanitation–Street Cleaning

This unit, a branch of the public works department, is responsible for collecting, hauling, and disposing of all limbs and leaves within the City and sweeping all City streets. Leaf and limb service is provided on an irregular basis to those areas where it is needed. The street sweepers follow the leaf and limb collection so they can completely clean the streets after debris has been removed.

Equipment

Manufacturer	Age (years)	Type of Vehicle
Dodge	2	Leaf truck
Dodge	2	Leaf truck
Ford	8	Leaf truck
Dodge	3	Boom truck
Dodge	6	Limb truck
Dodge	6	Limb truck
Dodge	5	Limb truck
Dodge	2	Limb truck
Dodge	4	Limb truck
Dodge	2	Limb truck
Dodge	2	Limb truck
Wayne	4	Street sweeper
Elgin	7	Street sweeper
Dodge	7	Pickup

Activity Indicators	FY V	FY V % Achieved	FY VI Estimate
Gutter miles swept	560	42%	1200
Average number of days per cleaning cycle	120	75%	90

Operating needs: One additional street sweeper crew (two positions).
Capital budget needs: Replacement of Elgin street sweeper ($85,000).

EXPENDITURE DATA

Sanitation-Street Cleaning

Object of Expenditure	Year I Budgeted	Year II Budgeted	Year III Budgeted	Year IV Budgeted	Year V Budgeted
Salaries	$195,174	$197,894	$244,364	$233,154	$193,726
Gas and oil	10,000	10,000	12,000	0	0
Equipment repair	24,000	32,000	2,160	0	0
Tires, tubes, and batteries	7,000	9,000	674	0	0
Claims	1,000	0	0	0	0
Freight and express	100	100	1,100	100	100
Tools and supplies	12,000	6,000	7,000	0	0
Diesel fuel	0	0	0	0	0
Clothing	200	200	1,000	0	0
Capital improvements	86,000	0	170,000	52,000	0
Contracts	0	1,000	0	0	0
Professional services	0	0	0	1,000	100
Office supplies	0	0	0	22,000	25,000
TOTAL	$335,474	$256,194	$438,298	$308,254	$218,926

Sanitation-Street Cleaning

Object of Expenditure	Year I Spent	Year II Spent	Year III Spent	Year IV Spent	Year V Spent
Salaries	$182,970	$180,262	$194,638	$181,172	$223,774
Gas and oil	7,444	17,948	17,612	0	0
Equipment repair	42,808	25,972	2,160	0	0
Tires, tubes, and batteries	13,408	8,450	674	0	0
Claims	500	0	0	0	0
Freight and express	20	0	600	38	24
Tools and supplies	7,066	6,824	11,990	0	0
Diesel fuel	178	0	0	0	0
Clothing	0	0	0	0	0
Capital improvements	70,866	0	151,048	84,410	0
Contracts	0	200	0	0	0
Professional services	0	0	0	100	0
Office supplies	0	0	0	23,746	28,036
TOTAL	$325,260	$239,656	$378,722	$289,466	$251,834

ACCOUNT TITLE: Service Garage

The service garage is responsible for maintaining the more than 200 vehicles owned by the City. The following services are performed on the equipment: electrical diagnostic testing, preventive maintenance, welding, transmission repair, and general maintenance (tuneups, wheel balancing, changing oil, and greasing). The service garage, located on a five-acre site in the north part of the City, is a concrete block structure with approximately 4,000 square feet of work area.

The following pieces of equipment are assigned to the service garage:

Manufacturer	Age (years)	Type of Equipment	Current Estimated Resale Value
Dodge	3	Generator	$2,650
Dodge	6	Generator	970
Dodge	5	100 Power wagon	1,400

The service garage billed departments for the cost of parts, tires, tubes and batteries, and the subcontracted repairs which the department coordinated in FY I and II. In subsequent years—III, IV, and V—the garage assumed all of these costs in its own budget, except for heavy equipment tires, tubes, and batteries (bulldozers and fire engines, for example) and subcontracted repairs. Gas and oil are provided through the service garage gas depot, but each department gets billed for the amount used.

Within three years the following items will be needed:

Portable air compressor	$ 2,500
Pickup truck	14,000
1-ton service truck	19,000

Activity Indicators	FY V	FY V % Achieved	FY VI Estimate
Average percentage of units disabled for 72 hours or longer, daily	12%	50%	5%
Equipment units receiving preventive maintenance	212	98%	220

Operating needs: Increased funding for overtime to reduce disabled vehicle rate by 50 percent.

Capital budget needs: Study to set up internal service fund by which user departments are billed for the costs of services provided by the service garage or contracting out garage services with departments paying directly for them (consultant, $15,000).

EXPENDITURE DATA

Service Garage

Object of Expenditure	Year I Budgeted	Year II Budgeted	Year III Budgeted	Year IV Budgeted	Year V Budgeted
Salaries	$136,980	$132,812	$144,618	$166,412	$164,566
Office supplies	450	0	0	50,000	3,000
Telephone and telegraph	1,000	1,250	2,000	0	1,400
Gas and oil	2,000	6,000	2,400	0	0
Truck and car repairs	400	400	0	0	0
Equipment repairs	0	500	316,882	275,186	326,000
Parts	64,000	80,000	100,000	0	0
Tires, tubes, and batteries	800	800	54,786	0	0
Travel expense	80	500	500	400	400
Janitorial supplies	1,800	1,800	8,000	0	0
Chemicals	2,000	4,000	0	0	0
Supplies	1,250	2,400	0	0	0
Sublet repairs	12,000	12,000	0	0	0
Real property repairs	2,000	2,000	3,000	400	0
Capital improvements	4,200	7,800	1,000	0	60,200
Printing	0	0	0	0	200
Advertising	0	0	0	0	0
Utilities	0	0	0	0	0
Equipment leasing	0	0	0	0	0
TOTAL	$228,960	$252,262	$633,186	$492,398	$555,766

Service Garage

Object of Expenditure	Year I Spent	Year II Spent	Year III Spent	Year IV Spent	Year V Spent
Salaries	$119,218	$119,086	$145,528	$145,972	$157,412
Office supplies	450	0	0	4,304	4,240
Telephone and telegraph	1,298	1,062	1,414	110	1,234
Gas and oil	5,250	3,314	2,720	0	0
Truck and car repairs	240	68	0	0	0
Equipment repairs	640	438	95,944	341,210	401,976
Parts	106,078	137,736	165,152	0	0
Tires, tubes, and batteries	1,288	0	61,220	0	0
Travel expense	454	714	160	52	180
Janitorial supplies	2,068	1,376	6,966	0	0
Chemicals	4,642	4,262	0	0	0
Supplies	2,314	3,554	0	0	0
Sublet repairs	11,250	12,818	0	0	0
Real property repairs	200	1,296	174	52	0
Capital improvements	3,590	7,234	0	600	0
Printing	0	0	0	146	115
Advertising	0	0	0	2,048	0
Utilities	0	0	0	0	126
Equipment leasing	0	0	0	0	398
TOTAL	$258,980	$292,958	$479,278	$494,494	$565,681

ACCOUNT TITLE: Stockade

The Police Department has direct responsibility for the operation of the City jail facility (stockade). It serves as a detention facility for persons (1) unable to make bond who are awaiting disposition of their cases before the magistrate's court and (2) sentenced by the magistrate's court for violation of City ordinances. All violators of state statutes within the City limits are processed by the county sheriff's office and are incarcerated (if necessary) in the county jail.

A detention facility's use is measured in "prisoner days." In FY V, the City jail averaged 4.36 prisoners per day. Of this total, approximately 1.88 were serving a sentence and 2.48 were awaiting disposition. Of the total number of people processed, approximately 36 percent were not detained more than four hours. Monthly or yearly averages do not reflect the daily population; also, the number of prisoners is usually higher on a weekend.

When scheduling demands require it, regular police department uniformed services staff supplement stockade staff as jailers. However, there are problems in such scheduling; in fact, the City faces a lawsuit over the adequacy of staffing coverage in the stockade.

Facility

The stockade is a masonry building with two sections. One section, having 16 bunks, is used primarily for persons awaiting trial or sentencing; the other, having 50 beds, is used for persons serving sentences. The total designed detention capacity is for 65 persons. However, the state-mandated limit is 40 inmates.

The extremely deteriorated condition of the facility, combined with its low use, has prompted discussion about the need to merge the City jail with the much larger county jail, located adjacent to the county courthouse and near the chambers of the magistrate's court. The City and county have been negotiating an arrangement to let City prisoners be housed in the county jail. In return, the City would pay a set amount per prisoner per day.

Following are some of the repairs needed:

Item	Cost
Sandblast, seal, paint	$16,000
New windows	8,000
Fire alarm system	6,000
Fire escape	7,000

Activity Indicators	FY V	FY V % Achieved	FY VI Estimate
Prisoners injured	0	100%	0
Prisoners escaped	0	100%	0

Operating needs: Continued negotiations with county for housing of City prisoners (City's current negotiating positions: $425,000 per year or $250 per prisoner day, whichever is most).

Capital budget needs: Merger of stockade with county jail.

City Prisoners:
"Awaiting Disposition" and "Sentenced"
FY V

Month	Total Entered on Record	Total Prisoners Serving Less Than 4 Hours
January	82	20
February	187	67
March	164	62
April	187	52
May	208	92
June	156	56
July	188	69
August	173	55
September	172	84
October	183	74
November	189	57
December	185	51
TOTAL	2,074	739

City Jail Population
FY V

Month	Total Prisoner Days Served "Awaiting Disposition"	Total Prisoner Days Served "Sentenced"	Total Prisoner Days Served
January	19	9	28
February	51	95	146
March	79	56	135
April	101	76	177
May	87	25	112
June	57	26	83
July	80	62	142
August	104	33	137
September	66	74	140
October	94	37	131
November	75	70	145
December	92	126	218
TOTAL	905	689	1,594
Percent	56.78%	43.22%	

Average prisoner population per day:
Total days served divided by 365 =   2.48   1.89   4.37

EXPENDITURE DATA

Stockade

Object of Expenditure	Year I Budgeted	Year II Budgeted	Year III Budgeted	Year IV Budgeted	Year V Budgeted
Salaries	$11,760	$14,496	$12,396	$ 77,600	$ 86,020
Groceries	9,000	7,000	8,000	8,000	7,000
Office supplies	0	0	0	0	0
Heat and power	8,600	10,000	9,600	0	0
Utilities	0	0	0	26,000	20,000
Communications	0	0	0	500	440
Telephone and telegraph	200	200	200	0	0
Equipment repairs	1,000	1,000	1,000	600	700
Janitorial supplies	1,500	900	1,000	3,400	2,600
Tools and supplies	1,000	1,000	1,000	0	0
Professional services	0	0	0	1,200	1,000
Real property repairs	6,000	14,272	15,000	1,600	1,800
Furnishings and bedding	1,000	500	1,000	0	0
Clothing	1,000	300	500	0	0
Uniform allowance	0	0	0	1,900	1,800
Medical	1,000	1,000	1,700	0	0
Capital improvements	6,000	0	0	0	1,176
TOTAL	$48,060	$50,668	$51,396	$120,800	$122,536

Stockade

Object of Expenditure	Year I Spent	Year II Spent	Year III Spent	Year IV Spent	Year V Spent
Salaries	$11,608	$ 1,264	$13,132	$ 67,162	$ 67,650
Groceries	6,730	8,158	6,302	8,006	7,062
Office supplies	0	0	0	0	16
Heat and power	11,404	15,728	11,794	0	0
Utilities	0	0	0	19,586	19,400
Communications	0	0	0	600	420
Telephone and telegraph	168	498	192	0	0
Equipment repairs	738	1,446	2,882	638	258
Janitorial supplies	796	1,904	922	2,186	2,442
Tools and supplies	1,634	654	1,426	0	0
Professional services	0	0	0	1,094	2,396
Real property repairs	3,298	14,122	366	2,026	12,996
Furnishings and bedding	126	1,522	326	0	0
Clothing	0	710	242	0	0
Uniform allowance	0	0	0	2,902	984
Medical	1,640	708	678	0	0
Capital improvements	4,180	0	0	0	1,006
TOTAL	$42,322	$46,714	$38,262	$104,200	$114,630

ACCOUNT TITLE: Streets Department

The following services are performed by the City Streets Department:

    Construction: Administering contracts with private contractors to construct new streets.

    Resurfacing: Administering contracts with private contractors to resurface. (Patching of streets is done by City crews before the surface is covered.

    Curb and gutter maintenance: Replacing and constructing curbs and gutters.

    Right-of-way maintenance: Cutting grass and picking up litter along the right-of-way.

    Surface and storm drain maintenance: Cleaning storm drains.

    Raising drains for resurfacing projects. Constructing new storm drains.

In the Streets Department, multiple accounts for drainage, street, and sidewalk improvements represent the different projects carried out during the year. The organizational chart of the Streets Department follows.

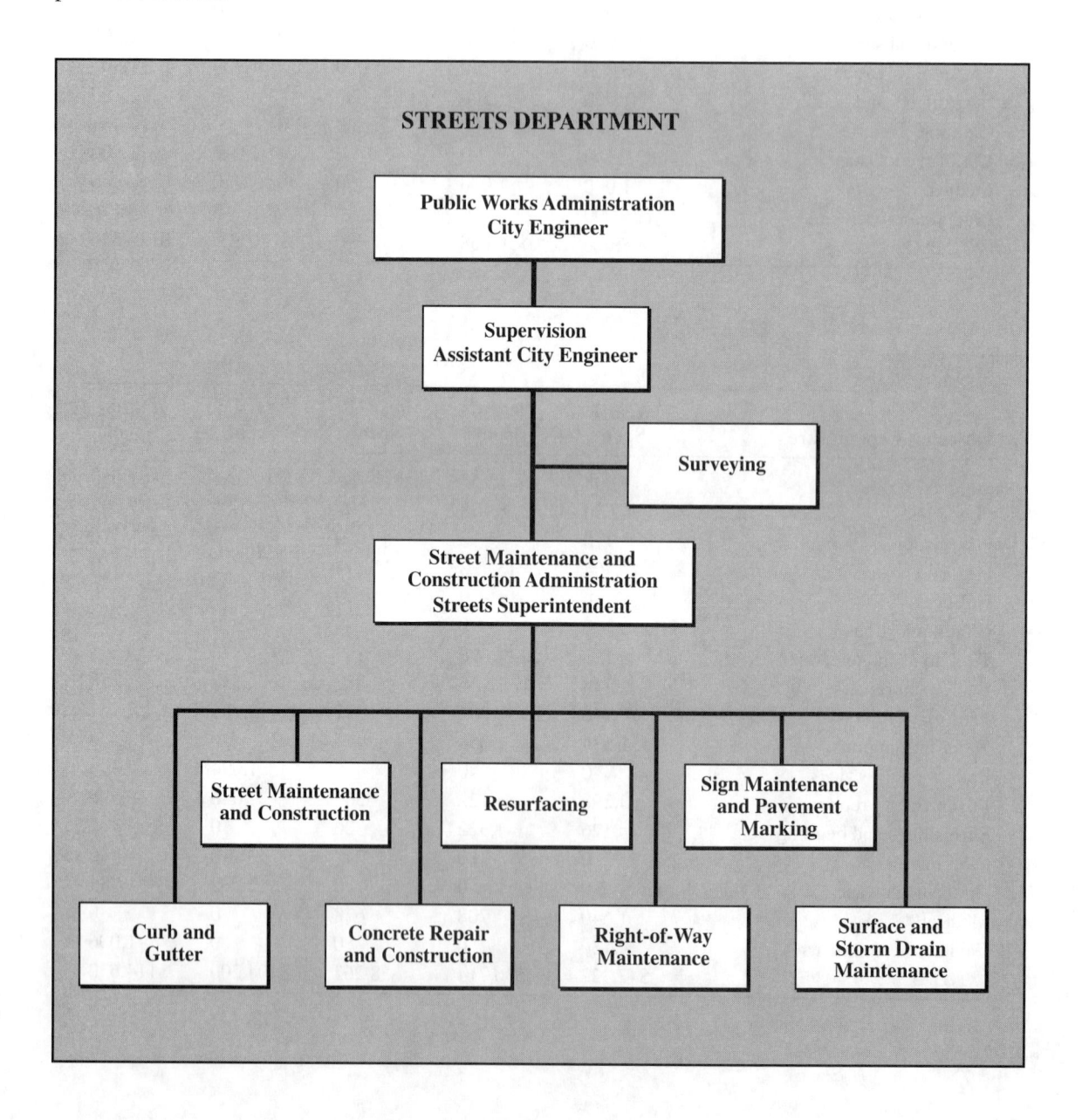

STREETS DEPARTMENT

- Public Works Administration — City Engineer
  - Supervision — Assistant City Engineer
    - Surveying
    - Street Maintenance and Construction Administration — Streets Superintendent
      - Street Maintenance and Construction
      - Resurfacing
      - Sign Maintenance and Pavement Marking
      - Curb and Gutter
      - Concrete Repair and Construction
      - Right-of-Way Maintenance
      - Surface and Storm Drain Maintenance

A current list of equipment assigned to the department includes the following:

Manufacturer (number)	Age (years)	Type of vehicle
Ford	3	Pickup
Ford	4	Pickup
Dodge	6	Pickup
Ford	3	Flatbed dump
Ford	3	Pickup
Dodge	5	Pickup
Ford (2)	7	Flatbed dump
Dodge	4	Tandem dump
Dodge	3	Tandem dump
Dodge	7	Dump truck
Dodge	9	Dump truck
Ford	4	Pickup
Dodge	3	Tandem dump
Dodge	12	Pickup
Dodge	2	Dump truck
Dodge	2	Paint machine
Phelan	2	Lowboy trailer
Tanker	Army surplus	5,000 gal. tanker
GMC	Army surplus	Tandem tractor
GMC	Army surplus	Water truck
GMC	Army surplus	Dump truck
Dodge	9	Slurry machine truck
	Army surplus	Lowboy trailer
GMC 6x6	Army surplus	Flatbed truck
Dodge	2	Do-Al
Dodge	2	Flatbed dump
Wald	10	Old paint machine
Gradall	5	Grading machine
Bantum Teleskoop	6	Grading machine
Dodge (2)	15	$^3/_4$-ton army surplus
Dodge	2	Pickup with club cab
Dodge	5	Pickup
Phelan	2	Lowboy trailer
Diamond	Army surplus	5-ton tandem
30-foot conveyor	2	Conveyor
Trailer, homemade	2	Mower carrier
Schramm (2)	Army surplus	Air compressor
Ford	12	$^1/_2$-ton pickup
Galion	13	Motor grader

A recently completed capital improvements program for the Streets Department indicated a need for the following equipment items within the next three years:

Item (number)	Cost per item*
Gradall	$220,000
Utility and storage shed	120,000
Flatbed dump truck (3)	24,000
Pickup truck (8)	15,000
Air compressor	80,000
Tractor mowers (6)	2,050
Small stump cutter	11,000
Jackhammer (2)	2,000
Motor grader	185,000
Tandem dump truck (3)	90,000
Small steel wheel roller	30,000
Backhoe/rubber tire	80,000
Mechanical tamp	10,000
Front-end loader/payloader	175,000

*The costs are estimated by the department head. Budget staff should determine actual costs based on local conditions.

Activity Indicators	FY V	FY V % Achieved	FY VI Estimate
Number of lane miles of flexible base streets penetration paved (7,627 square yds. 1 lane mile)	3.6	100%	5
Potholes patched	1,862	51%	5,000
Miles of curb and gutter installed	23	68%	50

Operating needs: Additional curb and gutter crew (8 positions = approx. $265,000); two additional pothole patching crews (12 positions = approximately $625,000).

EXPENDITURE DATA

Streets Department

Object of Expenditure	Year I Budgeted	Year II Budgeted	Year III Budgeted	Year IV Budgeted	Year V Budgeted
Salaries	$ 513,562	$ 551,500	$ 609,158	$ 628,000	$ 710,616
Office supplies	1,000	1,200	0	0	2,000
Heat and power	500	500	500	500	500
Telephone and telegraph	3,000	3,000	1,800	2,600	2,600
Gas and oil	16,000	24,000	36,000	44,000	56,000
Equipment repairs	99,000	102,000	10,072	9,000	9,000
Tires, tubes, and batteries	11,808	13,000	1,374	0	0
Claims	1,000	0	0	0	0
Legal	1,000	0	0	0	62,140
Travel expense	400	1,400	500	3,500	3,600
Janitorial supplies	1,000	1,500	58,000	22,700	8,000
Tools and supplies	36,504	36,500	0	36,000	71,860
Paint	20,000	17,000	24,000	30,000	0
Asphalt	200,000	200,000	140,000	356,000	200,000
Diesel fuel and oil	8,000	9,000	15,000	0	0
Other aggregate	24,000	20,000	30,000	20,000	20,000
Cement	2,000	2,000	3,000	0	0
Ready-mix concrete	80,000	50,000	30,000	54,000	54,000
Traffic signs	16,000	12,000	24,000	33,400	0
Rights of way	8,000	5,000	0	0	0
Concrete pipe materials	4,000	0	0	0	0
Pipe	16,000	16,000	10,000	74,000	30,000
Real property repairs	6,000	3,000	3,000	3,000	3,000
Clothing	200	600	0	0	0
Medical	200	200	0	0	0
Education and training	400	200	200	200	200
Dues and subscriptions	80	200	200	200	200
Car allowance	6,000	3,600	1,200	0	0
Capital improvements	88,800	178,060	211,950	51,060	123,244
Professional services	0	0	0	3,000	3,200
Freight and express	0	0	0	400	300
Printing	0	0	0	600	300
Equipment leasing	0	0	0	0	0
Chemicals	0	0	0	0	0
TOTAL	$1,164,454	$1,251,460	$1,209,954	$1,372,160	$1,360,760

Streets Department

Object of Expenditure	Year I Spent	Year II Spent	Year III Spent	Year IV Spent	Year V Spent
Salaries	$ 470,624	$ 563,576	$ 565,374	$ 550,708	$ 635,640
Office supplies	1,070	1,290	0	1,664	508
Heat and power	70	156	274	374	466
Telephone and telegraph	3,428	3,822	2,044	2,676	2,596
Gas and oil	53,108	33,784	32,598	55,686	38,788
Equipment repairs	100,630	75,508	0	64,490	1,264
Tires, tubes, and batteries	16,218	11,898	1,374	0	0
Claims	1,672	0	0	0	0
Legal	950	0	0	0	62,340
Travel expense	0	244	576	3,268	3,392
Janitorial supplies	2,490	1,858	52,028	6,584	1,538
Tools and supplies	52,172	52,048	0	33,124	71,826
Paint	13,978	12,164	24,034	33,872	0
Asphalt	211,412	331,830	347,464	238,170	207,528
Diesel fuel and oil	9,328	14,584	13,676	0	0
Other aggregate	17,202	39,956	14,464	36,320	38,202
Cement	1,832	4,228	2,178	48,790	69,570
Ready-mix concrete	11,440	81,592	55,264	0	0
Traffic signs	17,274	36,526	21,400	33,250	0
Rights of way	598	16	0	0	0
Concrete pipe materials	124	0	0	0	0
Pipe	20,130	23,596	4,594	9,800	34,206
Real property repairs	2,568	3,700	1,588	256	1,340
Clothing	632	206	0	0	0
Medical	0	0	0	0	0
Education and training	0	16	154	0	74
Dues and subscriptions	50	54	70	70	70
Car allowance	5,100	3,600	1,950	0	0
Capital improvements	106,562	151,172	203,070	49,376	238,440
Professional services	0	0	0	3,092	820
Freight and express	0	0	0	170	216
Printing	0	0	0	46	60
Equipment leasing	0	0	0	240	0
Chemicals	0	0	0	308	0
TOTAL	$1,120,662	$1,447,424	$1,344,174	$1,172,334	$1,408,884

Streets Department–Thomas Street Widening

Object of Expenditure	Year I Budgeted	Spent
Tools and supplies	$0	$ 2,494
Other aggregate	0	2,240
Cement	0	142
Ready-mix concrete	0	18,158
Traffic signs	0	142
Special contracts	0	130,364
Pipe	0	9,314
TOTAL	$0	$162,854

Streets Department–General Project

Object of Expenditure	Year I Budgeted	Spent
Tools and supplies	$0	$ 44
Other aggregate	0	892
Ready-mix concrete	0	626
Pipe	0	128,812
Cast iron pipe fittings	0	16,594
Hydrants	0	3,328
TOTAL	$0	$150,296

Streets Department–Madison Avenue, 1st Leg

Object of Expenditure	Year I Budgeted	Spent
Special contracts	$0	$16,240
TOTAL	$0	$16,240

Streets Department–Madison Avenue, 2d Leg

Object of Expenditure	Year II Budgeted	Spent
Special contracts	$0	$106,648
Other aggregate	0	68
TOTAL	$0	$106,716

Streets Department–Downtown Beautification

Object of Expenditure	Year III Budgeted	Spent
Consultants/Contract services	$200,000	$64,028
TOTAL	$200,000	$64,028

B. Water-Sewer Enterprise Fund

ACCOUNT TITLE: General Administrative

This section of the budget includes the nondepartmental costs for water and sewer service departments. It covers expenses that benefit all of these departments (such as group insurance and pensions) and those concerning some departments (such as bond repayment).

The City has a contractual agreement with an insurance company to provide pension benefits for City employees. A trust fund is maintained for the accumulation and payment of current City and employee contributions. The Water-Sewer Enterprise Fund pays pension contribution (employer share) costs, at present 10 percent of total annual salaries. The retirement system is presently fully funded.

The Water-Sewer Debt Service Fund and Renewal and Extension Fund hold moneys for payment to bondholders as bonds mature and, until payment, are invested in U.S. Treasury bills. Exhibit 4 presents a summary of outstanding water and sewer revenue bonds and interest payments. Exhibit 5 presents the legal agreement binding the City to specific steps in collecting revenue for the system, paying bondholders, and transferring money from account to account.

To compute Social Security, Medicare, workers' compensation, disability insurance, and unemployment insurance, a review of current federal and state law will be necessary.

Exhibit 6 is a form for identifying the relationship between water and sewer revenues and expenditures (including bond repayment). Information for FY VI should be obtained from revenue/receipt projections and from staff members responsible for the expense/expenditure estimates of the cited accounts/departments (e.g., Water Filter Plant).

EXHIBIT 4
Summary of Outstanding Water and Sewer Revenue Bonds and Interest Payments

Payment Date	Principal	Interest	Annual Debt Service	Principal Balance
I	$ 280,000	$ 2,560,000	$ 2,840,000	$31,720,000
II	305,000	2,537,600	2,842,600	31,415,000
III	330,000	2,513,200	2,843,200	31,085,000
IV	355,000	2,486,800	2,841,800	30,730,000
V	385,000	2,458,400	2,843,400	30,345,000
VI	415,000	2,427,600	2,842,600	29,930,000
VII	450,000	2,394,400	2,844,400	29,480,000
VIII	485,000	2,358,400	2,843,400	28,995,000
IX	525,000	2,319,600	2,844,600	28,470,000
X	565,000	2,277,600	2,842,600	27,905,000
XI	610,000	2,232,400	2,842,400	27,295,000
XII	660,000	2,183,600	2,843,600	26,635,000
XIII	710,000	2,130,800	2,840,800	25,925,000
XIV	770,000	2,074,000	2,844,000	25,155,000
XV	830,000	2,012,400	2,842,400	24,325,000
XVI	895,000	1,946,000	2,841,000	23,430,000
XVII	970,000	1,874,400	2,844,400	22,460,000
XVIII	1,045,000	1,796,800	2,841,800	21,415,000
XIX	1,130,000	1,713,200	2,843,200	20,285,000
XX	1,220,000	1,622,800	2,842,800	19,065,000
XXI	1,315,000	1,525,200	2,840,200	17,750,000
XXII	1,420,000	1,420,000	2,840,000	16,330,000
XXIII	1,535,000	1,306,400	2,841,400	14,795,000
XXIV	1,660,000	1,183,600	2,843,600	13,135,000
XXV	1,790,000	1,050,800	2,840,800	11,345,000
XXVI	1,935,000	907,600	2,842,600	9,410,000
XXVII	2,090,000	752,800	2,842,800	7,320,000
XXVIII	2,255,000	585,600	2,840,600	5,065,000
XXIX	2,435,000	405,200	2,840,200	2,630,000
XXX	2,630,000	210,400	2,840,400	0
TOTAL	$30,345,000	$40,711,600	$71,056,600	

EXHIBIT 5

THE INDENTURE OF MORTGAGE
WATER AND SEWER UTILITY SYSTEM

The Water and Sewer Bonds are issued pursuant to an Indenture. The Indenture grants a mortgage to the Trustee, in trust for the holders of the Bonds, on all the properties and assets of the Utility now owned or hereafter acquired by the City during the time any of the Bonds secured thereby remain outstanding and unpaid.

Covenants of the City

Rate Covenants. The City covenants that at all times it will prescribe and charge such rates and charges for the services to the Utility, and will so restrict Operating Expenses, as shall result in Net Revenues sufficient to provide for the greater of (i) (A) the payments required to be made into the Funds pursuant to the Indenture (see below), (B) sufficient earnings coverage to permit the issuance of any Additional Bonds required for the construction of necessary or advisable Improvements (being generally improvements, additions or extensions to the Utility) and (C) proper improvement and replacement reserves, or (ii) during each 12-month period ending December 31, an amount at least equal to 125 percent of the amount required to be paid into the Debt Service Fund during the period of Maximum Annual Debt Service. If Additional Bonds are issued to pay the cost of Improvements, the portion of that amount required to be paid into the Debt Service Fund with respect to interest to be included in this computation during the estimated construction period of the Improvements may equal only the portion of the interest on those Additional Bonds accruing during that period that has not been capitalized.

The City further covenants that if in any 12-month period ending December 31, the Net Revenues shall be less than the amount so required, it will, within 30 days following receipt of a written request of the Trustee, employ a recognized firm of independent management consultants knowledgeable and experienced in the operation and finances of municipal water and sewer systems or a similarly qualified firm of independent engineers (the "Consultant"), to make recommendations within 45 days as to a revision of the rates, fees and charges or Operating Expenses or methods of operations of the Utility, if any, that will result in producing the amount so required in the next succeeding such 12-month period; copies of such request and the recommendations of the Consultant shall be filed with the Trustee. The City covenants, promptly upon its receipt of such recommendations, to revise the rates, fees and charges or Operating Expenses or methods of operation of the Utility and to take such other action as shall be in conformity with such recommendations to the extent the City feasibly may do so.

If the City complies with all recommendations of the Consultant, the failure of the Net Revenues to meet the requirements described above will not in and of itself constitute an Event of Default under the Indenture unless such requirements are not met for two consecutive 12-month periods ending December 31.

Payment from General Utility Operating Fund. All Operating Expenses will be paid out of the General Utility Operating Fund. After that payment and after reserving therein an amount not less than one-sixth of the Operating Expenses of the preceding calendar year as a reserve in order to meet the current requirements for Operating Expenses, the following payments shall be made to the following funds and accounts and in the following order:

First, into the Debt Service Fund:

(i) Into the Interest Payment Account of the Debt Service Fund on or before the 15th day of each February, May, August, and November one-half of the amount of the interest due on all outstanding Bonds on the next Interest Payment Date; and

(ii) Into the Principal Payment Account of the Debt Service Fund on or before the 15th day of each February, May, August, and November one-fourth of the amount of the principal amount of outstanding Bonds due on the next principal payment date as state maturity or by mandatory sinking fund redemption.

Second: On or before the 15th day of each February, May, August, and November such amount in addition to any of the foregoing payments as may be necessary and available, after meeting the requirements of the preceding paragraphs, to make up any previous deficiency in any such quarterly payment.

Third: Into the Renewal and Extension Fund: annually on February 15 of each year the Revenues remaining in the General Utility Operating Fund, after (i) making all the payments required by the preceding paragraphs, (ii) providing necessary accruals against the current requirements of the preceding paragraphs, (iii) as stated above, reserving therein an amount not less than one-sixth of the Operating Expenses of the preceding calendar year as a working capital reserve in order to meet the current requirements for Operating Expenses, (iv) an administrative overhead allocation to the City's General Fund, and (v) only as available after meeting conditions (i), (ii), (iii) and (iv), an amount in the City's General Fund which the City Mayor and City Council will individually certify as excess of utility needs.

EXHIBIT 6
Water and Sewer Utility–
General Utility Operating Fund Statement of Operations (FY VI)

Operating Revenues
   Water revenue _____
   Sprinkler and hydrant rent _____
   Water and wastewater connection fees _____
   Tap and meter charges– water and wastewater _____
   Wastewater charges _____
   County supplement _____
     REVENUE SUBTOTAL _____

Current Expenses
   General administration _____
   Water filter plant _____
   Water and sewer distribution _____
   Water meter installation _____
   Waterworks commercial _____
   Pollution control plants _____
   Other: (specify) _____
     EXPENSE SUBTOTAL _____

Net Revenues
   Maximum annual debt service (1) _____
   Debt service coverage (2) _____
   Actual debt service (3) _____
   Balance available (4) _____

Notes:
1. The maximum annual debt service in any future year (i.e., Year IX from Exhibit 4).
2. Net Revenues divided by maximum Annual Debt Service.
3. See Exhibit 4 for next year's (Year VI's) debt service. The required funds are to be transferred into a Debt Service Fund from which bondholders will be paid.
4. Balance available for capital improvements, reserves, and other purposes (see "The Indenture of Mortgage").

EXPENDITURE DATA

Water–Sewer General Administrative

Object of Expenditure	Year I Budgeted	Year II Budgeted	Year III Budgeted	Year IV Budgeted	Year V Budgeted
Renewal and extension fund	$ 0	$ 120,000	$ 120,000	$ 60,000	$ 0
Water and sewer debt service fund					
Revenue bond principal	280,000	305,000	330,000	355,000	385,000
Revenue bond interest	2,560,000	2,537,600	2,513,200	2,486,600	2,458,400
Professional services					
Audit	20,000	24,000	24,000	40,000	40,000
Water-sewer trust fund					
Pension/Retirement system City share	60,000	70,000	100,000	100,000	100,000
Social security					
City share	50,000	55,000	75,000	80,000	85,000
Insurance					
General, property, and workers compensation	70,000	70,000	70,000	150,000	150,000
Group health insurance	50,000	50,000	75,000	125,000	140,000
TOTAL	$3,090,000	$3,231,600	$3,307,200	$3,396,600	$3,358,400

Water–Sewer General Administrative

Object of Expenditure	Year I Spent	Year II Spent	Year III Spent	Year IV Spent	Year V Spent
Renewal and extension fund	$ 40,000	$ 120,000	$ 120,000	$ 39,088	$ 0
Water and sewer debt service fund					
Revenue bond principal	280,000	305,000	330,000	355,000	385,000
Revenue bond interest	2,560,000	2,537,600	2,513,200	2,486,600	2,458,400
Professional services					
Audit	26,054	23,500	23,960	46,672	40,226
Water-sewer trust fund					
Pension/Retirement system City share	60,777	68,748	95,871	99,072	109,090
Social security					
City share	46,495	52,593	73,341	75,790	83,454
Insurance					
General, property, and workers compensation	67,401	70,426	86,163	145,184	169,289
Group health insurance	36,466	41,249	57,523	59,443	65,454
TOTAL	$3,117,194	$3,219,116	$3,300,058	$3,306,850	$3,310,912

ACCOUNT TITLE: Water Filter Plant

It is the responsibility of this office of the Public Works Department to ensure safe and clean water for water users through operating and maintaining the water filter plant.

Water for the City and the county comes from two rivers. Water is pumped from the rivers to the water filter plant in the northern part of the City through five river pumps at rates ranging from 900 gallons per minute to 8,600 gallons per minute. All or some of the pumps can be operated, depending on the rate of flow and water consumption.

The water filter plant is operated 24 hours a day, 365 days a year.

Once the water is at the plant, it is pumped through the prechemical building at which point chemicals are added for coagulation of the mud and so that bacteria and germs are killed. Once the mud has been removed, the water is filtered through eight dual-media filters, consisting of approximately five feet of graded gravel, graded silica sand, and anthracite media. When the water leaves the filters, it is continuously monitored from the control room with turbidimeters. After filtration, chemicals are added. Hydrated lime is added for pH adjustment, chlorine is added to maintain 1.5 parts per million in the finished water, and sodium silica fluoride is added in the amount of 1 part per million, as recommended by the American Waterworks Association and the state's environmental protection division.

The treated water is then stored in three storage reservoirs for finished water with a total capacity of 4 million gallons. The water is pumped from the reservoirs through 1 of 10 pumps or a combination thereof, ranging in pumping capacity from 1,200 gallons per minute to 10,500 gallons per minute. Most of the water is pumped directly from the plant through a network of water feeder mains, with pipes ranging from 10 to 24 inches in diameter. Pipes decrease gradually in size as the water moves into industrial areas (8 to 4 inches) and residential areas (1 inch to $1/2$ inch).

To maintain pressure in the distribution system, some of the water is pumped to elevated tanks: this water is used mostly for reserve and for peak demands. The four elevated tanks are the north industrial tank with a 750,000 gallon capacity, the twin university area tanks with a 500,000 gallon total capacity, and the west side tank with a 500,000 gallon capacity. The total elevated capacity is 1.75 million gallons. The City has one recirculating booster station in the southwestern area, which is a ground storage tank with a capacity of 1.5 million gallons. It has two pumps operated by remote control from the water filter plant. The City also has one in-line booster station in the county with two pumps operated by remote control. All pressures and tank levels are monitored through a telemetering system in the control room of the plant.

Water is tested at different stages of treatment to ensure that the proper concentrations of chemicals are maintained and that all bacteria and germs are killed. Samples of the raw, coagulated, and finished tap water, taken from different parts of the distribution system, are tested for the presence of bacteria. Water is also tested for physical properties and amounts of chlorine at the plant and in the distribution system. In addition, samples of water are collected and sent to the state lab once a month to test for fluoride content and bacteria. At the plant, two employees on each shift keep a careful check on pH control, amounts of all chemicals added, results of all tests, and strict records of the entire operation. In FY V, 57,938 samples of water were tested in various stages of the operation.

The filter plant has two half-ton pickup trucks available for use: one vehicle is two years old, the other is six years old.

Activity Indicators	FY V	FY V % Achieved	FY VI Estimate
Number of days water quality exceeded EPA standards	0	100%	0
Number of times pressure			
—fell below or	0	100%	0
—exceeded maximum	0	100%	0
Water samples tested	57,930	100%	59,000

Improvements for the upcoming three-year period have been estimated to require the following:

Electrical improvements in the plant area	$ 300,000
Ground elevation storage tank on the eastern side of the service area	450,000
Raw water intake and supply line from Middle River	4,000,000
Liquid alum storage tank	45,000
Parts storage building	2,500
Resurface service roadways at filter plant area	12,000
1/2-ton pickup truck	30,000
Elevated tank repair	25,000

EXPENDITURE DATA

Water Filter Plant

Object of Expenditure	Year I Budgeted	Year II Budgeted	Year III Budgeted	Year IV Budgeted	Year V Budgeted
Salaries	$180,600	$195,076	$241,028	$250,800	$255,706
Heat and power	150,000	164,250	263,680	0	0
Repairs to equipment	12,000	24,000	25,600	25,600	36,000
Chemicals	90,000	124,000	126,582	207,654	158,140
Tools and supplies	8,000	12,000	14,000	600	800
Telephone and telegraph	1,400	2,050	2,400	0	0
Gas and oil	400	500	700	800	1,450
Tires, tubes, and batteries	200	250	34	0	0
Janitorial supplies	800	1,100	1,300	1,300	1,300
Laboratory supplies	2,000	3,000	5,000	5,000	0
Real property repairs	2,000	48,000	40,000	30,000	0
Clothing and uniforms	100	100	200	300	500
Medical expenses	0	0	0	0	0
Education expenses	400	600	800	0	0
Dues and subscriptions	100	150	200	200	200
Capital improvements	12,820	12,268	19,830	13,150	0
Training	0	0	0	270	480
Travel	0	0	0	900	1,100
Communications	0	0	0	2,600	2,200
Freight and express	0	0	0	200	200
Utilities	0	0	0	312,792	296,000
Printing	0	0	0	600	550
Parts	0	0	0	16,000	0
Paint	0	0	0	2,000	1,300
Charts	0	0	0	4,000	6,000
Pipe and fittings	0	0	0	3,000	2,000
Concrete	0	0	0	1,000	0
Aggregate	0	0	0	0	0
Office supplies	0	0	0	0	400
Car supplies	0	0	0	0	10,000
Professional services	0	0	0	0	1,000
TOTAL	$460,820	$587,344	$741,354	$878,766	$775,326

Water Filter Plant

Object of Expenditure	Year I Spent	Year II Spent	Year III Spent	Year IV Spent	Year V Spent
Salaries	$168,052	$198,436	$237,640	$244,320	$260,748
Heat and power	174,670	251,384	330,694	0	0
Repairs to equipment	22,096	14,804	23,018	25,274	43,408
Chemicals	121,800	143,512	170,266	163,904	218,500
Tools and supplies	11,744	10,030	12,704	776	1,186
Telephone and telegraph	2,064	1,926	1,928	0	0
Gas and oil	86	476	1,018	1,264	1,772
Tires, tubes, and batteries	158	146	34	0	0
Janitorial supplies	1,506	1,240	1,250	1,504	2,052
Laboratory supplies	2,284	4,330	2,290	4,110	0
Real property repairs	236	42,210	35,810	28,304	0
Clothing and uniforms	0	42	74	728	610
Medical expenses	10	0	0	0	0
Education expenses	180	144	822	0	0
Dues and subscriptions	0	0	50	140	66
Capital improvements	1,598	8,204	11,578	3,454	0
Training	0	0	0	182	358
Travel	0	0	0	1,292	1,530
Communications	0	0	0	2,210	2,488
Freight and express	0	0	0	160	146
Utilities	0	0	0	297,204	419,410
Printing	0	0	0	374	314
Parts	0	0	0	13,384	0
Paint	0	0	0	884	160
Charts	0	0	0	3,124	5,362
Pipe and fittings	0	0	0	986	48
Concrete	0	0	0	0	0
Aggregate	0	0	0	14,632	0
Office supplies	0	0	0	0	474
Car supplies	0	0	0	0	5,400
Professional services	0	0	0	0	840
TOTAL	$506,484	$676,884	$829,176	$808,210	$964,872

Water Filter Plant Expansion (Federal Grant Supported)

Object of Expenditure	Year III Budgeted	Spent	Year V Budgeted	Spent
Consultants and contract services	$1,000,000	$61,174	$5,000,000	$4,972,602
Relocation payments	0	16,000	0	0
Acquisition	0	22,500	0	0
TOTAL	$1,000,000	$99,674	$5,000,000	$4,972,602

ACCOUNT TITLE: Water Meters

This office, within the Public Works Department, installs and maintains water meters. The City requires a new water user to pay for a water meter, which is then installed by this division's personnel.

Activity Indicators	FY V	FY V % Achieved	FY VI Estimate
Water meters installed	322	N/A	350
Customer complaints checked	83	100%	100

EXPENDITURE DATA

Water Meters

Object of Expenditure	Year I Budgeted	Year II Budgeted	Year III Budgeted	Year IV Budgeted	Year V Budgeted
Salaries	$ 46,200	$ 50,300	$ 75,338	$ 76,000	$ 76,692
Social security	0	0	0	0	0
Printing	0	0	0	400	200
Tools and supplies	20,000	0	0	10,000	5,000
Janitorial supplies	200	200	0	0	0
Vehicle and equipment parts	6,000	9,000	0	0	0
Clothing, uniforms, and badges	0	0	0	0	0
Freight and express	0	0	0	400	300
Communications	0	0	0	500	800
Utilities	500	500	500	0	0
Diesel fuel	0	0	0	0	0
Gas and oil	6,000	5,000	4,000	5,000	4,000
Truck and car repairs	0	0	0	0	0
Equipment repair	3,000	3,000	1,070	1,400	1,000
Equipment rental/Purchase	0	0	0	0	0
Tires, tubes, and batteries	1,000	1,200	8	0	0
New meters	60,000	70,000	60,000	26,000	30,000
Meter castings	15,000	10,000	13,000	10,000	20,000
Cement	0	0	0	0	0
Service pipe	44,000	0	0	0	0
Concrete	0	0	0	8,000	30,000
Cast iron pipe and fittings	0	0	0	28,000	0
Service pipe	0	44,000	52,000	0	0
Tools and supplies	0	30,000	30,000	0	0
Professional services	0	0	0	200	200
Medical	0	0	0	0	0
Capital improvements	8,400	0	10,400	8,400	15,000
TOTAL	$210,300	$223,200	$246,316	$174,300	$183,192

Water Meters

Object of Expenditure	Year I Spent	Year II Spent	Year III Spent	Year IV Spent	Year V Spent
Salaries	$ 46,862	$ 46,824	$ 73,318	$ 67,960	$ 80,322
Social security	0	0	0	0	0
Printing	0	0	0	152	70
Tools and supplies	0	0	0	5,178	5,098
Janitorial supplies	74	214	0	0	0
Vehicle and equipment parts	7,454	5,192	0	0	0
Clothing, uniforms, and badges	76	0	0	0	0
Freight and express	0	0	0	0	10
Communications	0	0	0	980	1,360
Utilities	382	262	510	0	18
Diesel fuel	0	0	0	0	0
Gas and oil	15,560	850	7,734	3,320	3,300
Truck and car repairs	0	0	0	0	0
Equipment repair	2,853	2,666	1,616	658	226
Equipment rental/Purchase	0	0	0	0	0
Tires, tubes, and batteries	684	360	10	0	0
New meters	106,508	66,904	23,128	30,136	60,048
Meter castings	4,282	18,292	8,148	14,164	22,078
Cement	100	0	0	0	0
Service pipe	61,554	0	0	0	0
Concrete	0	0	0	8,226	46,194
Cast iron pipe and fittings	0	0	0	37,164	0
Service pipe	0	80,038	0	0	0
Tools and supplies	37,052	24,188	16,674	0	0
Professional services	0	0	0	0	0
Medical	0	0	0	0	0
Capital improvements	5,660	0	7,398	8,102	11,010
TOTAL	$289,101	$245,790	$138,536	$176,040	$229,734

ACCOUNT TITLE: Water Pollution Control Plant

It is the responsibility of this office of the Public Works Department to ensure that sewer wastes are treated and that legal guidelines are followed.

The City operates two water pollution control plants. Both treat the sewage prior to returning the water to the local rivers.

The north plant was built 16 years ago. It has been expanded during the last few years. The "design average flow" of the plant was doubled from 5 million gallons per day (MGD) to 10 MGD during the expansion. Secondary treatment is also provided by this facility. A sludge dewater process, which uses a centrifuge operation instead of a drying bed, has been added. This facility is designed to accommodate the service area for the next 13 years.

The south plant was built 13 years ago but was expanded in FY V. The newly expanded facility will start operation during FY VI. During the expansion, a new laboratory and administrative complex were constructed. In addition, the expansion program doubled the "design average flow" from 2 MGD to 4 MGD. Tertiary treatment is provided by this facility, designed to accommodate the service area for the next 15 years. The City has also taken over the operation of the oxidation ponds, which serve a population of approximately 3,500 in the non-City part of the county. In FY V, accounts were separated to allow a distinction to be made in the costs among the two sanitary sewer treatment plants and the oxidation pond operation.

An inventory list of the equipment assigned to these facilities includes the following items:

Manufacturer (number)	Age (years)	Type of Vehicle
Dodge	5	Dumpster
Ford	7	Dump truck
Dodge (3)	2	Pickup truck
Dodge	7	Pickup truck
Dodge (2)	1	Dump truck

Activity Indicators	FY V	FY V % Achieved	FY VI Estimate
Number of days water quality did not meet federal standards	5	−500%	0

A recent study indicated that the following would be needed by the department within the next three years:

Item (number)	Cost per Item
Rebuild south plant access road	$ 44,000
Resurface road and parking area at the north plant	5,000
Storage building for oil, grease, and chemicals (1)	40,000
Mobile communications system	19,600
Low center of gravity tractor and mower (1)	30,000
Grit container and screening boxes	20,000
Automatic samplers and flow recorders (2)	9,000
$2^1/_2$-ton flatbed dump truck (1)	25,000
Rebuild primary lines and final lines at the north plant	2,250,000
Van for industrial sampling operation (1)	26,000
$1/_2$-ton pickup truck (1)	10,600
Midsize vehicle for laboratory (1)	15,600
Set of bar screen chains for the north plant	3,600
Handrails for primary and final tanks at the north plant	92,000

Operating needs: Ongoing consultant services for keeping up with changing clean water standards and regulations ($25,000).

EXPENDITURE DATA

Water Pollution Control Plant

Object of Expenditure	Year I Budgeted	Year II Budgeted	Year III Budgeted	Year IV Budgeted
Salaries	$190,050	$223,220	$300,048	$ 270,100
Heat and power	40,000	44,000	96,920	0
Utilities	0	0	0	200,000
Communications	0	0	0	2,000
Telephone and telegraph	1,000	1,000	1,400	0
Equipment repair	26,000	28,000	89,000	129,000
Gas and oil	4,000	4,800	13,000	48,000
Tires, tubes, and batteries	600	600	0	0
Travel	200	0	0	3,402
Janitorial supplies	3,600	4,320	0	2,700
Chemicals	40,000	44,000	119,600	164,700
Supplies	0	0	24,000	0
Laboratory supplies	2,000	2,000	0	5,200
Tools and supplies	7,500	7,500	0	4,784
Diesel fuel	4,500	6,000	0	0
Paint	0	600	0	0
Cement	0	0	0	0
Property repair and improvement	1,200	600	600	40,000
Education and training	300	300	1,000	340
Clothing, badges, and uniforms	100	100	0	1,752
Medical	100	100	0	0
Car allowance	0	0	0	0
Dues and subscriptions	0	0	0	130
Parts	0	0	0	15,566
Capital improvements	14,170	211,172	185,474	238,768
TOTAL	$335,320	$578,312	$831,042	$1,126,442

Water Pollution Control Plant

Object of Expenditure	Year I Spent	Year II Spent	Year III Spent	Year IV Spent
Salaries	$206,830	$244,112	$275,162	$260,583
Heat and power	41,654	67,132	96,362	0
Utilities	0	0	0	121,364
Communications	0	0	0	1,960
Telephone and telegraph	1,106	1,304	1,628	0
Equipment repair	30,784	35,364	41,002	78,420
Gas and oil	4,732	5,416	14,050	30,228
Tires, tubes, and batteries	438	742	0	0
Travel	0	0	0	1,404
Janitorial supplies	4,536	4,194	0	2,952
Chemicals	37,114	66,428	116,152	84,876
Supplies	0	0	19,638	0
Laboratory supplies	500	2,966	0	7,482
Tools and supplies	9,148	25,572	0	5,598
Diesel fuel	3,974	4,138	0	0
Paint	378	0	0	0
Cement	8	0	0	0
Property repair and improvement	0	394	228	59,250
Education and training	250	520	854	234
Clothing, badges, and uniforms	170	176	0	2,050
Medical	48	0	0	0
Car allowance	1,500	1,720	0	0
Dues and subscriptions	0	0	0	16
Parts	0	0	0	14,680
Capital improvements	3,038	183,558	100,142	181,526
TOTAL	$346,208	$643,736	$665,218	$852,623

South Water Pollution Control Plant

Object of Expenditure	Year V Budgeted	Spent
Salaries	$ 85,000	$ 81,218
Heat and power	0	0
Utilities	44,800	34,164
Communications	1,000	884
Telephone and telegraph	0	0
Equipment repair	42,000	37,438
Gas and oil	16,000	1,446
Tires, tubes, and batteries	0	0
Travel	0	0
Janitorial supplies	2,000	1,822
Chemicals	31,226	30,394
Supplies	0	0
Laboratory supplies	0	0
Tools and supplies	2,400	2,600
Diesel fuel	0	0
Paint	0	0
Cement	0	0
Property repair and improvement	3,000	1,186
Education and training	0	0
Clothing, badges, and uniforms	1,000	1,032
Medical	0	0
Car allowance	0	0
Dues and subscriptions	0	0
Parts	0	0
Capital improvements	0	0
TOTAL	$228,426	$192,184

North Water Pollution Control Plant

Object of Expenditure	Year V Budgeted	Spent
Salaries	$183,148	$170,072
Heat and power	0	0
Utilities	140,000	158,702
Communications	1,920	2,548
Telephone and telegraph	0	0
Equipment repair	92,000	104,140
Gas and oil	25,000	15,414
Tires, tubes, and batteries	0	0
Travel	3,250	1,464
Janitorial supplies	3,000	2,316
Chemicals	100,000	126,666
Supplies	400	594
Laboratory supplies	6,000	4,544
Tools and supplies	5,000	5,554
Diesel fuel	0	0
Paint	0	0
Cement	0	0
Property repair and improvement	8,000	7,334
Education and training	360	114
Clothing, badges, and uniforms	2,000	2,216
Medical	0	0
Car allowance	0	0
Dues and subscriptions	0	0
Parts	0	0
Capital improvements	0	0
TOTAL	$570,078	$601,678

Oxidation Pond Operations

Object of Expenditure	Year V Budgeted	Spent
Salaries	$34,912	$36,026
Utilities	6,120	6,356
Repairs to equipment	8,000	6,288
Chemicals	16,000	11,020
Tools	0	16
TOTAL	$65,032	$59,706

ACCOUNT TITLE: Water–Sewer Distribution

The function of this office, which is under the Public Works Department, is to maintain the water and sewer lines. There is a total of 408,249 miles of water mains in the system. In FY III, 2,197 miles were added to the water main system; in FY II, 21,047 miles; in FY I, 20,025 miles.

The budgets for water and sewer distribution were combined after FY I.

Information about the distribution of treated water from the filter plant is found in the section on the "Water Filter Plant," page 110.

Equipment assigned to the water and sewer distribution system includes the following items:

Manufacturer	Age (years)	Type of Vehicle
Ford	5	Pickup
Ford	3	250 utility
Dodge	5	200 utility
Dodge	5	D-800 flatbed with winch
Dodge	8	D-800 dump
Ford	14	Pickup
Dodge	2	D-600 flatbed dump
Dodge	8	300 utility
Ford	3	350 utility
Dodge	2	200 utility
Dodge	2	300 utility
Dodge	4	D-800 dump
Dodge	8	D-500 water wagon
Chevrolet	18	Utility
Dodge	23	Army surplus pickup
Hobart	15	Welder
	15	Hydro-Rotor
Ingersoll Rand	15	Air compressor
Solair	15	Air compressor
Schramm	15	Air compressor
	15	Utility trailer

Activity Indicators	FY V	FY V % Achieved	FY VI Estimate
Preliminary design (feet) surveyed	15,000	35%	36,000
Number of cost estimates deviating plus/minus 10%	2	–200%	0

A recent study indicated the following items would be needed within the next three years:

Item (number)	Cost per Item
Hydraulic excavator (1)	$110,000
Front-end loader (1)	175,000
1-ton utility truck (3)	40,000
Utility and storage shed (1)	120,000
Trash pump (1)	8,000
Boring equipment (1)	9,200
Steam cleaner (1)	3,000
Utility hoist (1)	2,200
Backhoe (1)	48,000
1½-ton truck/air compressor (1)	17,000
Hydraulic tamp (1)	37,800
Power sewer rudder/4-wheel drive carrier (1)	27,000
Dump truck (2)	90,000
¾-ton utility truck (2)	11,000
Multipurpose saw (2)	2,800
Sand blaster (1)	3,500
2½-ton flatbed truck with winch	24,000

EXPENDITURE DATA

Sewer Distribution

Object of Expenditure	Year I Budgeted	Spent
Salaries	$ 2,100	$ 0
Heat and power	4,000	3,416
Janitorial supplies	0	230
Office supplies	0	0
Printing	0	0
Communications	0	0
Telephone and telegraph	0	34
Gas and oil	0	0
Truck and car repairs	0	0
Equipment repairs	800	68
Tires, tubes, and batteries	200	78
Claims	0	64
Tools and supplies	6,000	8,974
Capital improvements	0	0
TOTAL	$13,100	$12,864

Water Distribution

Object of Expenditure	Year I Budgeted	Spent
Salaries	$ 53,550	$ 43,036
Janitorial supplies	200	0
Office supplies	500	0
Telephone and telegraph	1,000	1,410
Fuel	5,000	8,560
Equipment repairs	10,000	3,302
Tires, tubes, and batteries	4,000	2,384
Claims	400	364
Service pipe	1,000	3,630
Cast iron pipe fittings	6,000	2,244
Hydrants	6,000	6,570
Real property repairs	6,000	0
Clothing, badges, and uniforms	0	48
Medical	100	0
Tools and supplies	12,000	25,406
Capital improvements	19,000	32,590
TOTAL	$124,750	$129,544

EXPENDITURE DATA

Water–Sewer Distribution

Object of Expenditure	Year II Budgeted	Year III Budgeted	Year IV Budgeted	Year V Budgeted
Salaries	$ 71,650	$344,400	$357,500	$369,382
Training	0	0	0	600
Travel	0	0	400	200
Professional services	0	0	400	200
Janitorial supplies	6,200	0	0	0
Office supplies	500	0	0	0
Printing	0	0	600	200
Freight and express	0	0	600	800
Communications	0	0	1,600	1,700
Telephone and telegraph	1,200	1,400	0	0
Diesel fuel	1,000	1,000	0	0
Gas and oil	5,000	3,600	14,000	14,000
Truck and car repairs	0	0	0	0
Equipment repairs	10,000	6,000	5,000	5,000
Tires, tubes, and batteries	4,200	466	0	0
Real property maintenance	0	0	2,000	2,000
Claims	0	0	0	0
Meter castings	0	0	0	0
Hydrants	6,000	2,000	4,000	5,000
Concrete	0	0	20,000	16,000
Cast iron pipe and fittings	6,000	4,000	12,000	20,000
Service pipe	1,600	0	0	0
Tools and supplies	27,000	32,000	31,000	24,000
Contracts	400	0	0	0
Medical	200	0	0	0
Capital improvements	31,138	29,900	17,000	48,000
TOTAL	$172,088	$424,766	$466,100	$507,082

Water–Sewer Distribution

Object of Expenditure	Year II Spent	Year III Spent	Year IV Spent	Year V Spent
Salaries	$44,138	$238,704	$264,464	$326,126
Training	0	0	46	92
Travel	0	0	380	142
Professional services	0	0	0	2,094
Janitorial supplies	38	0	0	0
Office supplies	18	0	0	70
Printing	0	0	14	292
Freight and express	0	0	662	532
Communications	0	0	1,648	1,956
Telephone and telegraph	1,738	1,980	0	0
Diesel fuel	0	302	0	0
Gas and oil	2,696	10,222	15,264	17,630
Truck and car repairs	0	0	0	0
Equipment repairs	6,718	0	5,304	5,046
Tires, tubes, and batteries	1,024	66	0	0
Real property maintenance	0	0	830	578
Claims	0	0	0	0
Meter castings	0	0	630	0
Hydrants	0	2,538	1,342	2,844
Concrete	0	0	14,474	24,802
Cast iron pipe and fittings	938	8,520	70,902	146,166
Service pipe	312	0	0	0
Tools and supplies	30,348	40,228	31,168	37,000
Contracts	386	0	0	0
Medical	0	0	0	0
Capital improvements	3,790	29,512	17,480	34,590
TOTAL	$92,144	$332,072	$424,608	$599,960

Water-Sewer Improvements (Federal Grant Supported)

Object of Expenditure	Year I Budgeted	Year II Budgeted	Year III Budgeted	Year IV Budgeted
Salaries	$51,000	$49,614	$ 60,426	$ 0
Social security	0	0	0	0
Workers compensation	0	0	0	0
Consumable supplies	0	0	0	0
Janitorial supplies	0	0	0	0
Legal	0	0	0	0
Printing	0	0	0	0
Freight and express	0	0	0	0
Communications	0	0	0	0
Telephone and telegraph	0	0	0	0
Diesel fuel	0	0	0	0
Gas and oil	0	0	0	0
Truck and car repairs	0	0	0	0
Equipment rental/Purchase	0	0	0	0
Tires, tubes, and batteries	0	0	0	0
Real property maintenance	0	0	0	0
Claims	0	0	0	0
Cement	0	0	0	0
Other aggregate	0	0	0	0
Concrete	0	0	0	0
Cast iron pipe and fittings	0	0	0	0
Service pipe	0	0	0	0
Tools and supplies	0	0	0	0
Consultants and contracts	0	0	0	4,000,000
Medical	0	0	0	0
State assisted projects	0	0	100,000	0
TOTAL	$51,000	$49,614	$160,426	$4,000,000

Water-Sewer Improvements (Federal Grant Supported)

Object of Expenditure	Year I Spent	Year II Spent	Year III Spent	Year IV Spent
Salaries	$ 1,190	$ 0	$ 60,426	$ 0
Social security	0	62	780	0
Workers compensation	0	0	2,234	0
Consumable supplies	1,824	1,824	0	0
Janitorial supplies	0	0	0	0
Legal	0	0	400	0
Printing	0	0	0	0
Freight and express	0	0	0	0
Communications	0	0	0	0
Telephone and telegraph	0	0	0	0
Diesel fuel	0	0	0	0
Gas and oil	0	0	0	0
Truck and car repairs	0	0	0	0
Equipment rental/Purchase	37,812	37,812	13,712	0
Tires, tubes, and batteries	0	0	0	0
Real property maintenance	0	0	0	0
Claims	0	0	0	0
Cement	442	442	0	0
Other aggregate	78	78	0	0
Concrete	110	110	60	0
Cast iron pipe and fittings	0	0	0	0
Service pipe	0	0	0	0
Tools and supplies	0	0	0	0
Consultants and contracts	0	0	0	3,975,272
Medical	0	0	0	0
State assisted projects	0	0	241,588	0
TOTAL	$41,456	$40,328	$319,200	$3,975,272

ACCOUNT TITLE: Waterworks Commercial

The City water utility serves parts of five counties in the area. The waterworks commercial office reads meters, bills accounts, collects payments, maintains records, and prepares reports for various offices concerned with the waterworks' activities.

The City marshal supervises the collection of water-sewer bills and the reading of water meters. Meter reading in the residential sections occurs on a rotating basis; that is, each home's water use is not recorded every month.

An inventory of the vehicles used by the waterworks commercial office follows:

Manufacturer	Age (years)	Type of Vehicle	Salvage Value (each vehicle)
Ford (3)	3	2-door sedan	$4,000
Chevrolet	10	2-door sedan	500
Chevrolet	11	$\frac{1}{2}$-ton pickup	500
Dodge	8	2-door sedan	750
Plymouth	4	2-door sedan	1,000

Activity Indicators	FY V	FY V % Achieved	FY VI Estimate
Customer calls processed	8,235	100%	8,400
Percentage of meters used found to be in error	0.45%	100%	0.40%
Customer-requested investigations	152	100%	100

Operating needs: One additional meter reader; a hand-held computer for each meter reader for meter reading ($2,200 each).

Capital budget needs: Replacement of two vehicles that are 10 years or older.

EXPENDITURE DATA

Waterworks Commercial

Object of Expenditure	Year I Budgeted	Year II Budgeted	Year III Budgeted	Year IV Budgeted	Year V Budgeted
Salaries	$135,662	$151,560	$168,122	$148,634	$144,244
Professional services	0	0	0	200	200
Office supplies	5,600	5,600	6,000	8,400	5,400
Printing	0	0	0	5,000	6,000
Communications	0	0	0	20	20
Telephone and telegraph	60	60	60	0	0
Gas and oil	2,400	3,600	5,000	0	0
Truck and car repairs	2,800	3,600	1,182	0	0
Equipment repairs	3,200	3,600	2,400	1,100	1,000
Tires, tubes, and batteries	1,400	1,400	244	0	0
Claims	200	200	200	0	0
Tools and supplies	0	0	0	0	0
Capital improvements	1,000	17,640	2,400	0	0
TOTAL	$152,322	$187,260	$185,608	$163,354	$156,864

Waterworks Commercial

Object of Expenditure	Year I Spent	Year II Spent	Year III Spent	Year IV Spent	Year V Spent
Salaries	$142,994	$153,974	$133,886	$153,394	$136,384
Professional services	0	0	0	110	20
Office supplies	3,842	5,696	5,130	8,208	8,112
Printing	0	0	0	4,926	2,142
Communications	0	0	0	0	0
Telephone and telegraph	56	56	16	0	0
Gas and oil	1,350	4,224	6,216	0	0
Truck and car repairs	3,934	2,062	1,182	0	0
Equipment repairs	2,980	2,208	894	632	1,056
Tires, tubes, and batteries	1,226	726	244	0	0
Claims	0	0	100	0	0
Tools and supplies	8	0	0	0	0
Capital improvements	1,788	19,424	1,444	0	0
TOTAL	$158,178	$188,370	$149,112	$167,270	$147,714

PART 3

CITY PERSONNEL DATA

City Employee Information, FY V

This table lists positions authorized by ordinance, including those filled for the entire year or only part of the year, and certain information about City employees. Positions are listed by department for FY V. The "Retired" entries under "General Administrative" refer to persons who retired from City government work who receive City retirement pay under an old retirement system.

The information included with the classification is abbreviated as follows:

1. JOB CODE: A four-digit number corresponding to numbers for class code in the "Classification Index" data.
2. RANGE: A two-digit pay range keyed to the "40-Hour Personnel Pay Schedule" (which is the following table).
3. STEP: A letter also keyed to the "40-Hour Personnel Pay Schedule."
4. SALARY: Annual salary for those not listed in the "40-Hour Personnel Pay Schedule."
5. YE: Years of employment. If the number is zero, the employee was hired during FY V. If the number is left blank, the position is vacant.
6. YTRA: Years to age 65. If the number is left blank, the position is vacant.

Note: Employees may move from one department to another, and even change job classifications (if qualified), confounding the use of years in service to confirm seniority or payrolls for past years in a specific department.

Forecasting personnel expenditures calls for calculating all positions authorized at the start of the year times their respective yearly pay. While this is the maximum amount to budget, actual expenditures reflect positions vacated during the year and replaced at different salary levels. This makes it difficult to use a staffing profile on a single day to recalculate payroll expenses for past periods.

City Employee Information, FY V

Job Code	Title	Department	Range	Step	Salary	YE	YTRA
6114	Animal Services Officer	Animal Services	12	1		3	40
6114	Animal Services Officer	Animal Services	12	2		4	36
6118	Director of Animal Services	Animal Services	22	1		4	22
0132	Secretary II	Building Inspection	14	5		0	9
2335	Heating & Air Conditioning Inspector	Building Inspection	21	2		4	38
2315	Housing Inspector	Building Inspection	21	3		8	37
2345	Building Inspector	Building Inspection	21	3		3	15
2345	Building Inspector	Building Inspection	21	5		25	20
2325	Plumbing Inspector	Building Inspection	22	5		22	21
9119	Director, Permits and Inspection	Building Inspection			38,174	14	23
5211	Custodial Worker I	City Hall	7	3		7	38
5211	Custodial Worker I	City Hall	7	5		10	7
0113	Clerk III	City Marshal	14	3		6	35
0334	Assistant to City Marshal	City Marshal	15	0		2	10
9108	City Marshal	City Marshal			37,080	30	0
0132	Secretary II	Clerk-Treasurer	14	0			
0113	Clerk III	Clerk-Treasurer	14	2		5	24
0132	Secretary II	Clerk-Treasurer	14	4		5	35
0323	Accounting Clerk II	Clerk-Treasurer	15	5		17	13
0345	Supervisor, Tax Collection	Clerk-Treasurer	17	5		19	22
0325	Accountant	Clerk-Treasurer	20	0			
0655	Deputy City Clerk	Clerk-Treasurer	20	4		7	23
0635	Administrative Assistant	Clerk-Treasurer	22	0			
9102	Secretary	Clerk-Treasurer			7,994	2	41
9104	Admin. Assistant to the Mayor	Clerk-Treasurer			47,250	6	8
9105	City Attorney	Clerk-Treasurer			34,689	3	26
9106	City Clerk-Treasurer	Clerk-Treasurer			41,160	7	19
9122	Secretary to the Mayor	Clerk-Treasurer			20,459	6	28
0412	Data Entry Operator II	Computer and Data Processing	14	3		9	30
0412	Data Entry Operator II	Computer and Data Processing	14	5		20	22
0414	Computer Operator	Computer and Data Processing	15	0			
0415	Computer Programmer	Computer and Data Processing	20	0		0	40
9113	Director, Computer Services	Computer and Data Processing			36,338	6	28
8100	Council Member	Elective			7,400	12	
8100	Council Member	Elective			7,400	3	
8100	Council Member	Elective			7,400	15	
8100	Council Member	Elective			7,400	7	
8100	Council Member	Elective			7,400	2	
8100	Council Member	Elective			7,400	3	
8100	Council Member	Elective			7,400	2	
8100	Council Member	Elective			7,400	3	
8100	Council Member	Elective			7,400	4	
8100	Council Member	Elective			7,400	8	
8101	Mayor	Elective			28,650	0	
9100	Recorder	Elective			14,500		

Job Code	Title	Department	Range	Step	Salary	YE	YTRA
5513	Electrician's Assistant	Electrical	16	1		3	35
5518	City Electrician	Electrical	22	4		4	30
4214	Firefighter	Fire	17	0			
4214	Firefighter	Fire	17	0			
4214	Firefighter	Fire	17	0			
4214	Firefighter	Fire	17	0			
4214	Firefighter	Fire	17	0			
4214	Firefighter	Fire	17	0			
4214	Firefighter	Fire	17	1		4	41
4214	Firefighter	Fire	17	1		4	39
4214	Firefighter	Fire	17	1		3	41
4214	Firefighter	Fire	17	1		3	39
4214	Firefighter	Fire	17	1		4	40
4214	Firefighter	Fire	17	1		5	40
4214	Firefighter	Fire	17	1		6	39
4214	Firefighter	Fire	17	1		4	40
4214	Firefighter	Fire	17	1		4	32
4214	Firefighter	Fire	17	1		3	39
4214	Firefighter	Fire	17	2		4	36
4214	Firefighter	Fire	17	2		4	38
4214	Firefighter	Fire	17	2		4	40
4214	Firefighter	Fire	17	2		4	39
4214	Firefighter	Fire	17	2		4	40
4214	Firefighter	Fire	17	2		4	40
4214	Firefighter	Fire	17	2		4	41
4214	Firefighter	Fire	17	2		4	41
4214	Firefighter	Fire	17	2		8	34
4214	Firefighter	Fire	17	3		5	37
4213	Fire Dispatcher	Fire	17	4		11	34
4214	Firefighter	Fire	17	4		11	34
4213	Fire Dispatcher	Fire	17	5		23	20
4215	Fire Driver-Engineer	Fire	19	2		4	40
4215	Fire Driver-Engineer	Fire	19	2		4	40
4235	Fire Prevention Officer	Fire	19	2		8	36
4215	Fire Driver-Engineer	Fire	19	3		5	39
4215	Fire Driver-Engineer	Fire	19	3		8	35
4215	Fire Driver-Engineer	Fire	19	3		6	38
4215	Fire Driver-Engineer	Fire	19	3		20	25
4215	Fire Driver-Engineer	Fire	19	3		8	35
4215	Fire Driver-Engineer	Fire	19	3		6	39
4215	Fire Driver-Engineer	Fire	19	3		16	23
4215	Fire Driver-Engineer	Fire	19	3		11	28
4215	Fire Driver-Engineer	Fire	19	3		6	36
4215	Fire Driver-Engineer	Fire	19	3		19	25
4215	Fire Driver-Engineer	Fire	19	3		6	38
4215	Fire Driver-Engineer	Fire	19	3		10	35
4215	Fire Driver-Engineer	Fire	19	3		6	39
4215	Fire Driver-Engineer	Fire	19	4		7	35
4216	Fire Lieutenant	Fire	21	3		19	23

Job Code	Title	Department	Range	Step	Salary	YE	YTRA
4216	Fire Lieutenant	Fire	21	3		6	33
4216	Fire Lieutenant	Fire	21	3		8	34
4216	Fire Lieutenant	Fire	21	3		13	30
4216	Fire Lieutenant	Fire	21	3		9	29
4216	Fire Lieutenant	Fire	21	3		25	20
4216	Fire Lieutenant	Fire	21	3		6	37
4216	Fire Lieutenant	Fire	21	3		25	20
4216	Fire Lieutenant	Fire	21	3		11	34
4216	Fire Lieutenant	Fire	21	3		19	23
4216	Fire Lieutenant	Fire	21	3		6	39
4216	Fire Lieutenant	Fire	21	3		11	34
4216	Fire Lieutenant	Fire	21	3		14	31
4216	Fire Lieutenant	Fire	21	3		11	30
2345	Building Inspector	Fire	21	5		25	20
4237	Fire Marshal	Fire	23	1		8	35
4257	Fire Alarm Superintendent	Fire	23	2		20	25
4217	Fire Captain	Fire	23	3		16	22
4217	Fire Captain	Fire	23	3		20	20
4217	Fire Captain	Fire	23	3		20	24
4217	Fire Captain	Fire	23	3		25	20
4217	Fire Captain	Fire	23	3		32	13
4217	Fire Captain	Fire	23	3		12	30
4217	Fire Captain	Fire	23	3		17	20
4217	Fire Captain	Fire	23	3		14	30
4227	Fire Training Chief	Fire	23	3		16	28
4217	Fire Captain	Fire	23	4		15	29
4217	Fire Captain	Fire	23	4		25	15
4217	Fire Captain	Fire	23	4		13	22
4268	Assistant Fire Chief	Fire	26	3		30	15
4268	Assistant Fire Chief	Fire	26	3		26	18
4268	Assistant Fire Chief	Fire	26	3		36	8
9126	Fire Chief	Fire			40,136	31	9
4214	Firefighter	Fire Station, County	17	0		2	40
4214	Firefighter	Fire Station, County	17	0		2	41
4214	Firefighter	Fire Station, County	17	0		2	36
4214	Firefighter	Fire Station, County	17	0		2	32
4214	Firefighter	Fire Station, County	17	0		0	38
4214	Firefighter	Fire Station, County	17	1		11	32
4214	Firefighter	Fire Station, County	17	1		9	36
4214	Firefighter	Fire Station, County	17	2		6	32
4235	Fire Prevention Officer	Fire Station, County	19	1		11	30
4215	Fire Driver-Engineer	Fire Station, County	19	2		5	39
4215	Fire Driver-Engineer	Fire Station, County	19	3		6	37
4215	Fire Driver-Engineer	Fire Station, County	19	3		11	34
4215	Fire Driver-Engineer	Fire Station, County	19	3		11	29
4216	Fire Lieutenant	Fire Station, County	21	1		12	33
4216	Fire Lieutenant	Fire Station, County	21	3		13	31
4217	Fire Captain	Fire Station, County	23	3		23	16
4217	Fire Captain	Fire Station, County	23	3		35	1

Job Code	Title	Department	Range	Step	Salary	YE	YTRA
4217	Fire Captain	Fire Station, County	23	3		16	23
7100	Retired	General Administrative			240		
7100	Retired	General Administrative			600		
7100	Retired	General Administrative			120		
7100	Retired	General Administrative			480		
7100	Retired	General Administrative			600		
7100	Retired	General Administrative			900		
7100	Retired	General Administrative			600		
7100	Retired	General Administrative			900		
7100	Retired	General Administrative			600		
7100	Retired	General Administrative			900		
7100	Retired	General Administrative			900		
7100	Retired	General Administrative			360		
7100	Retired	General Administrative			600		
7100	Retired	General Administrative			720		
7100	Retired	General Administrative			600		
7100	Retired	General Administrative			480		
7100	Retired	General Administrative			600		
7100	Retired	General Administrative			600		
7100	Retired	General Administrative			600		
7100	Retired	General Administrative			900		
7100	Retired	General Administrative			600		
7100	Retired	General Administrative			600		
6312	Recreation Leader	Human Resources	8	0			
0112	Clerk II	Human Resources	11	0			
5312	Equipment Operator I	Human Resources	11	0		2	32
0123	Clerk Typist III	Human Resources	13	2		3	42
0123	Clerk Typist III	Human Resources	13	2		6	30
1133	Information and Referral Specialist	Human Resources	17	0			
1144	Social Service Specialist	Human Resources	17	0			
1133	Information and Referral Specialist	Human Resources	17	4		8	13
1133	Information and Referral Specialist	Human Resources	17	4		7	38
1133	Information and Referral Specialist	Human Resources	17	4		22	9
0325	Accountant	Human Resources	20	0			
1145	Child-Care Coordinator	Human Resources	20	2		4	40
1135	Information and Referral Coordinator	Human Resources	22	5		6	29
9115	Director of Human Resources	Human Resources			32,491	8	23
5211	Custodial Worker I	Parks and Recreation	7	3		5	24
5111	Laborer I	Parks and Recreation	8	0		2	38
5212	Custodial Worker II	Parks and Recreation	8	0		2	37
5212	Custodial Worker II	Parks and Recreation	8	0		2	43
5212	Custodial Worker II	Parks and Recreation	8	0		2	28
6312	Recreation Leader	Parks and Recreation	8	0		2	39
6312	Recreation Leader	Parks and Recreation	8	0		2	37
6312	Recreation Leader	Parks and Recreation	8	0		2	41
6312	Recreation Leader	Parks and Recreation	8	0		2	38
6312	Recreation Leader	Parks and Recreation	8	0		2	43
6312	Recreation Leader	Parks and Recreation	8	1		3	40

Job Code	Title	Department	Range	Step	Salary	YE	YTRA
6312	Recreation Leader	Parks and Recreation	8	1		3	42
5212	Custodial Worker II	Parks and Recreation	8	2		4	35
6312	Recreation Leader	Parks and Recreation	8	2		4	38
6312	Recreation Leader	Parks and Recreation	8	2		4	41
6312	Recreation Leader	Parks and Recreation	8	2		4	41
5111	Laborer I	Parks and Recreation	8	3		11	4
0121	Clerk Typist I	Parks and Recreation	9	1		3	42
5112	Laborer II	Parks and Recreation	10	0		2	43
5112	Laborer II	Parks and Recreation	10	0		2	41
5112	Laborer II	Parks and Recreation	10	0		2	15
5112	Laborer II	Parks and Recreation	10	2		3	40
0131	Secretary I	Parks and Recreation	11	0		2	40
5312	Equipment Operator I	Parks and Recreation	11	0		2	42
0131	Secretary I	Parks and Recreation	11	1		3	40
5312	Equipment Operator I	Parks and Recreation	11	1		3	40
5312	Equipment Operator I	Parks and Recreation	11	1		3	38
6313	Neighborhood Center Leader	Parks and Recreation	12	0		2	29
6313	Neighborhood Center Leader	Parks and Recreation	12	0		6	39
6313	Neighborhood Center Leader	Parks and Recreation	12	0		6	36
6313	Neighborhood Center Leader	Parks and Recreation	12	1		3	37
6313	Neighborhood Center Leader	Parks and Recreation	12	1		5	17
6313	Neighborhood Center Leader	Parks and Recreation	12	1		9	20
6313	Neighborhood Center Leader	Parks and Recreation	12	1		5	26
5113	Laborer III	Parks and Recreation	12	2		3	40
6313	Neighborhood Center Leader	Parks and Recreation	12	4		5	40
5313	Equipment Operator II	Parks and Recreation	13	2		3	42
5313	Equipment Operator II	Parks and Recreation	13	2		3	38
5714	Labor Supervisor I	Parks and Recreation	14	0		2	40
5714	Labor Supervisor I	Parks and Recreation	14	0		2	40
6214	Animal Caretaker	Parks and Recreation	14	0		2	41
6375	Maintenance Service Center Supervisor	Parks and Recreation	14	0		2	38
6325	Assistant Community Center Director	Parks and Recreation	14	1		3	39
6325	Assistant Community Center Director	Parks and Recreation	14	1		9	31
5735	Custodial Supervisor	Parks and Recreation	14	2		3	35
6214	Animal Caretaker	Parks and Recreation	14	2		4	38
6325	Assistant Community Center Director	Parks and Recreation	14	2		5	35
5714	Labor Supervisor I	Parks and Recreation	14	3		6	36
6315	Neighborhood Centers Supervisor	Parks and Recreation	14	3		7	36
0132	Secretary II	Parks and Recreation	14	5		6	39
5714	Labor Supervisor I	Parks and Recreation	14	5		6	37
6365	Assistant Park Manager	Parks and Recreation	16	0		3	36
6345	Cultural Arts Supervisor	Parks and Recreation	16	1		4	41
6345	Cultural Arts Supervisor	Parks and Recreation	16	1		3	40
5725	General Maintenance Supervisor	Parks and Recreation	16	2		5	40
6343	Dance Instructor	Parks and Recreation	16	4		5	26
6334	Assistant Sports Coordinator	Parks and Recreation	17	1		3	40
6326	Community Center Director	Parks and Recreation	18	1		6	39
6326	Community Center Director	Parks and Recreation	18	2		4	38

Job Code	Title	Department	Range	Step	Salary	YE	YTRA
6316	Coordinator, Neighborhood Centers	Parks and Recreation	18	3		16	24
6346	Coordinator for Special Activities	Parks and Recreation	18	4		6	35
6366	Park Manager	Parks and Recreation	19	3		5	40
6336	Sports Coordinator	Parks and Recreation	19	4		4	41
6376	Coordinator for Grounds Development	Parks and Recreation	21	2		2	39
6388	Superintendent of Parks	Parks and Recreation	24	2		4	38
6358	Superintendent of Recreation	Parks and Recreation	24	3		9	29
9116	Director, Parks and Recreation	Parks and Recreation			36,408	7	35
0112	Clerk II	Personnel	11	2			
0131	Secretary I	Personnel	11	3		0	40
0132	Secretary II	Personnel	14	1			
0645	Personnel Technician	Personnel	17	4		6	39
0515	Graphics and Printing Coordinator	Personnel	19	3		5	36
0325	Accountant	Personnel	20	5			
1128	Program Specialist	Personnel	24	3			
1127	Program Coordinator	Personnel	27	2		7	38
0648	Assistant Personnel Director	Personnel	27	3		7	31
9101	Personnel Board Member	Personnel			1,000	6	
9101	Personnel Board Member	Personnel			1,000	6	
9101	Personnel Board Member	Personnel			1,000	3	
9101	Personnel Board Member	Personnel			1,000	6	
9101	Personnel Board Member	Personnel			1,000	4	
9112	Director of Personnel	Personnel			36,225	3	40
9114	Director of Community Development	Planning Commission			36,338	7	32
2211	Cartographer I	Planning Commission	10	0		0	40
2211	Cartographer I	Planning Commission	10	0			
0132	Secretary II	Planning Commission	14	1		6	33
2212	Cartographer II	Planning Commission	14	2		5	40
1116	Environmental Planner	Planning Commission	24	5		7	35
1118	Assistant Director of Planning	Planning Commission	24	5			
9120	Director, Planning Commission	Planning Commission			41,315	7	32
2375	Administrator, Zoning and Subdivision	Planning Commission	20	3		8	35
4121	School Crossing Guard	Police	6	2		8	37
4121	School Crossing Guard	Police	6	2		4	30
4121	School Crossing Guard	Police	6	2		4	29
4121	School Crossing Guard	Police	6	2		7	29
4121	School Crossing Guard	Police	6	2		11	16
4121	School Crossing Guard	Police	6	2		7	35
4121	School Crossing Guard	Police	6	2		6	4
4121	School Crossing Guard	Police	6	2		2	31
4121	School Crossing Guard	Police	6	2		16	28
4121	School Crossing Guard	Police	6	2		7	33
4121	School Crossing Guard	Police	6	2		6	21
4121	School Crossing Guard	Police	6	2		7	36
4142	Neighborhood Service Officer	Police	8	0			
4142	Neighborhood Service Officer	Police	8	0		2	39
5111	Laborer I	Police	8	0		2	34
4142	Neighborhood Service Officer	Police	8	1		3	42

Job Code	Title	Department	Range	Step	Salary	YE	YTRA
0121	Clerk Typist I	Police	9	0		2	22
0112	Clerk II	Police	11	0		2	38
0122	Clerk Typist II	Police	11	0		2	39
0131	Secretary I	Police	11	0		2	36
0112	Clerk II	Police	11	1		3	37
0112	Clerk II	Police	11	1		3	39
0131	Secretary I	Police	11	1		3	42
0112	Clerk II	Police	11	4		8	16
4122	Parking Violations Officer	Police	13	0			
4122	Parking Violations Officer	Police	13	3		11	31
4122	Parking Violations Officer	Police	13	3		14	27
4122	Parking Violations Officer	Police	13	3		19	12
4122	Parking Violations Officer	Police	13	3		6	25
4122	Parking Violations Officer	Police	13	3		13	19
0312	Parking Meter Repairer	Police	13	5		20	10
0113	Clerk III	Police	14	0			
0113	Clerk III	Police	14	1		3	30
0113	Clerk III	Police	14	2		3	40
0132	Secretary II	Police	14	2		6	34
0113	Clerk III	Police	14	5		21	19
4123	Police Radio Dispatcher	Police	15	0			
4123	Police Radio Dispatcher	Police	15	0			
4123	Police Radio Dispatcher	Police	15	0			
4123	Police Radio Dispatcher	Police	15	0		2	22
4123	Police Radio Dispatcher	Police	15	0		2	39
4123	Police Radio Dispatcher	Police	15	1		3	45
4123	Police Radio Dispatcher	Police	15	1		3	26
4123	Police Radio Dispatcher	Police	15	2		4	36
4133	Police Officer	Police	18	0			
4133	Police Officer	Police	18	0			
4133	Police Officer	Police	18	0			
4133	Police Officer	Police	18	0			
4133	Police Officer	Police	18	1		2	42
4133	Police Officer	Police	18	1		3	42
4133	Police Officer	Police	18	1		3	39
4133	Police Officer	Police	18	1		3	40
4133	Police Officer	Police	18	1		6	37
4133	Police Officer	Police	18	2		2	21
4133	Police Officer	Police	18	2		2	40
4133	Police Officer	Police	18	2		9	36
4133	Police Officer	Police	18	2		2	40
4133	Police Officer	Police	18	2		3	41
4133	Police Officer	Police	18	2		2	43
4133	Police Officer	Police	18	2		3	42
4133	Police Officer	Police	18	2		2	36
4133	Police Officer	Police	18	2		3	42
4133	Police Officer	Police	18	2		3	40
4133	Police Officer	Police	18	2		3	42
4133	Police Officer	Police	18	2		4	37

Job Code	Title	Department	Range	Step	Salary	YE	YTRA
4133	Police Officer	Police	18	2		4	38
4133	Police Officer	Police	18	3		8	35
4133	Police Officer	Police	18	3		3	40
4133	Police Officer	Police	18	3		7	38
4133	Police Officer	Police	18	3		3	40
4133	Police Officer	Police	18	3		5	40
4133	Police Officer	Police	18	3		7	37
4133	Police Officer	Police	18	3		6	39
4133	Police Officer	Police	18	3		7	37
4133	Police Officer	Police	18	3		3	41
4133	Police Officer	Police	18	3		3	33
4133	Police Officer	Police	18	3		3	41
4133	Police Officer	Police	18	4		7	38
4133	Police Officer	Police	18	4		7	38
4133	Police Officer	Police	18	4		9	30
4133	Police Officer	Police	18	4		10	35
4133	Police Officer	Police	18	4		10	34
4133	Police Officer	Police	18	4		18	22
4133	Police Officer	Police	18	4		7	38
4133	Police Officer	Police	18	5		8	35
4133	Police Officer	Police	18	5		20	25
4134	Police Corporal	Police	19	4		4	41
4134	Police Corporal	Police	19	4		7	38
4134	Police Corporal	Police	19	4		3	31
4134	Police Corporal	Police	19	5		13	29
4175	Police Detective	Police	20	2			
4175	Police Detective	Police	20	3			
4175	Police Detective	Police	20	3			
4175	Police Detective	Police	20	3		5	37
4175	Police Detective	Police	20	4		10	35
4175	Police Detective	Police	20	4		10	34
4175	Police Detective	Police	20	4		4	40
4175	Police Detective	Police	20	4		4	41
4175	Police Detective	Police	20	5		5	39
4175	Police Detective	Police	20	5		7	38
4135	Police Sergeant	Police	21	3			
4135	Police Sergeant	Police	21	3			
4135	Police Sergeant	Police	21	5			
4135	Police Sergeant	Police	21	5		30	13
4135	Police Sergeant	Police	21	5		10	35
4135	Police Sergeant	Police	21	5		25	20
4135	Police Sergeant	Police	21	5		28	16
4135	Police Sergeant	Police	21	5		25	19
4135	Police Sergeant	Police	21	5		15	25
4135	Police Sergeant	Police	21	5			
4135	Police Sergeant	Police	21	5		12	33
4136	Police Lieutenant	Police	24	1		9	35
4137	Police Shift Commander	Police	24	1		35	10
4136	Police Lieutenant	Police	24	2		15	30

Job Code	Title	Department	Range	Step	Salary	YE	YTRA
4137	Police Shift Commander	Police	24	2		31	14
4125	Supervisor, Special Services	Police	24	3		39	3
4136	Police Lieutenant	Police	24	4			
4136	Police Lieutenant	Police	24	4		27	14
4136	Police Lieutenant	Police	24	4		31	12
4136	Police Lieutenant	Police	24	4		29	13
4136	Police Lieutenant	Police	24	4		22	18
4136	Police Lieutenant	Police	24	4		9	35
4136	Police Lieutenant	Police	24	4		27	14
4138	Police Captain	Police	25	3		31	14
4138	Police Captain	Police	25	5		31	12
4139	Police Major	Police	27	2		2	33
4139	Police Major	Police	27	4		3	34
4139	Police Major	Police	27	4		3	28
4198	Assistant Police Chief	Police	28	5		31	14
9121	Police Chief	Police			44,940	4	
2114	Engineering Aide IV	Public Works	20	5		0	35
0635	Administrative Assistant	Public Works	22	5		35	7
2128	Special Projects Engineer	Public Works	27	0		4	40
2118	Assistant City Engineer	Public Works	29	3		6	39
9107	City Engineer	Public Works			42,062	19	13
5314	Equipment Operator III	Sanitation-Garbage Collection	14	0		2	31
5221	Security Guard	Sanitation-Garbage Collection	8	1		3	26
5221	Security Guard	Sanitation-Garbage Collection	8	1		3	6
5221	Security Guard	Sanitation-Garbage Collection	8	5		11	13
5611	Refuse Collector	Sanitation-Garbage Collection	9	0		2	40
5611	Refuse Collector	Sanitation-Garbage Collection	9	0		2	20
5611	Refuse Collector	Sanitation-Garbage Collection	9	0		2	43
5611	Refuse Collector	Sanitation-Garbage Collection	9	0		2	38
5611	Refuse Collector	Sanitation-Garbage Collection	9	0		2	43
5611	Refuse Collector	Sanitation-Garbage Collection	9	0		2	43
5611	Refuse Collector	Sanitation-Garbage Collection	9	1		3	38
5611	Refuse Collector	Sanitation-Garbage Collection	9	1		9	12
5611	Refuse Collector	Sanitation-Garbage Collection	9	1		2	43
5611	Refuse Collector	Sanitation-Garbage Collection	9	2		4	36
5611	Refuse Collector	Sanitation-Garbage Collection	9	2		4	35
5411	Automotive Servicer	Sanitation-Garbage Collection	9	3		13	6
5611	Refuse Collector	Sanitation-Garbage Collection	9	3		5	19
5611	Refuse Collector	Sanitation-Garbage Collection	9	3		7	27
5611	Refuse Collector	Sanitation-Garbage Collection	9	3		6	11
5611	Refuse Collector	Sanitation-Garbage Collection	9	5		11	29
5611	Refuse Collector	Sanitation-Garbage Collection	9	5		14	27
5611	Refuse Collector	Sanitation-Garbage Collection	9	5		16	25
5612	Refuse Collection Driver I	Sanitation-Garbage Collection	10	3		9	28
5612	Refuse Collection Driver I	Sanitation-Garbage Collection	10	3		7	30
5612	Refuse Collection Driver I	Sanitation-Garbage Collection	10	4		5	24
5612	Refuse Collection Driver I	Sanitation-Garbage Collection	10	4		23	20
5612	Refuse Collection Driver I	Sanitation-Garbage Collection	10	4		5	32

Job Code	Title	Department	Range	Step	Salary	YE	YTRA
5612	Refuse Collection Driver I	Sanitation-Garbage Collection	10	5		5	37
5613	Refuse Collection Driver II	Sanitation-Garbage Collection	11	0		2	43
5613	Refuse Collection Driver II	Sanitation-Garbage Collection	11	0		2	32
5613	Refuse Collection Driver II	Sanitation-Garbage Collection	11	0		2	30
5613	Refuse Collection Driver II	Sanitation-Garbage Collection	11	0		2	41
5613	Refuse Collection Driver II	Sanitation-Garbage Collection	11	1		3	42
5613	Refuse Collection Driver II	Sanitation-Garbage Collection	11	1		3	35
5613	Refuse Collection Driver II	Sanitation-Garbage Collection	11	2		4	29
5613	Refuse Collection Driver II	Sanitation-Garbage Collection	11	2		5	40
5613	Refuse Collection Driver II	Sanitation-Garbage Collection	11	2		6	36
5613	Refuse Collection Driver II	Sanitation-Garbage Collection	11	2		4	36
5613	Refuse Collection Driver II	Sanitation-Garbage Collection	11	3		7	14
5613	Refuse Collection Driver II	Sanitation-Garbage Collection	11	3		11	32
5614	Refuse Collection Driver III	Sanitation-Garbage Collection	13	2		4	40
5614	Refuse Collection Driver III	Sanitation-Garbage Collection	13	3		13	11
5614	Refuse Collection Driver III	Sanitation-Garbage Collection	13	3		5	40
5614	Refuse Collection Driver III	Sanitation-Garbage Collection	13	3		32	8
5614	Refuse Collection Driver III	Sanitation-Garbage Collection	13	3		11	8
5614	Refuse Collection Driver III	Sanitation-Garbage Collection	13	3		5	40
5614	Refuse Collection Driver III	Sanitation-Garbage Collection	13	3		5	39
0123	Clerk Typist III	Sanitation-Garbage Collection	13	4		8	33
5755	Sanitation Supervisor	Sanitation-Garbage Collection	14	2		5	35
5314	Equipment Operator III	Sanitation-Garbage Collection	14	3		6	10
5414	Automotive Mechanic	Sanitation-Garbage Collection	14	3		12	19
5314	Equipment Operator III	Sanitation-Garbage Collection	14	5		16	12
5755	Sanitation Supervisor	Sanitation-Garbage Collection	14	5		39	3
5758	Assistant Director of Sanitation	Sanitation-Garbage Collection	20	3		22	8
9118	Director of Sanitation	Sanitation-Garbage Collection			36,166	7	9
5111	Laborer I	Sanitation-Street Cleaning	8	0			
5111	Laborer I	Sanitation-Street Cleaning	8	0			
5111	Laborer I	Sanitation-Street Cleaning	8	0		9	12
5111	Laborer I	Sanitation-Street Cleaning	8	0		2	38
5111	Laborer I	Sanitation-Street Cleaning	8	1		7	36
5111	Laborer I	Sanitation-Street Cleaning	8	3		15	11
5613	Refuse Collection Driver II	Sanitation-Street Cleaning	11	0		2	31
5613	Refuse Collection Driver II	Sanitation-Street Cleaning	11	1		3	42
5613	Refuse Collection Driver II	Sanitation-Street Cleaning	11	2		4	19
5613	Refuse Collection Driver II	Sanitation-Street Cleaning	11	2		7	37
5613	Refuse Collection Driver II	Sanitation-Street Cleaning	11	4		5	36
5313	Equipment Operator II	Sanitation-Street Cleaning	13	3		23	6
5313	Equipment Operator II	Sanitation-Street Cleaning	13	3		7	16
5314	Equipment Operator III	Sanitation-Street Cleaning	14	2		12	12
5314	Equipment Operator III	Sanitation-Street Cleaning	14	2		8	32
5755	Sanitation Supervisor	Sanitation-Street Cleaning	14	5		15	19
5755	Sanitation Supervisor	Sanitation-Street Cleaning	14	5		12	16
5412	Automotive Mechanic Helper	Service Garage	10	0		0	41
5412	Automotive Mechanic Helper	Service Garage	10	1		3	42
5414	Automotive Mechanic	Service Garage	14	0		2	35

Job Code	Title	Department	Range	Step	Salary	YE	YTRA
5414	Automotive Mechanic	Service Garage	14	1		3	42
0113	Clerk III	Service Garage	14	3		5	31
5414	Automotive Mechanic	Service Garage	14	3		6	26
5415	Automotive Mechanic Technician	Service Garage	16	2		5	37
5416	Automotive Technician II	Service Garage	18	0		4	8
9109	City Shop Manager	Service Garage			30,000	25	26
4111	Jailer	Stockade	14	0		2	43
4111	Jailer	Stockade	14	0		2	25
4111	Jailer	Stockade	14	0		2	14
4115	Head Jailer	Stockade	16	2		4	18
5111	Laborer I	Streets	8	0		2	37
5111	Laborer I	Streets	8	0		2	21
5111	Laborer I	Streets	8	0		0	39
5111	Laborer I	Streets	8	1		4	7
5111	Laborer I	Streets	8	2		9	31
2111	Engineering Aide I	Streets	10	0		2	38
5112	Laborer II	Streets	10	0		2	43
5112	Laborer II	Streets	10	0		2	16
5112	Laborer II	Streets	10	0		2	43
5112	Laborer II	Streets	10	3		9	6
5112	Laborer II	Streets	10	3		10	18
5112	Laborer II	Streets	10	4		14	29
5312	Equipment Operator I	Streets	11	0		2	39
5312	Equipment Operator I	Streets	11	0		2	43
5312	Equipment Operator I	Streets	11	0		2	34
5312	Equipment Operator I	Streets	11	0		2	41
5312	Equipment Operator I	Streets	11	1		2	40
5312	Equipment Operator I	Streets	11	2		3	42
5312	Equipment Operator I	Streets	11	2		4	31
5312	Equipment Operator I	Streets	11	2		6	39
5312	Equipment Operator I	Streets	11	2		4	31
0131	Secretary I	Streets	11	3		4	37
5312	Equipment Operator I	Streets	11	3		8	37
5312	Equipment Operator I	Streets	11	3		6	39
5312	Equipment Operator I	Streets	11	3		12	5
5312	Equipment Operator I	Streets	11	4		16	16
5113	Laborer III	Streets	12	2		15	11
5113	Laborer III	Streets	12	3		9	36
5313	Equipment Operator II	Streets	13	3		6	22
5714	Labor Supervisor I	Streets	14	4		6	39
2112	Engineering Aide II	Streets	15	0		3	41
5715	Labor Supervisor II	Streets	16	3		11	30
5315	Equipment Operator IV	Streets	16	5		18	27
5315	Equipment Operator IV	Streets	16	5		40	5
5716	Labor Supervisor III	Streets	17	3		31	11
0324	Accounting Clerk III	Streets	17	4		10	25
5716	Labor Supervisor III	Streets	17	4		23	17
5716	Labor Supervisor III	Streets	17	4		12	28

Job Code	Title	Department	Range	Step	Salary	YE	YTRA
2113	Engineering Aide III	Streets	18	2		5	40
5768	Street Superintendent	Streets	22	3		7	30
9102	Secretary	Streets			21,000	4	
5212	Custodial Worker II	Water Filter Plant	8	2		4	21
3121	Water Plant Operator Trainee	Water Filter Plant	12	0		2	40
3121	Water Plant Operator Trainee	Water Filter Plant	12	0		0	21
3121	Water Plant Operator Trainee	Water Filter Plant	12	0		0	37
3121	Water Plant Operator Trainee	Water Filter Plant	12	2		4	37
3121	Water Plant Operator Trainee	Water Filter Plant	14	1		3	40
3121	Water Plant Operator Trainee	Water Filter Plant	14	2		3	42
3122	Water Plant Operator	Water Filter Plant	14	2		5	40
3123	Senior Water Filter Operator	Water Filter Plant	16	5		6	27
3123	Senior Water Filter Operator	Water Filter Plant	16	5		7	36
3134	Laboratory Technician	Water Filter Plant	16	5		12	33
3124	Chief Maintenance Operator	Water Filter Plant	18	4		10	35
3126	Chief Water Filter Operator	Water Filter Plant	20	3		28	12
3317	Assistant Superintendent, Water Filter Plant	Water Filter Plant	21	3		31	14
3318	Superintendent, Water Filter Plant	Water Filter Plant	23	5		17	23
5112	Laborer II	Water Meters	10	3		12	18
5423	Water Meter Repairer	Water Meters	12	3		8	23
5314	Equipment Operator III	Water Meters	14	3		23	18
5778	Water-Sewer Superintendent	Water Meters	27	0		23	18
3131	Laboratory Aide	Water Pollution Control Plant	10	1		0	36
3131	Laboratory Aide	Water Pollution Control Plant	10	2		4	35
3131	Laboratory Aide	Water Pollution Control Plant	10	3		5	34
5312	Equipment Operator I	Water Pollution Control Plant	11	3		8	37
3111	Wastewater Plant Operator Trainee	Water Pollution Control Plant	12	0			
3111	Wastewater Plant Operator Trainee	Water Pollution Control Plant	12	0			
3111	Wastewater Plant Operator Trainee	Water Pollution Control Plant	12	0			
3142	Maintenance Mechanic I WPC	Water Pollution Control Plant	13	0			
3143	Maintenance Mechanic II	Water Pollution Control Plant	14	1		8	35
3112	Wastewater Plant Operator	Water Pollution Control Plant	14	2		5	28
3112	Wastewater Plant Operator	Water Pollution Control Plant	14	3		6	27
3112	Wastewater Plant Operator	Water Pollution Control Plant	14	3		6	27
3112	Wastewater Plant Operator	Water Pollution Control Plant	14	5		10	15
3134	Laboratory Technician	Water Pollution Control Plant	16	1		6	38
3113	Senior Wastewater Plant Operator	Water Pollution Control Plant	16	2		4	34
3134	Laboratory Technician	Water Pollution Control Plant	16	2		7	38
3113	Senior Wastewater Plant Operator	Water Pollution Control Plant	16	3		6	32
3114	Chief Maintenance Operator WPC	Water Pollution Control Plant	18	5		0	35
3114	Chief Maintenance Operator WPC	Water Pollution Control Plant	18	5		0	35
3114	Chief Maintenance Operator WPC	Water Pollution Control Plant	18	5		0	34
3218	Superintendent, Water Pollution Control	Water Pollution Control Plant	23	5		17	23
5111	Laborer I	Water-Sewer Distribution	8	0		2	24
5111	Laborer I	Water-Sewer Distribution	8	0		2	17
5111	Laborer I	Water-Sewer Distribution	8	0		2	36

Job Code	Title	Department	Range	Step	Salary	YE	YTRA
5111	Laborer I	Water-Sewer Distribution	8	0		2	15
5111	Laborer I	Water-Sewer Distribution	8	1		5	40
5111	Laborer I	Water-Sewer Distribution	8	1		5	18
5112	Laborer II	Water-Sewer Distribution	10	2		5	21
5112	Laborer II	Water-Sewer Distribution	10	3		18	24
0112	Clerk II	Water Sewer Distribution	11	1		3	37
5312	Equipment Operator I	Water-Sewer Distribution	11	1		8	9
5312	Equipment Operator I	Water-Sewer Distribution	11	3		7	26
5113	Laborer III	Water-Sewer Distribution	12	0		2	35
5113	Laborer III	Water-Sewer Distribution	12	3		10	18
5313	Equipment Operator II	Water-Sewer Distribution	13	3		8	36
5313	Equipment Operator II	Water-Sewer Distribution	13	3		18	5
5314	Equipment Operator III	Water-Sewer Distribution	14	0		5	34
5714	Labor Supervisor I	Water Sewer Distribution	14	2		18	26
5715	Labor Supervisor II	Water-Sewer Distribution	16	3		13	30
5715	Labor Supervisor II	Water-Sewer Distribution	16	3		27	9
5716	Labor Supervisor III	Water-Sewer Distribution	17	5		24	18
0321	Cashier	Waterworks Commercial	11	2		5	36
0212	Meter Reader II	Waterworks Commercial	12	0		0	39
0212	Meter Reader II	Waterworks Commercial	12	0		0	42
0212	Meter Reader II	Waterworks Commercial	12	2		9	36
0212	Meter Reader II	Waterworks Commercial	12	4		7	10
0212	Meter Reader II	Waterworks Commercial	12	5		22	3
0323	Accounting Clerk II	Waterworks Commercial	15	4		17	23
0215	Meter Reader Supervisor	Waterworks Commercial	17	5		29	14
0225	Supervisor, Customer Service	Waterworks Commercial	19	4		26	17
9102	Secretary				14,076	4	

40-Hour Personnel Pay Schedule, Effective FY V

Pay Range		Step 0	Step 1	Step 2	Step 3	Step 4	Step 5
3	Hourly	4.250	4.462	4.685	4.919	5.164	5.422
	Weekly	170.000	178.483	187.390	196.741	206.559	216.867
	Semi-monthly	368.333	386.714	406.012	426.272	447.544	469.878
	Monthly	736.667	773.428	812.023	852.545	895.089	939.755
	Annually	8,840.000	9,281.134	9,744.281	10,230.540	10,741.064	11,277.065
4	Hourly	4.462	4.685	4.919	5.164	5.422	5.692
	Weekly	178.483	187.390	196.741	206.559	216.867	227.689
	Semi-monthly	386.714	406.012	426.272	447.544	469.878	493.326
	Monthly	773.428	812.023	852.545	895.089	939.755	986.651
	Annually	9,281.134	9,744.281	10,230.540	10,741.064	11,277.065	11,839.813
5	Hourly	4.685	4.919	5.164	5.422	5.692	5.976
	Weekly	187.390	196.741	206.559	216.867	227.689	239.051
	Semi-monthly	406.012	426.272	447.544	469.878	493.326	517.943
	Monthly	812.023	852.545	895.089	939.755	986.651	1,035.887
	Annually	9,744.281	10,230.540	10,741.064	11,277.065	11,839.813	12,430.643
6	Hourly	4.919	5.164	5.422	5.692	5.976	6.274
	Weekly	196.741	206.559	216.867	227.689	239.051	250.980
	Semi-monthly	426.272	447.544	469.878	493.326	517.943	543.790
	Monthly	852.545	895.089	939.755	986.651	1,035.887	1,087.580
	Annually	10,230.540	10,741.064	11,277.065	11,839.813	12,430.643	13,050.957
7	Hourly	5.164	5.422	5.692	5.976	6.274	6.588
	Weekly	206.559	216.867	227.689	239.051	250.980	263.504
	Semi-monthly	447.544	469.878	493.326	517.943	543.790	570.926
	Monthly	895.089	939.755	986.651	1,035.887	1,087.580	1,141.852
	Annually	10,741.064	11,277.065	11,839.813	12,430.643	13,050.957	13,702.226
8	Hourly	5.422	5.692	5.976	6.274	6.588	6.916
	Weekly	216.867	227.689	239.051	250.980	263.504	276.654
	Semi-monthly	469.878	493.326	517.943	543.790	570.926	599.416
	Monthly	939.755	986.651	1,035.887	1,087.580	1,141.852	1,198.833
	Annually	11,277.065	11,839.813	12,430.643	13,050.957	13,702.226	14,385.995
9	Hourly	5.692	5.976	6.274	6.588	6.916	7.261
	Weekly	227.689	239.051	250.980	263.504	276.654	290.459
	Semi-monthly	493.326	517.943	543.790	570.926	599.416	629.329
	Monthly	986.651	1,035.887	1,087.580	1,141.852	1,198.833	1,258.657
	Annually	11,839.813	12,430.643	13,050.957	13,702.226	14,385.995	15,103.885
10	Hourly	5.976	6.274	6.588	6.916	7.261	7.624
	Weekly	239.051	250.980	263.504	276.654	290.459	304.954
	Semi-monthly	517.943	543.790	570.926	599.416	629.329	660.733
	Monthly	1,035.887	1,087.580	1,141.852	1,198.833	1,258.657	1,321.467
	Annually	12,430.643	13,050.957	13,702.226	14,385.995	15,103.885	15,857.599

Pay Range		Step 0	Step 1	Step 2	Step 3	Step 4	Step 5
11	Hourly	6.274	6.588	6.916	7.261	7.624	8.004
	Weekly	250.980	263.504	276.654	290.459	304.954	320.172
	Semi-monthly	543.790	570.926	599.416	629.329	660.733	693.705
	Monthly	1,087.580	1,141.852	1,198.833	1,258.657	1,321.467	1,387.410
	Annually	13,050.957	13,702.226	14,385.995	15,103.885	15,857.599	16,648.925
12	Hourly	6.588	6.916	7.261	7.624	8.004	8.404
	Weekly	263.504	276.654	290.459	304.954	320.172	336.149
	Semi-monthly	570.926	599.416	629.329	660.733	693.705	728.322
	Monthly	1,141.852	1,198.833	1,258.657	1,321.467	1,387.410	1,456.645
	Annually	13,702.226	14,385.995	15,103.885	15,857.599	16,648.925	17,479.739
13	Hourly	6.916	7.261	7.624	8.004	8.404	8.823
	Weekly	276.654	290.459	304.954	320.172	336.149	352.923
	Semi-monthly	599.416	629.329	660.733	693.705	728.322	764.667
	Monthly	1,198.833	1,258.657	1,321.467	1,387.410	1,456.645	1,529.334
	Annually	14,385.995	15,103.885	15,857.599	16,648.925	17,479.739	18,352.013
14	Hourly	7.261	7.624	8.004	8.404	8.823	9.263
	Weekly	290.459	304.954	320.172	336.149	352.923	370.535
	Semi-monthly	629.329	660.733	693.705	728.322	764.667	802.826
	Monthly	1,258.657	1,321.467	1,387.410	1,456.645	1,529.334	1,605.651
	Annually	15,103.885	15,857.599	16,648.925	17,479.739	18,352.013	19,267.815
15	Hourly	7.624	8.004	8.404	8.823	9.263	9.726
	Weekly	304.954	320.172	336.149	352.923	370.535	389.025
	Semi-monthly	660.733	693.705	728.322	764.667	802.826	842.888
	Monthly	1,321.467	1,387.410	1,456.645	1,529.334	1,605.651	1,685.776
	Annually	15,857.599	16,648.925	17,479.739	18,352.013	19,267.815	20,229.318
16	Hourly	8.004	8.404	8.823	9.263	9.726	10.211
	Weekly	320.172	336.149	352.923	370.535	389.025	408.438
	Semi-monthly	693.705	728.322	764.667	802.826	842.888	884.950
	Monthly	1,387.410	1,456.645	1,529.334	1,605.651	1,685.776	1,769.900
	Annually	16,648.925	17,479.739	18,352.013	19,267.815	20,229.318	21,238.801
17	Hourly	8.404	8.823	9.263	9.726	10.211	10.721
	Weekly	336.149	352.923	370.535	389.025	408.438	428.820
	Semi-monthly	728.322	764.667	802.826	842.888	884.950	929.111
	Monthly	1,456.645	1,529.334	1,605.651	1,685.776	1,769.900	1,858.222
	Annually	17,479.739	18,352.013	19,267.815	20,229.318	21,238.801	22,298.660
18	Hourly	8.823	9.263	9.726	10.211	10.721	11.255
	Weekly	352.923	370.535	389.025	408.438	428.820	450.219
	Semi-monthly	764.667	802.826	842.888	884.950	929.111	975.475
	Monthly	1,529.334	1,605.651	1,685.776	1,769.900	1,858.222	1,950.951
	Annually	18,352.013	19,267.815	20,229.318	21,238.801	22,298.660	23,411.408

Pay Range		Step 0	Step 1	Step 2	Step 3	Step 4	Step 5
19	Hourly	9.263	9.726	10.211	10.721	11.255	11.817
	Weekly	370.535	389.025	408.438	428.820	450.219	472.686
	Semi-monthly	802.826	842.888	884.950	929.111	975.475	1,024.153
	Monthly	1,605.651	1,685.776	1,769.900	1,858.222	1,950.951	2,048.307
	Annually	19,267.815	20,229.318	21,238.801	22,298.660	23,411.408	24,579.684
20	Hourly	9.726	10.211	10.721	11.255	11.817	12.407
	Weekly	389.025	408.438	428.820	450.219	472.686	496.274
	Semi-monthly	842.888	884.950	929.111	975.475	1,024.153	1,075.261
	Monthly	1,685.776	1,769.900	1,858.222	1,950.951	2,048.307	2,150.522
	Annually	20,229.318	21,238.801	22,298.660	23,411.408	24,579.684	25,806.259
21	Hourly	10.211	10.721	11.255	11.817	12.407	13.026
	Weekly	408.438	428.820	450.219	472.686	496.274	521.039
	Semi-monthly	884.950	929.111	975.475	1,024.153	1,075.261	1,128.918
	Monthly	1,769.900	1,858.222	1,950.951	2,048.307	2,150.522	2,257.837
	Annually	21,238.801	22,298.660	23,411.408	24,579.684	25,806.259	27,094.043
22	Hourly	10.721	11.255	11.817	12.407	13.026	13.676
	Weekly	428.820	450.219	472.686	496.274	521.039	547.040
	Semi-monthly	929.111	975.475	1,024.153	1,075.261	1,128.918	1,185.254
	Monthly	1,858.222	1,950.951	2,048.307	2,150.522	2,257.837	2,370.507
	Annually	22,298.660	23,411.408	24,579.684	25,806.259	27,094.043	28,446.090
23	Hourly	11.255	11.817	12.407	13.026	13.676	14.358
	Weekly	450.219	472.686	496.274	521.039	547.040	574.339
	Semi-monthly	975.475	1,024.153	1,075.261	1,128.918	1,185.254	1,244.400
	Monthly	1,950.951	2,048.307	2,150.522	2,257.837	2,370.507	2,488.801
	Annually	23,411.408	24,579.684	25,806.259	27,094.043	28,446.090	29,865.607
24	Hourly	11.817	12.407	13.026	13.676	14.358	15.075
	Weekly	472.686	496.274	521.039	547.040	574.339	602.999
	Semi-monthly	1,024.153	1,075.261	1,128.918	1,185.254	1,244.400	1,306.498
	Monthly	2,048.307	2,150.522	2,257.837	2,370.507	2,488.801	2,612.997
	Annually	24,579.684	25,806.259	27,094.043	28,446.090	29,865.607	31,355.960
25	Hourly	12.407	13.026	13.676	14.358	15.075	15.827
	Weekly	496.274	521.039	547.040	574.339	602.999	633.090
	Semi-monthly	1,075.261	1,128.918	1,185.254	1,244.400	1,306.498	1,371.695
	Monthly	2,150.522	2,257.837	2,370.507	2,488.801	2,612.997	2,743.390
	Annually	25,806.259	27,094.043	28,446.090	29,865.607	31,355.960	32,920.685
26	Hourly	13.026	13.676	14.358	15.075	15.827	16.617
	Weekly	521.039	547.040	574.339	602.999	633.090	664.683
	Semi-monthly	1,128.918	1,185.254	1,244.400	1,306.498	1,371.695	1,440.146
	Monthly	2,257.837	2,370.507	2,488.801	2,612.997	2,743.390	2,880.291
	Annually	27,094.043	28,446.090	29,865.607	31,355.960	32,920.685	34,563.493

Pay Range		Step 0	Step 1	Step 2	Step 3	Step 4	Step 5
27	Hourly	13.676	14.358	15.075	15.827	16.617	17.446
	Weekly	547.040	574.339	602.999	633.090	664.683	697.852
	Semi-monthly	1,185.254	1,244.400	1,306.498	1,371.695	1,440.146	1,512.012
	Monthly	2,370.507	2,488.801	2,612.997	2,743.390	2,880.291	3,024.023
	Annually	28,446.090	29,865.607	31,355.960	32,920.685	34,563.493	36,288.281
28	Hourly	14.358	15.075	15.827	16.617	17.446	18.317
	Weekly	574.339	602.999	633.090	664.683	697.852	732.676
	Semi-monthly	1,244.400	1,306.498	1,371.695	1,440.146	1,512.012	1,587.464
	Monthly	2,488.801	2,612.997	2,743.390	2,880.291	3,024.023	3,174.928
	Annually	29,865.607	31,355.960	32,920.685	34,563.493	36,288.281	38,099.139
29	Hourly	15.075	15.827	16.617	17.446	18.317	19.231
	Weekly	602.999	633.090	664.683	697.852	732.676	769.238
	Semi-monthly	1,306.498	1,371.695	1,440.146	1,512.012	1,587.464	1,666.682
	Monthly	2,612.997	2,743.390	2,880.291	3,024.023	3,174.928	3,333.363
	Annually	31,355.960	32,920.685	34,563.493	36,288.281	38,099.139	40,000.362
30	Hourly	15.827	16.617	17.446	18.317	19.231	20.191
	Weekly	633.090	664.683	697.852	732.676	769.238	807.624
	Semi-monthly	1,371.695	1,440.146	1,512.012	1,587.464	1,666.682	1,749.852
	Monthly	2,743.390	2,880.291	3,024.023	3,174.928	3,333.363	3,499.705
	Annually	32,920.685	34,563.493	36,288.281	38,099.139	40,000.362	41,996.460

Alphabetical Classification Index by Title
(Pay data corresponding with ranges and steps is shown on pp. 146-49.)

Job Code	Title	Department	Range	Step	Salary
0325	Accountant	Clerk-Treasurer	20	0	
0325	Accountant	Human Resources	20	0	
0325	Accountant	Personnel	20	5	
0323	Accounting Clerk II	Clerk-Treasurer	15	5	
0323	Accounting Clerk II	Waterworks Commercial	15	4	
0324	Accounting Clerk III	Streets	17	4	
0635	Administrative Assistant	Clerk-Treasurer	22	0	
0635	Administrative Assistant	Public Works	22	5	
9104	Administrative Assistant to the Mayor	Clerk-Treasurer			47,250
2375	Administrator, Zoning and Subdivision	Planning Commission	20	3	
6214	Animal Caretaker	Parks and Recreation	14	0	
6214	Animal Caretaker	Parks and Recreation	14	2	
6114	Animal Services Officer	Animal Services	12	1	
6114	Animal Services Officer	Animal Services	12	2	
2118	Assistant City Engineer	Public Works	29	3	
6325	Assistant Community Center Director	Parks and Recreation	14	1	
6325	Assistant Community Center Director	Parks and Recreation	14	1	
6325	Assistant Community Center Director	Parks and Recreation	14	2	
1118	Assistant Director of Planning	Planning Commission	24	5	
5758	Assistant Director of Sanitation	Sanitation-Garbage Collection	20	3	
4268	Assistant Fire Chief	Fire	26	3	
4268	Assistant Fire Chief	Fire	26	3	
4268	Assistant Fire Chief	Fire	26	3	
6365	Assistant Park Manager	Parks and Recreation	16	0	
0648	Assistant Personnel Director	Personnel	27	3	
4198	Assistant Police Chief	Police	28	5	
6334	Assistant Sports Coordinator	Parks and Recreation	17	1	
3317	Assistant Superintendent, Water Filter Plant	Water Filter Plant	21	3	
0334	Assistant to City Marshal	City Marshal	15	0	
5415	Automotive Mechanic Technician	Service Garage	16	2	
5414	Automotive Mechanic	Sanitation-Garbage Collection	14	3	
5414	Automotive Mechanic	Service Garage	14	0	
5414	Automotive Mechanic	Service Garage	14	1	
5414	Automotive Mechanic	Service Garage	14	3	
5412	Automotive Mechanic Helper	Service Garage	10	0	
5412	Automotive Mechanic Helper	Service Garage	10	1	
5411	Automotive Servicer	Sanitation-Garbage Collection	9	3	
5416	Automotive Technician II	Service Garage	18	0	
2345	Building Inspector	Fire	21	5	
2345	Building Inspector	Building Inspection	21	3	
2345	Building Inspector	Building Inspection	21	5	
2211	Cartographer I	Planning Commission	10	0	
2211	Cartographer I	Planning Commission	10	0	
2212	Cartographer II	Planning Commission	14	2	
0321	Cashier	Waterworks Commercial	11	2	
3124	Chief Maintenance Operator	Water Filter Plant	18	4	
3114	Chief Maintenance Operator WPC	Water Pollution Control Plant	18	5	
3114	Chief Maintenance Operator WPC	Water Pollution Control Plant	18	5	

Job Code	Title	Department	Range	Step	Salary
3126	Chief Water Filter Operator	Water Filter Plant	20	3	
1145	Child-Care Coordinator	Human Resources	20	2	
9105	City Attorney	Clerk-Treasurer			34,689
9106	City Clerk-Treasurer	Clerk-Treasurer			41,160
5518	City Electrician	Electrical	22	4	
9107	City Engineer	Public Works			42,062
9108	City Marshal	City Marshal			37,080
9109	City Shop Manager	Service Garage			30,000
0112	Clerk II	Human Resources	11	0	
0112	Clerk II	Personnel	11	2	
0112	Clerk II	Police	11	0	
0112	Clerk II	Police	11	1	
0112	Clerk II	Police	11	1	
0112	Clerk II	Police	11	4	
0112	Clerk II	Water-Sewer Distribution	11	1	
0113	Clerk III	City Marshal	14	3	
0113	Clerk III	Clerk-Treasurer	14	2	
0113	Clerk III	Police	14	0	
0113	Clerk III	Police	14	1	
0113	Clerk III	Police	14	2	
0113	Clerk III	Police	14	5	
0113	Clerk III	Service Garage	14	3	
0121	Clerk Typist I	Parks and Recreation	9	1	
0121	Clerk Typist I	Police	9	0	
0122	Clerk Typist II	Police	11	0	
0123	Clerk Typist III	Human Resources	13	2	
0123	Clerk Typist III	Human Resources	13	2	
0123	Clerk Typist III	Sanitation-Garbage Collection	13	4	
6326	Community Center Director	Parks and Recreation	18	1	
6326	Community Center Director	Parks and Recreation	18	2	
0414	Computer Operator	Computer	15	0	
0415	Computer Programmer	Computer	20	0	
6376	Coordinator for Grounds Development	Parks and Recreation	21	2	
6346	Coordinator for Special Activities	Parks and Recreation	18	4	
6316	Coordinator, Neighborhood Centers	Parks and Recreation	18	3	
8100	Council Member	Elective			6,000
8100	Council Member	Elective			6,000
8100	Council Member	Elective			6,000
8100	Council Member	Elective			6,000
8100	Council Member	Elective			6,000
8100	Council Member	Elective			6,000
8100	Council Member	Elective			6,000
8100	Council Member	Elective			6,000
8100	Council Member	Elective			6,000
8100	Council Member	Elective			6,000
6345	Cultural Arts Supervisor	Parks and Recreation	16	1	
6345	Cultural Arts Supervisor	Parks and Recreation	16	1	
5735	Custodial Supervisor	Parks and Recreation	14	2	
5211	Custodial Worker I	City Hall	7	3	
5211	Custodial Worker I	City Hall	7	5	

Job Code	Title	Department	Range	Step	Salary
5211	Custodial Worker I	Parks and Recreation	7	3	
5212	Custodial Worker II	Parks and Recreation	8	0	
5212	Custodial Worker II	Parks and Recreation	8	0	
5212	Custodial Worker II	Parks and Recreation	8	0	
5212	Custodial Worker II	Parks and Recreation	8	2	
5212	Custodial Worker II	Water Filter Plant	8	2	
6343	Dance Instructor	Parks and Recreation	16	4	
0412	Data Entry Operator II	Computer	14	3	
0412	Data Entry Operator II	Computer	14	5	
0655	Deputy City Clerk	Clerk-Treasurer	20	4	
6118	Director of Animal Services	Animal Services	22	1	
9114	Director of Community Development	Personnel			36,338
9115	Director of Human Resources	Human Resources			32,491
9112	Director of Personnel	Personnel			36,225
9118	Director of Sanitation	Sanitation-Garbage Collection			36,166
9113	Director, Computer Services	Computer and Data Processing			36,338
9116	Director, Parks and Recreation	Parks and Recreation			36,408
9119	Director, Permits and Inspection	Building Inspection			38,174
9120	Director, Planning Commission	Planning Commission			41,315
5513	Electrician's Assistant	Electrical	16	1	
2111	Engineering Aide I	Streets	10	0	
2112	Engineering Aide II	Streets	15	0	
2113	Engineering Aide III	Streets	18	2	
2114	Engineering Aide IV	Public Works	20	5	
1116	Environmental Planner	Planning Commission	24	5	
5312	Equipment Operator I	Human Resources	11	0	
5312	Equipment Operator I	Parks and Recreation	11	0	
5312	Equipment Operator I	Parks and Recreation	11	1	
5312	Equipment Operator I	Parks and Recreation	11	1	
5312	Equipment Operator I	Streets	11	0	
5312	Equipment Operator I	Streets	11	0	
5312	Equipment Operator I	Streets	11	0	
5312	Equipment Operator I	Streets	11	0	
5312	Equipment Operator I	Streets	11	1	
5312	Equipment Operator I	Streets	11	2	
5312	Equipment Operator I	Streets	11	2	
5312	Equipment Operator I	Streets	11	2	
5312	Equipment Operator I	Streets	11	2	
5312	Equipment Operator I	Streets	11	3	
5312	Equipment Operator I	Streets	11	3	
5312	Equipment Operator I	Streets	11	3	
5312	Equipment Operator I	Streets	11	4	
5312	Equipment Operator I	Water Pollution Control Plant	11	3	
5312	Equipment Operator I	Water-Sewer Distribution	11	1	
5312	Equipment Operator I	Water-Sewer Distribution	11	3	
5313	Equipment Operator II	Parks and Recreation	13	2	
5313	Equipment Operator II	Parks and Recreation	13	2	
5313	Equipment Operator II	Sanitation-Street Cleaning	13	3	
5313	Equipment Operator II	Sanitation-Street Cleaning	13	3	
5313	Equipment Operator II	Streets	13	3	

Job Code	Title	Department	Range	Step	Salary
5313	Equipment Operator II	Water-Sewer Distribution	13	3	
5313	Equipment Operator II	Water-Sewer Distribution	13	3	
5314	Equipment Operator III	Sanitation-Garbage Collection	14	0	
5314	Equipment Operator III	Sanitation-Garbage Collection	14	3	
5314	Equipment Operator III	Sanitation-Garbage Collection	14	5	
5314	Equipment Operator III	Sanitation-Street Cleaning	14	2	
5314	Equipment Operator III	Sanitation-Street Cleaning	14	2	
5314	Equipment Operator III	Water Meters	14	3	
5314	Equipment Operator III	Water-Sewer Distribution	14	0	
5315	Equipment Operator IV	Streets	16	5	
5315	Equipment Operator IV	Streets	16	5	
0656	Federal Aid Coordinator	Clerk-Treasurer	28	5	
4257	Fire Alarm Superintendent	Fire	23	2	
4217	Fire Captain	Fire	23	3	
4217	Fire Captain	Fire	23	3	
4217	Fire Captain	Fire	23	3	
4217	Fire Captain	Fire	23	3	
4217	Fire Captain	Fire	23	3	
4217	Fire Captain	Fire	23	3	
4217	Fire Captain	Fire	23	3	
4217	Fire Captain	Fire	23	3	
4217	Fire Captain	Fire	23	4	
4217	Fire Captain	Fire	23	4	
4217	Fire Captain	Fire	23	4	
4217	Fire Captain	Fire Station, County	23	3	
4217	Fire Captain	Fire Station, County	23	3	
4217	Fire Captain	Fire Station, County	23	3	
9126	Fire Chief	Fire			40,136
4213	Fire Dispatcher	Fire	17	4	
4213	Fire Dispatcher	Fire	17	5	
4215	Fire Driver-Engineer	Fire	19	2	
4215	Fire Driver-Engineer	Fire	19	2	
4215	Fire Driver-Engineer	Fire	19	3	
4215	Fire Driver-Engineer	Fire	19	3	
4215	Fire Driver-Engineer	Fire	19	3	
4215	Fire Driver-Engineer	Fire	19	3	
4215	Fire Driver-Engineer	Fire	19	3	
4215	Fire Driver-Engineer	Fire	19	3	
4215	Fire Driver-Engineer	Fire	19	3	
4215	Fire Driver-Engineer	Fire	19	3	
4215	Fire Driver-Engineer	Fire	19	3	
4215	Fire Driver-Engineer	Fire	19	3	
4215	Fire Driver-Engineer	Fire	19	3	
4215	Fire Driver-Engineer	Fire	19	4	
4215	Fire Driver-Engineer	Fire Station, County	19	2	
4215	Fire Driver-Engineer	Fire Station, County	19	3	
4215	Fire Driver-Engineer	Fire Station, County	19	3	
4215	Fire Driver-Engineer	Fire Station, County	19	3	

Job Code	Title	Department	Range	Step	Salary
4216	Fire Lieutenant	Fire	21	3	
4216	Fire Lieutenant	Fire	21	3	
4216	Fire Lieutenant	Fire	21	3	
4216	Fire Lieutenant	Fire	21	3	
4216	Fire Lieutenant	Fire	21	3	
4216	Fire Lieutenant	Fire	21	3	
4216	Fire Lieutenant	Fire	21	3	
4216	Fire Lieutenant	Fire	21	3	
4216	Fire Lieutenant	Fire	21	3	
4216	Fire Lieutenant	Fire	21	3	
4216	Fire Lieutenant	Fire	21	3	
4216	Fire Lieutenant	Fire	21	3	
4216	Fire Lieutenant	Fire	21	3	
4216	Fire Lieutenant	Fire	21	3	
4216	Fire Lieutenant	Fire Station, County	21	1	
4216	Fire Lieutenant	Fire Station, County	21	3	
4237	Fire Marshal	Fire	23	1	
4235	Fire Prevention Officer	Fire	19	2	
4235	Fire Prevention Officer	Fire Station, County	19	1	
4227	Fire Training Chief	Fire	23	3	
4214	Firefighter	Fire	17	0	
4214	Firefighter	Fire	17	0	
4214	Firefighter	Fire	17	0	
4214	Firefighter	Fire	17	0	
4214	Firefighter	Fire	17	0	
4214	Firefighter	Fire	17	0	
4214	Firefighter	Fire	17	1	
4214	Firefighter	Fire	17	1	
4214	Firefighter	Fire	17	1	
4214	Firefighter	Fire	17	1	
4214	Firefighter	Fire	17	1	
4214	Firefighter	Fire	17	1	
4214	Firefighter	Fire	17	1	
4214	Firefighter	Fire	17	1	
4214	Firefighter	Fire	17	1	
4214	Firefighter	Fire	17	2	
4214	Firefighter	Fire	17	2	
4214	Firefighter	Fire	17	2	
4214	Firefighter	Fire	17	2	
4214	Firefighter	Fire	17	2	
4214	Firefighter	Fire	17	2	
4214	Firefighter	Fire	17	2	
4214	Firefighter	Fire	17	2	
4214	Firefighter	Fire	17	2	
4214	Firefighter	Fire	17	3	
4214	Firefighter	Fire	17	4	
4214	Firefighter	Fire Station, County	17	0	
4214	Firefighter	Fire Station, County	17	0	
4214	Firefighter	Fire Station, County	17	0	

Job Code	Title	Department	Range	Step	Salary
4214	Firefighter	Fire Station, County	17	0	
4214	Firefighter	Fire Station, County	17	0	
4214	Firefighter	Fire Station, County	17	1	
4214	Firefighter	Fire Station, County	17	1	
4214	Firefighter	Fire Station, County	17	2	
5725	General Maintenance Supervisor	Parks and Recreation	16	2	
0515	Graphics and Printing Coordinator	Personnel	19	3	
4115	Head Jailer	Stockade	16	2	
2335	Heating and Air Conditioning Inspector	Building Inspection	21	2	
2315	Housing Inspector	Building Inspection	21	3	
1135	Information and Referral Coordinator	Human Resources	22	5	
1133	Information and Referral Specialist	Human Resources	17	0	
1133	Information and Referral Specialist	Human Resources	17	4	
1133	Information and Referral Specialist	Human Resources	17	4	
1133	Information and Referral Specialist	Human Resources	17	4	
4111	Jailer	Stockade	14	0	
4111	Jailer	Stockade	14	0	
4111	Jailer	Stockade	14	0	
5714	Labor Supervisor I	Parks and Recreation	14	0	
5714	Labor Supervisor I	Parks and Recreation	14	0	
5714	Labor Supervisor I	Parks and Recreation	14	3	
5714	Labor Supervisor I	Parks and Recreation	14	5	
5714	Labor Supervisor I	Streets	14	4	
5714	Labor Supervisor I	Water-Sewer Distribution	14	2	
5715	Labor Supervisor II	Streets	16	3	
5715	Labor Supervisor II	Water-Sewer Distribution	16	3	
5715	Labor Supervisor II	Water-Sewer Distribution	16	3	
5716	Labor Supervisor III	Streets	17	3	
5716	Labor Supervisor III	Streets	17	4	
5716	Labor Supervisor III	Streets	17	4	
5716	Labor Supervisor III	Water-Sewer Distribution	17	5	
3131	Laboratory Aide	Water Pollution Control Plant	10	1	
3134	Laboratory Technician	Water Filter Plant	16	5	
3134	Laboratory Technician	Water Pollution Control Plant	16	1	
5111	Laborer I	Parks and Recreation	8	0	
5111	Laborer I	Parks and Recreation	8	3	
5111	Laborer I	Police	8	0	
5111	Laborer I	Sanitation-Street Cleaning	8	0	
5111	Laborer I	Sanitation-Street Cleaning	8	0	
5111	Laborer I	Sanitation-Street Cleaning	8	0	
5111	Laborer I	Sanitation-Street Cleaning	8	0	
5111	Laborer I	Sanitation-Street Cleaning	8	1	
5111	Laborer I	Sanitation-Street Cleaning	8	3	
5111	Laborer I	Streets	8	0	
5111	Laborer I	Streets	8	0	
5111	Laborer I	Streets	8	0	
5111	Laborer I	Streets	8	1	
5111	Laborer I	Streets	8	2	
5111	Laborer I	Water-Sewer Distribution	8	0	
5111	Laborer I	Water-Sewer Distribution	8	0	

Job Code	Title	Department	Range	Step	Salary
5111	Laborer I	Water-Sewer Distribution	8	0	
5111	Laborer I	Water-Sewer Distribution	8	0	
5111	Laborer I	Water-Sewer Distribution	8	1	
5111	Laborer I	Water-Sewer Distribution	8	1	
5112	Laborer II	Parks and Recreation	10	0	
5112	Laborer II	Parks and Recreation	10	0	
5112	Laborer II	Parks and Recreation	10	0	
5112	Laborer II	Parks and Recreation	10	2	
5112	Laborer II	Streets	10	0	
5112	Laborer II	Streets	10	0	
5112	Laborer II	Streets	10	0	
5112	Laborer II	Streets	10	3	
5112	Laborer II	Streets	10	3	
5112	Laborer II	Streets	10	4	
5112	Laborer II	Water Meters	10	3	
5112	Laborer II	Water-Sewer Distribution	10	2	
5112	Laborer II	Water-Sewer Distribution	10	3	
5113	Laborer III	Parks and Recreation	12	2	
5113	Laborer III	Streets	12	2	
5113	Laborer III	Streets	12	3	
5113	Laborer III	Water-Sewer Distribution	12	0	
5113	Laborer III	Water-Sewer Distribution	12	3	
3142	Maintenance Mechanic I WPC	Water Pollution Control Plant	13	0	
3143	Maintenance Mechanic II	Water Pollution Control Plant	14	1	
6375	Maintenance Service Center Supervisor	Parks and Recreation	14	0	
8101	Mayor	Elective			24,000
0212	Meter Reader II	Waterworks Commercial	12	0	
0212	Meter Reader II	Waterworks Commercial	12	0	
0212	Meter Reader II	Waterworks Commercial	12	2	
0212	Meter Reader II	Waterworks Commercial	12	4	
0212	Meter Reader II	Waterworks Commercial	12	5	
0215	Meter Reader Supervisor	Waterworks Commercial	17	5	
6313	Neighborhood Center Leader	Parks and Recreation	12	0	
6313	Neighborhood Center Leader	Parks and Recreation	12	0	
6313	Neighborhood Center Leader	Parks and Recreation	12	0	
6313	Neighborhood Center Leader	Parks and Recreation	12	1	
6313	Neighborhood Center Leader	Parks and Recreation	12	1	
6313	Neighborhood Center Leader	Parks and Recreation	12	1	
6313	Neighborhood Center Leader	Parks and Recreation	12	1	
6313	Neighborhood Center Leader	Parks and Recreation	12	4	
6315	Neighborhood Centers Supervisor	Parks and Recreation	14	3	
4142	Neighborhood Service Officer	Police	8	0	
4142	Neighborhood Service Officer	Police	8	0	
4142	Neighborhood Service Officer	Police	8	1	
6366	Park Manager	Parks and Recreation	19	3	
0312	Parking Meter Repairer	Police	13	5	
4122	Parking Violations Officer	Police	13	0	
4122	Parking Violations Officer	Police	13	3	
4122	Parking Violations Officer	Police	13	3	
4122	Parking Violations Officer	Police	13	3	

Job Code	Title	Department	Range	Step	Salary
4122	Parking Violations Officer	Police	13	3	
4122	Parking Violations Officer	Police	13	3	
9101	Personnel Board Member	Personnel			1,000
9101	Personnel Board Member	Personnel			1,000
9101	Personnel Board Member	Personnel			1,000
9101	Personnel Board Member	Personnel			1,000
9101	Personnel Board Member	Personnel			1,000
0645	Personnel Technician	Personnel	17	4	
1127	Physical Program Coordinator	Personnel	27	2	
1128	Physical Program Specialist	Personnel	24	3	
2325	Plumbing Inspector	Inspection	22	5	
4138	Police Captain	Police	25	3	
4138	Police Captain	Police	25	5	
9121	Police Chief	Police			44,940
4134	Police Corporal	Police	19	4	
4134	Police Corporal	Police	19	4	
4134	Police Corporal	Police	19	4	
4134	Police Corporal	Police	19	5	
4175	Police Detective	Police	20	2	
4175	Police Detective	Police	20	3	
4175	Police Detective	Police	20	3	
4175	Police Detective	Police	20	3	
4175	Police Detective	Police	20	4	
4175	Police Detective	Police	20	4	
4175	Police Detective	Police	20	4	
4175	Police Detective	Police	20	4	
4175	Police Detective	Police	20	5	
4175	Police Detective	Police	20	5	
4136	Police Lieutenant	Police	24	1	
4136	Police Lieutenant	Police	24	2	
4136	Police Lieutenant	Police	24	4	
4136	Police Lieutenant	Police	24	4	
4136	Police Lieutenant	Police	24	4	
4136	Police Lieutenant	Police	24	4	
4136	Police Lieutenant	Police	24	4	
4136	Police Lieutenant	Police	24	4	
4136	Police Lieutenant	Police	24	4	
4139	Police Major	Police	27	2	
4139	Police Major	Police	27	4	
4139	Police Major	Police	27	4	
4133	Police Officer	Police	18	0	
4133	Police Officer	Police	18	0	
4133	Police Officer	Police	18	0	
4133	Police Officer	Police	18	0	
4133	Police Officer	Police	18	1	
4133	Police Officer	Police	18	1	
4133	Police Officer	Police	18	1	
4133	Police Officer	Police	18	1	
4133	Police Officer	Police	18	1	
4133	Police Officer	Police	18	2	

Job Code	Title	Department	Range	Step	Salary
4133	Police Officer	Police	18	2	
4133	Police Officer	Police	18	2	
4133	Police Officer	Police	18	2	
4133	Police Officer	Police	18	2	
4133	Police Officer	Police	18	2	
4133	Police Officer	Police	18	2	
4133	Police Officer	Police	18	2	
4133	Police Officer	Police	18	2	
4133	Police Officer	Police	18	2	
4133	Police Officer	Police	18	2	
4133	Police Officer	Police	18	2	
4133	Police Officer	Police	18	2	
4133	Police Officer	Police	18	3	
4133	Police Officer	Police	18	3	
4133	Police Officer	Police	18	3	
4133	Police Officer	Police	18	3	
4133	Police Officer	Police	18	3	
4133	Police Officer	Police	18	3	
4133	Police Officer	Police	18	3	
4133	Police Officer	Police	18	3	
4133	Police Officer	Police	18	3	
4133	Police Officer	Police	18	3	
4133	Police Officer	Police	18	3	
4133	Police Officer	Police	18	4	
4133	Police Officer	Police	18	4	
4133	Police Officer	Police	18	4	
4133	Police Officer	Police	18	4	
4133	Police Officer	Police	18	4	
4133	Police Officer	Police	18	4	
4133	Police Officer	Police	18	4	
4133	Police Officer	Police	18	5	
4133	Police Officer	Police	18	5	
4123	Police Radio Dispatcher	Police	15	0	
4123	Police Radio Dispatcher	Police	15	0	
4123	Police Radio Dispatcher	Police	15	0	
4123	Police Radio Dispatcher	Police	15	0	
4123	Police Radio Dispatcher	Police	15	0	
4123	Police Radio Dispatcher	Police	15	1	
4123	Police Radio Dispatcher	Police	15	1	
4123	Police Radio Dispatcher	Police	15	2	
4135	Police Sergeant	Police	21	3	
4135	Police Sergeant	Police	21	3	
4135	Police Sergeant	Police	21	5	
4135	Police Sergeant	Police	21	5	
4135	Police Sergeant	Police	21	5	
4135	Police Sergeant	Police	21	5	
4135	Police Sergeant	Police	21	5	
4135	Police Sergeant	Police	21	5	
4135	Police Sergeant	Police	21	5	
4135	Police Sergeant	Police	21	5	

Job Code	Title	Department	Range	Step	Salary
4135	Police Sergeant	Police	21	5	
4137	Police Shift Commander	Police	24	1	
4137	Police Shift Commander	Police	24	2	
9100	Recorder	Elective			14,500
6312	Recreation Leader	Human Resources	8	0	
6312	Recreation Leader	Parks and Recreation	8	0	
6312	Recreation Leader	Parks and Recreation	8	0	
6312	Recreation Leader	Parks and Recreation	8	0	
6312	Recreation Leader	Parks and Recreation	8	0	
6312	Recreation Leader	Parks and Recreation	8	0	
6312	Recreation Leader	Parks and Recreation	8	1	
6312	Recreation Leader	Parks and Recreation	8	1	
6312	Recreation Leader	Parks and Recreation	8	2	
6312	Recreation Leader	Parks and Recreation	8	2	
6312	Recreation Leader	Parks and Recreation	8	2	
5612	Refuse Collection Driver I	Sanitation-Garbage Collection	10	3	
5612	Refuse Collection Driver I	Sanitation-Garbage Collection	10	3	
5612	Refuse Collection Driver I	Sanitation-Garbage Collection	10	4	
5612	Refuse Collection Driver I	Sanitation-Garbage Collection	10	4	
5612	Refuse Collection Driver I	Sanitation-Garbage Collection	10	4	
5612	Refuse Collection Driver I	Sanitation-Garbage Collection	10	5	
5613	Refuse Collection Driver II	Sanitation-Garbage Collection	11	0	
5613	Refuse Collection Driver II	Sanitation-Garbage Collection	11	0	
5613	Refuse Collection Driver II	Sanitation-Garbage Collection	11	0	
5613	Refuse Collection Driver II	Sanitation-Garbage Collection	11	0	
5613	Refuse Collection Driver II	Sanitation-Garbage Collection	11	1	
5613	Refuse Collection Driver II	Sanitation-Garbage Collection	11	1	
5613	Refuse Collection Driver II	Sanitation-Garbage Collection	11	2	
5613	Refuse Collection Driver II	Sanitation-Garbage Collection	11	2	
5613	Refuse Collection Driver II	Sanitation-Garbage Collection	11	2	
5613	Refuse Collection Driver II	Sanitation-Garbage Collection	11	2	
5613	Refuse Collection Driver II	Sanitation-Garbage Collection	11	3	
5613	Refuse Collection Driver II	Sanitation-Garbage Collection	11	3	
5613	Refuse Collection Driver II	Sanitation-Street Cleaning	11	0	
5613	Refuse Collection Driver II	Sanitation-Street Cleaning	11	1	
5613	Refuse Collection Driver II	Sanitation-Street Cleaning	11	2	
5613	Refuse Collection Driver II	Sanitation-Street Cleaning	11	2	
5613	Refuse Collection Driver II	Sanitation-Street Cleaning	11	4	
5614	Refuse Collection Driver III	Sanitation-Garbage Collection	13	2	
5614	Refuse Collection Driver III	Sanitation-Garbage Collection	13	3	
5614	Refuse Collection Driver III	Sanitation-Garbage Collection	13	3	
5614	Refuse Collection Driver III	Sanitation-Garbage Collection	13	3	
5614	Refuse Collection Driver III	Sanitation-Garbage Collection	13	3	
5614	Refuse Collection Driver III	Sanitation-Garbage Collection	13	3	
5614	Refuse Collection Driver III	Sanitation-Garbage Collection	13	3	
5611	Refuse Collector	Sanitation-Garbage Collection	9	0	
5611	Refuse Collector	Sanitation-Garbage Collection	9	0	
5611	Refuse Collector	Sanitation-Garbage Collection	9	0	
5611	Refuse Collector	Sanitation-Garbage Collection	9	0	
5611	Refuse Collector	Sanitation-Garbage Collection	9	0	

Job Code	Title	Department	Range	Step	Salary
5611	Refuse Collector	Sanitation-Garbage Collection	9	0	
5611	Refuse Collector	Sanitation-Garbage Collection	9	1	
5611	Refuse Collector	Sanitation-Garbage Collection	9	1	
5611	Refuse Collector	Sanitation-Garbage Collection	9	1	
5611	Refuse Collector	Sanitation-Garbage Collection	9	2	
5611	Refuse Collector	Sanitation-Garbage Collection	9	2	
5611	Refuse Collector	Sanitation-Garbage Collection	9	3	
5611	Refuse Collector	Sanitation-Garbage Collection	9	3	
5611	Refuse Collector	Sanitation-Garbage Collection	9	3	
5611	Refuse Collector	Sanitation-Garbage Collection	9	5	
5611	Refuse Collector	Sanitation-Garbage Collection	9	5	
5611	Refuse Collector	Sanitation-Garbage Collection	9	5	
7100	Retired	General Administrative			240
7100	Retired	General Administrative			600
7100	Retired	General Administrative			120
7100	Retired	General Administrative			480
7100	Retired	General Administrative			600
7100	Retired	General Administrative			900
7100	Retired	General Administrative			600
7100	Retired	General Administrative			900
7100	Retired	General Administrative			600
7100	Retired	General Administrative			900
7100	Retired	General Administrative			900
7100	Retired	General Administrative			360
7100	Retired	General Administrative			600
7100	Retired	General Administrative			720
7100	Retired	General Administrative			600
7100	Retired	General Administrative			480
7100	Retired	General Administrative			600
7100	Retired	General Administrative			600
7100	Retired	General Administrative			600
7100	Retired	General Administrative			900
7100	Retired	General Administrative			600
7100	Retired	General Administrative			600
5755	Sanitation Supervisor	Sanitation-Garbage Collection	14	2	
5755	Sanitation Supervisor	Sanitation-Garbage Collection	14	5	
5755	Sanitation Supervisor	Sanitation-Street Cleaning	14	5	
5755	Sanitation Supervisor	Sanitation-Street Cleaning	14	5	
4121	School Crossing Guard	Police	6	2	
4121	School Crossing Guard	Police	6	2	
4121	School Crossing Guard	Police	6	2	
4121	School Crossing Guard	Police	6	2	
4121	School Crossing Guard	Police	6	2	
4121	School Crossing Guard	Police	6	2	
4121	School Crossing Guard	Police	6	2	
4121	School Crossing Guard	Police	6	2	
4121	School Crossing Guard	Police	6	2	
4121	School Crossing Guard	Police	6	2	
4121	School Crossing Guard	Police	6	2	
4121	School Crossing Guard	Police	6	2	

Job Code	Title	Department	Range	Step	Salary
9102	Secretary	Clerk-Treasurer			7,994
9102	Secretary	Streets			21,000
9102	Secretary				14,076
0131	Secretary I	Parks and Recreation	11	0	
0131	Secretary I	Parks and Recreation	11	1	
0131	Secretary I	Personnel	11	3	
0131	Secretary I	Police	11	0	
0131	Secretary I	Police	11	1	
0131	Secretary I	Streets	11	3	
0132	Secretary II	Clerk-Treasurer	14	0	
0132	Secretary II	Clerk-Treasurer	14	4	
0132	Secretary II	Building Inspection	14	5	
0132	Secretary II	Parks and Recreation	14	5	
0132	Secretary II	Personnel	14	1	
0132	Secretary II	Planning Commission	14	1	
0132	Secretary II	Police	14	2	
9122	Secretary to the Mayor	Clerk-Treasurer			20,459
5221	Security Guard	Sanitation-Garbage Collection	8	1	
5221	Security Guard	Sanitation-Garbage Collection	8	1	
5221	Security Guard	Sanitation-Garbage Collection	8	5	
3113	Senior Waste Water Plant Operator	Water Pollution Control Plant	16	2	
3123	Senior Water Filter Operator	Water Filter Plant	16	5	
3123	Senior Water Filter Operator	Water Filter Plant	16	5	
1144	Social Service Specialist	Human Resources	17	0	
2128	Special Projects Engineer	Public Works	27	0	
6336	Sports Coordinator	Parks and Recreation	19	4	
5768	Street Superintendent	Streets	22	3	
6388	Superintendent of Parks	Parks and Recreation	24	2	
6358	Superintendent of Recreation	Parks and Recreation	24	3	
3318	Superintendent, Water Filter Plant	Water Filter Plant	23	5	
3218	Superintendent, Water Pollution Control	Water Pollution Control Plant	23	5	
0225	Supervisor, Customer Service	Waterworks Commercial	19	4	
4125	Supervisor, Special Services	Police	24	3	
0345	Supervisor, Tax Collection	Clerk-Treasurer	17	5	
3112	Wastewater Plant Operator	Water Pollution Control Plant	14	2	
3112	Wastewater Plant Operator	Water Pollution Control Plant	14	5	
3111	Wastewater Plant Operator Trainee	Water Pollution Control Plant	12	0	
3111	Wastewater Plant Operator Trainee	Water Pollution Control Plant	12	0	
3111	Wastewater Plant Operator Trainee	Water Pollution Control Plant	12	0	
5423	Water Meter Repairer	Water Meters	12	3	
3122	Water Plant Operator	Water Filter Plant	14	2	
3121	Water Plant Operator Trainee	Water Filter Plant	12	0	
3121	Water Plant Operator Trainee	Water Filter Plant	12	0	
3121	Water Plant Operator Trainee	Water Filter Plant	12	0	
3121	Water Plant Operator Trainee	Water Filter Plant	12	2	
3121	Water Plant Operator Trainee	Water Filter Plant	14	1	
3121	Water Plant Operator Trainee	Water Filter Plant	14	2	
5778	Water-Sewer Superintendent	Water Meters	27	0	

Classification Index by Job Code

(Pay data corresponding with ranges and steps is shown on pp. 146-49.)

Job Code	Title	Department	Range	Step	Salary
0112	Clerk II	Human Resources	11	0	
0112	Clerk II	Police	11	0	
0112	Clerk II	Police	11	1	
0112	Clerk II	Police	11	1	
0112	Clerk II	Water-Sewer Distribution	11	1	
0112	Clerk II	Personnel	11	2	
0112	Clerk II	Police	11	4	
0113	Clerk III	Police	14	0	
0113	Clerk III	Police	14	1	
0113	Clerk III	Police	14	2	
0113	Clerk III	Clerk-Treasurer	14	2	
0113	Clerk III	City Marshal	14	3	
0113	Clerk III	Service Garage	14	3	
0113	Clerk III	Police	14	5	
0121	Clerk Typist I	Police	9	0	
0121	Clerk Typist I	Parks and Recreation	9	1	
0122	Clerk Typist II	Police	11	0	
0123	Clerk Typist III	Human Resources	13	2	
0123	Clerk Typist III	Human Resources	13	2	
0123	Clerk Typist III	Sanitation-Garbage Collection	13	4	
0131	Secretary I	Parks and Recreation	11	0	
0131	Secretary I	Police	11	0	
0131	Secretary I	Parks and Recreation	11	1	
0131	Secretary I	Police	11	1	
0131	Secretary I	Personnel	11	3	
0131	Secretary I	Streets	11	3	
0132	Secretary II	Clerk-Treasurer	14	0	
0132	Secretary II	Personnel	14	1	
0132	Secretary II	Planning Commission	14	1	
0132	Secretary II	Police	14	2	
0132	Secretary II	Clerk-Treasurer	14	4	
0132	Secretary II	Building Inspection	14	5	
0132	Secretary II	Parks and Recreation	14	5	
0212	Meter Reader II	Waterworks Commercial	12	0	
0212	Meter Reader II	Waterworks Commercial	12	0	
0212	Meter Reader II	Waterworks Commercial	12	2	
0212	Meter Reader II	Waterworks Commercial	12	4	
0212	Meter Reader II	Waterworks Commercial	12	5	
0215	Meter Reader Supervisor	Waterworks Commercial	17	5	
0225	Supervisor, Customer Service	Waterworks Commercial	19	4	
0312	Parking Meter Repairer	Police	13	5	
0321	Cashier	Waterworks Commercial	11	2	
0323	Accounting Clerk II	Waterworks Commercial	15	4	
0323	Accounting Clerk II	Clerk-Treasurer	15	5	
0324	Accounting Clerk III	Streets	17	4	
0325	Accountant	Clerk-Treasurer	20	0	
0325	Accountant	Human Resources	20	0	
0325	Accountant	Personnel	20	5	

Job Code	Title	Department	Range	Step	Salary
0334	Assistant to City Marshal	City Marshal	15	0	
0345	Supervisor, Tax Collection	Clerk-Treasurer	17	5	
0412	Data Entry Operator II	Computer and Data Processing	14	3	
0412	Data Entry Operator II	Computer and Data Processing	14	5	
0414	Computer Operator	Computer and Data Processing	15	0	
0415	Computer Programmer	Computer and Data Processing	20	0	
0515	Graphics and Printing Coordinator	Personnel	19	3	
0635	Administrative Assistant	Clerk-Treasurer	22	0	
0635	Administrative Assistant	Public Works	22	5	
0645	Personnel Technician	Personnel	17	4	
0648	Assistant Personnel Director	Personnel	27	3	
0655	Deputy City Clerk	Clerk-Treasurer	20	4	
0656	Federal Aid Coordinator	Clerk-Treasurer	28	5	
1116	Environmental Planner	Planning Commission	24	5	
1118	Assistant Director of Planning	Planning Commission	24	5	
1127	Physical Program Coordinator	Personnel	27	2	
1128	Physical Program Specialist	Personnel	24	3	
1133	Information and Referral Specialist	Human Resources	17	0	
1133	Information and Referral Specialist	Human Resources	17	4	
1133	Information and Referral Specialist	Human Resources	17	4	
1133	Information and Referral Specialist	Human Resources	17	4	
1135	Information and Referral Coordinator	Human Resources	22	5	
1144	Social Service Specialist	Human Resources	17	0	
1145	Child-Care Coordinator	Human Resources	20	2	
2111	Engineering Aide I	Streets	10	0	
2112	Engineering Aide II	Streets	15	0	
2113	Engineering Aide III	Streets	18	2	
2114	Engineering Aide IV	Public Works	20	5	
2118	Assistant City Engineer	Public Works	29	3	
2128	Special Projects Engineer	Public Works	27	0	
2211	Cartographer I	Planning Commission	10	0	
2211	Cartographer I	Planning Commission	10	0	
2212	Cartographer II	Planning Commission	14	2	
2315	Housing Inspector	Building Inspection	21	3	
2325	Plumbing Inspector	Building Inspection	22	5	
2335	Heating and Air Conditioning Inspector	Building Inspection	21	2	
2345	Building Inspector	Building Inspection	21	3	
2345	Building Inspector	Building Inspection	21	5	
2345	Building Inspector	Fire	21	5	
2375	Administrator, Zoning and Subdivision	Planning Commission	20	3	
3111	Wastewater Plant Operator Trainee	Water Pollution Control Plant	12	0	
3111	Wastewater Plant Operator Trainee	Water Pollution Control Plant	12	0	
3111	Wastewater Plant Operator Trainee	Water Pollution Control Plant	12	0	
3112	Wastewater Plant Operator	Water Pollution Control Plant	14	2	
3112	Wastewater Plant Operator	Water Pollution Control Plant	14	5	
3113	Senior Wastewater Plant Operator	Water Pollution Control Plant	16	2	
3114	Chief Maintenance Operator WPC	Water Pollution Control Plant	18	5	
3114	Chief Maintenance Operator WPC	Water Pollution Control Plant	18	5	
3121	Water Plant Operator Trainee	Water Filter Plant	12	0	
3121	Water Plant Operator Trainee	Water Filter Plant	12	0	

Job Code	Title	Department	Range	Step	Salary
3121	Water Plant Operator Trainee	Water Filter Plant	12	0	
3121	Water Plant Operator Trainee	Water Filter Plant	12	2	
3121	Water Plant Operator Trainee	Water Filter Plant	14	1	
3121	Water Plant Operator Trainee	Water Filter Plant	14	2	
3122	Water Plant Operator	Water Filter Plant	14	2	
3123	Senior Water Filter Operator	Water Filter Plant	16	5	
3123	Senior Water Filter Operator	Water Filter Plant	16	5	
3124	Chief Maintenance Operator	Water Filter Plant	18	4	
3126	Chief Water Filter Operator	Water Filter Plant	20	3	
3131	Laboratory Aide	Water Pollution Control Plant	10	1	
3134	Laboratory Technician	Water Pollution Control Plant	16	1	
3134	Laboratory Technician	Water Filter Plant	16	5	
3142	Maintenance Mechanic I WPC	Water Pollution Control Plant	13	0	
3143	Maintenance Mechanic II	Water Pollution Control Plant	14	1	
3218	Superintendent, Water Pollution Control	Water Pollution Control Plant	23	5	
3317	Assistant Superintendent, Water Filter Plant	Water Filter Plant	21	3	
3318	Superintendent, Water Filter Plant	Water Filter Plant	23	5	
4111	Jailer	Stockade	14	0	
4111	Jailer	Stockade	14	0	
4111	Jailer	Stockade	14	0	
4115	Head Jailer	Stockade	16	2	
4121	School Crossing Guard	Police	6	2	
4121	School Crossing Guard	Police	6	2	
4121	School Crossing Guard	Police	6	2	
4121	School Crossing Guard	Police	6	2	
4121	School Crossing Guard	Police	6	2	
4121	School Crossing Guard	Police	6	2	
4121	School Crossing Guard	Police	6	2	
4121	School Crossing Guard	Police	6	2	
4121	School Crossing Guard	Police	6	2	
4121	School Crossing Guard	Police	6	2	
4121	School Crossing Guard	Police	6	2	
4121	School Crossing Guard	Police	6	2	
4122	Parking Violations Officer	Police	13	0	
4122	Parking Violations Officer	Police	13	3	
4122	Parking Violations Officer	Police	13	3	
4122	Parking Violations Officer	Police	13	3	
4122	Parking Violations Officer	Police	13	3	
4122	Parking Violations Officer	Police	13	3	
4123	Police Radio Dispatcher	Police	15	0	
4123	Police Radio Dispatcher	Police	15	0	
4123	Police Radio Dispatcher	Police	15	0	
4123	Police Radio Dispatcher	Police	15	0	
4123	Police Radio Dispatcher	Police	15	0	
4123	Police Radio Dispatcher	Police	15	1	
4123	Police Radio Dispatcher	Police	15	1	
4123	Police Radio Dispatcher	Police	15	2	
4125	Supervisor, Special Services	Police	24	3	
4133	Police Officer	Police	18	0	
4133	Police Officer	Police	18	0	

Job Code	Title	Department	Range	Step	Salary
4133	Police Officer	Police	18	0	
4133	Police Officer	Police	18	0	
4133	Police Officer	Police	18	1	
4133	Police Officer	Police	18	1	
4133	Police Officer	Police	18	1	
4133	Police Officer	Police	18	1	
4133	Police Officer	Police	18	1	
4133	Police Officer	Police	18	2	
4133	Police Officer	Police	18	2	
4133	Police Officer	Police	18	2	
4133	Police Officer	Police	18	2	
4133	Police Officer	Police	18	2	
4133	Police Officer	Police	18	2	
4133	Police Officer	Police	18	2	
4133	Police Officer	Police	18	2	
4133	Police Officer	Police	18	2	
4133	Police Officer	Police	18	2	
4133	Police Officer	Police	18	2	
4133	Police Officer	Police	18	2	
4133	Police Officer	Police	18	3	
4133	Police Officer	Police	18	3	
4133	Police Officer	Police	18	3	
4133	Police Officer	Police	18	3	
4133	Police Officer	Police	18	3	
4133	Police Officer	Police	18	3	
4133	Police Officer	Police	18	3	
4133	Police Officer	Police	18	3	
4133	Police Officer	Police	18	3	
4133	Police Officer	Police	18	3	
4133	Police Officer	Police	18	4	
4133	Police Officer	Police	18	4	
4133	Police Officer	Police	18	4	
4133	Police Officer	Police	18	4	
4133	Police Officer	Police	18	4	
4133	Police Officer	Police	18	4	
4133	Police Officer	Police	18	4	
4133	Police Officer	Police	18	5	
4133	Police Officer	Police	18	5	
4134	Police Corporal	Police	19	4	
4134	Police Corporal	Police	19	4	
4134	Police Corporal	Police	19	4	
4134	Police Corporal	Police	19	5	
4135	Police Sergeant	Police	21	3	
4135	Police Sergeant	Police	21	3	
4135	Police Sergeant	Police	21	5	
4135	Police Sergeant	Police	21	5	
4135	Police Sergeant	Police	21	5	
4135	Police Sergeant	Police	21	5	

Job Code	Title	Department	Range	Step	Salary
4135	Police Sergeant	Police	21	5	
4135	Police Sergeant	Police	21	5	
4135	Police Sergeant	Police	21	5	
4135	Police Sergeant	Police	21	5	
4135	Police Sergeant	Police	21	5	
4136	Police Lieutenant	Police	24	1	
4136	Police Lieutenant	Police	24	2	
4136	Police Lieutenant	Police	24	4	
4136	Police Lieutenant	Police	24	4	
4136	Police Lieutenant	Police	24	4	
4136	Police Lieutenant	Police	24	4	
4136	Police Lieutenant	Police	24	4	
4136	Police Lieutenant	Police	24	4	
4136	Police Lieutenant	Police	24	4	
4137	Police Shift Commander	Police	24	1	
4137	Police Shift Commander	Police	24	2	
4138	Police Captain	Police	25	3	
4138	Police Captain	Police	25	5	
4139	Police Major	Police	27	2	
4139	Police Major	Police	27	4	
4139	Police Major	Police	27	4	
4142	Neighborhood Service Officer	Police	8	0	
4142	Neighborhood Service Officer	Police	8	0	
4142	Neighborhood Service Officer	Police	8	1	
4175	Police Detective	Police	20	2	
4175	Police Detective	Police	20	3	
4175	Police Detective	Police	20	3	
4175	Police Detective	Police	20	3	
4175	Police Detective	Police	20	4	
4175	Police Detective	Police	20	4	
4175	Police Detective	Police	20	4	
4175	Police Detective	Police	20	4	
4175	Police Detective	Police	20	5	
4175	Police Detective	Police	20	5	
4198	Assistant Police Chief	Police	28	5	
4213	Fire Dispatcher	Fire	17	4	
4213	Fire Dispatcher	Fire	17	5	
4214	Firefighter	Fire	17	0	
4214	Firefighter	Fire	17	0	
4214	Firefighter	Fire	17	0	
4214	Firefighter	Fire	17	0	
4214	Firefighter	Fire	17	0	
4214	Firefighter	Fire	17	0	
4214	Firefighter	Fire Station, County	17	0	
4214	Firefighter	Fire Station, County	17	0	
4214	Firefighter	Fire Station, County	17	0	
4214	Firefighter	Fire Station, County	17	0	
4214	Firefighter	Fire Station, County	17	0	
4214	Firefighter	Fire	17	1	
4214	Firefighter	Fire	17	1	

Job Code	Title	Department	Range	Step	Salary
4214	Firefighter	Fire	17	1	
4214	Firefighter	Fire	17	1	
4214	Firefighter	Fire	17	1	
4214	Firefighter	Fire	17	1	
4214	Firefighter	Fire	17	1	
4214	Firefighter	Fire	17	1	
4214	Firefighter	Fire	17	1	
4214	Firefighter	Fire	17	1	
4214	Firefighter	Fire Station, County	17	1	
4214	Firefighter	Fire Station, County	17	1	
4214	Firefighter	Fire	17	2	
4214	Firefighter	Fire	17	2	
4214	Firefighter	Fire	17	2	
4214	Firefighter	Fire	17	2	
4214	Firefighter	Fire	17	2	
4214	Firefighter	Fire	17	2	
4214	Firefighter	Fire	17	2	
4214	Firefighter	Fire	17	2	
4214	Firefighter	Fire	17	2	
4214	Firefighter	Fire Station, County	17	2	
4214	Firefighter	Fire	17	3	
4214	Firefighter	Fire	17	4	
4215	Fire Driver-Engineer	Fire	19	2	
4215	Fire Driver-Engineer	Fire	19	2	
4215	Fire Driver-Engineer	Fire Station, County	19	2	
4215	Fire Driver-Engineer	Fire	19	3	
4215	Fire Driver-Engineer	Fire	19	3	
4215	Fire Driver-Engineer	Fire	19	3	
4215	Fire Driver-Engineer	Fire	19	3	
4215	Fire Driver-Engineer	Fire	19	3	
4215	Fire Driver-Engineer	Fire	19	3	
4215	Fire Driver-Engineer	Fire	19	3	
4215	Fire Driver-Engineer	Fire	19	3	
4215	Fire Driver-Engineer	Fire	19	3	
4215	Fire Driver-Engineer	Fire	19	3	
4215	Fire Driver-Engineer	Fire	19	3	
4215	Fire Driver-Engineer	Fire	19	3	
4215	Fire Driver-Engineer	Fire Station, County	19	3	
4215	Fire Driver-Engineer	Fire Station, County	19	3	
4215	Fire Driver-Engineer	Fire Station, County	19	3	
4215	Fire Driver-Engineer	Fire	19	4	
4216	Fire Lieutenant	Fire Station, County	21	1	
4216	Fire Lieutenant	Fire	21	3	
4216	Fire Lieutenant	Fire	21	3	
4216	Fire Lieutenant	Fire	21	3	
4216	Fire Lieutenant	Fire	21	3	
4216	Fire Lieutenant	Fire	21	3	
4216	Fire Lieutenant	Fire	21	3	
4216	Fire Lieutenant	Fire	21	3	

Job Code	Title	Department	Range	Step	Salary
4216	Fire Lieutenant	Fire	21	3	
4216	Fire Lieutenant	Fire	21	3	
4216	Fire Lieutenant	Fire	21	3	
4216	Fire Lieutenant	Fire	21	3	
4216	Fire Lieutenant	Fire	21	3	
4216	Fire Lieutenant	Fire	21	3	
4216	Fire Lieutenant	Fire	21	3	
4216	Fire Lieutenant	Fire Station, County	21	3	
4217	Fire Captain	Fire	23	3	
4217	Fire Captain	Fire	23	3	
4217	Fire Captain	Fire	23	3	
4217	Fire Captain	Fire	23	3	
4217	Fire Captain	Fire	23	3	
4217	Fire Captain	Fire	23	3	
4217	Fire Captain	Fire	23	3	
4217	Fire Captain	Fire	23	3	
4217	Fire Captain	Fire Station, County	23	3	
4217	Fire Captain	Fire Station, County	23	3	
4217	Fire Captain	Fire Station, County	23	3	
4217	Fire Captain	Fire	23	4	
4217	Fire Captain	Fire	23	4	
4217	Fire Captain	Fire	23	4	
4227	Fire Training Chief	Fire	23	3	
4235	Fire Prevention Officer	Fire Station, County	19	1	
4235	Fire Prevention Officer	Fire	19	2	
4237	Fire Marshal	Fire	23	1	
4257	Fire Alarm Superintendent	Fire	23	2	
4268	Assistant Fire Chief	Fire	26	3	
4268	Assistant Fire Chief	Fire	26	3	
4268	Assistant Fire Chief	Fire	26	3	
5111	Laborer I	Sanitation-Street Cleaning	8	0	
5111	Laborer I	Water-Sewer Distribution	8	0	
5111	Laborer I	Parks and Recreation	8	0	
5111	Laborer I	Police	8	0	
5111	Laborer I	Sanitation-Street Cleaning	8	0	
5111	Laborer I	Sanitation-Street Cleaning	8	0	
5111	Laborer I	Sanitation-Street Cleaning	8	0	
5111	Laborer I	Streets	8	0	
5111	Laborer I	Streets	8	0	
5111	Laborer I	Streets	8	0	
5111	Laborer I	Water-Sewer Distribution	8	0	
5111	Laborer I	Water-Sewer Distribution	8	0	
5111	Laborer I	Water-Sewer Distribution	8	0	
5111	Laborer I	Sanitation-Street Cleaning	8	1	
5111	Laborer I	Streets	8	1	
5111	Laborer I	Water-Sewer Distribution	8	1	
5111	Laborer I	Water-Sewer Distribution	8	1	
5111	Laborer I	Streets	8	2	
5111	Laborer I	Parks and Recreation	8	3	
5111	Laborer I	Sanitation-Street Cleaning	8	3	

Job Code	Title	Department	Range	Step	Salary
5112	Laborer II	Parks and Recreation	10	0	
5112	Laborer II	Parks and Recreation	10	0	
5112	Laborer II	Parks and Recreation	10	0	
5112	Laborer II	Streets	10	0	
5112	Laborer II	Streets	10	0	
5112	Laborer II	Streets	10	0	
5112	Laborer II	Parks and Recreation	10	2	
5112	Laborer II	Water-Sewer Distribution	10	2	
5112	Laborer II	Streets	10	3	
5112	Laborer II	Streets	10	3	
5112	Laborer II	Water Meters	10	3	
5112	Laborer II	Water-Sewer Distribution	10	3	
5112	Laborer II	Streets	10	4	
5113	Laborer III	Water-Sewer Distribution	12	0	
5113	Laborer III	Parks and Recreation	12	2	
5113	Laborer III	Streets	12	2	
5113	Laborer III	Streets	12	3	
5113	Laborer III	Water-Sewer Distribution	12	3	
5211	Custodial Worker I	City Hall	7	3	
5211	Custodial Worker I	Parks and Recreation	7	3	
5211	Custodial Worker I	City Hall	7	5	
5212	Custodial Worker II	Parks and Recreation	8	0	
5212	Custodial Worker II	Parks and Recreation	8	0	
5212	Custodial Worker II	Parks and Recreation	8	0	
5212	Custodial Worker II	Parks and Recreation	8	2	
5212	Custodial Worker II	Water Filter Plant	8	2	
5221	Security Guard	Sanitation-Garbage Collection	8	1	
5221	Security Guard	Sanitation-Garbage Collection	8	1	
5221	Security Guard	Sanitation-Garbage Collection	8	5	
5312	Equipment Operator I	Streets	11	0	
5312	Equipment Operator I	Streets	11	0	
5312	Equipment Operator I	Streets	11	0	
5312	Equipment Operator I	Streets	11	0	
5312	Equipment Operator I	Human Resources	11	0	
5312	Equipment Operator I	Parks and Recreation	11	0	
5312	Equipment Operator I	Parks and Recreation	11	1	
5312	Equipment Operator I	Parks and Recreation	11	1	
5312	Equipment Operator I	Streets	11	1	
5312	Equipment Operator I	Water-Sewer Distribution	11	1	
5312	Equipment Operator I	Streets	11	2	
5312	Equipment Operator I	Streets	11	2	
5312	Equipment Operator I	Streets	11	2	
5312	Equipment Operator I	Streets	11	2	
5312	Equipment Operator I	Streets	11	3	
5312	Equipment Operator I	Streets	11	3	
5312	Equipment Operator I	Streets	11	3	
5312	Equipment Operator I	Water-Sewer Distribution	11	3	
5312	Equipment Operator I	Water Pollution Control Plant	11	3	
5312	Equipment Operator I	Streets	11	4	
5313	Equipment Operator II	Parks and Recreation	13	2	

Job Code	Title	Department	Range	Step	Salary
5313	Equipment Operator II	Parks and Recreation	13	2	
5313	Equipment Operator II	Sanitation-Street Cleaning	13	3	
5313	Equipment Operator II	Sanitation-Street Cleaning	13	3	
5313	Equipment Operator II	Streets	13	3	
5313	Equipment Operator II	Water-Sewer Distribution	13	3	
5313	Equipment Operator II	Water-Sewer Distribution	13	3	
5314	Equipment Operator III	Sanitation-Garbage Collection	14	0	
5314	Equipment Operator III	Water-Sewer Distribution	14	0	
5314	Equipment Operator III	Sanitation-Street Cleaning	14	2	
5314	Equipment Operator III	Sanitation-Street Cleaning	14	2	
5314	Equipment Operator III	Sanitation-Garbage Collection	14	3	
5314	Equipment Operator III	Water Meters	14	3	
5314	Equipment Operator III	Sanitation-Garbage Collection	14	5	
5315	Equipment Operator IV	Streets	16	5	
5315	Equipment Operator IV	Streets	16	5	
5411	Automotive Servicer	Sanitation-Garbage Collection	9	3	
5412	Automotive Mechanic Helper	Service Garage	10	0	
5412	Automotive Mechanic Helper	Service Garage	10	1	
5414	Automotive Mechanic	Service Garage	14	0	
5414	Automotive Mechanic	Service Garage	14	1	
5414	Automotive Mechanic	Sanitation-Garbage Collection	14	3	
5414	Automotive Mechanic	Service Garage	14	3	
5415	Automotive Mechanic Technician	Service Garage	16	2	
5416	Automotive Technician II	Service Garage	18	0	
5423	Water Meter Repairer	Water Meters	12	3	
5513	Electrician's Assistant	Electrical	16	1	
5518	City Electrician	Electrical	22	4	
5611	Refuse Collector	Sanitation-Garbage Collection	9	0	
5611	Refuse Collector	Sanitation-Garbage Collection	9	0	
5611	Refuse Collector	Sanitation-Garbage Collection	9	0	
5611	Refuse Collector	Sanitation-Garbage Collection	9	0	
5611	Refuse Collector	Sanitation-Garbage Collection	9	0	
5611	Refuse Collector	Sanitation-Garbage Collection	9	0	
5611	Refuse Collector	Sanitation-Garbage Collection	9	1	
5611	Refuse Collector	Sanitation-Garbage Collection	9	1	
5611	Refuse Collector	Sanitation-Garbage Collection	9	1	
5611	Refuse Collector	Sanitation-Garbage Collection	9	2	
5611	Refuse Collector	Sanitation-Garbage Collection	9	2	
5611	Refuse Collector	Sanitation-Garbage Collection	9	3	
5611	Refuse Collector	Sanitation-Garbage Collection	9	3	
5611	Refuse Collector	Sanitation-Garbage Collection	9	3	
5611	Refuse Collector	Sanitation-Garbage Collection	9	5	
5611	Refuse Collector	Sanitation-Garbage Collection	9	5	
5611	Refuse Collector	Sanitation-Garbage Collection	9	5	
5612	Refuse Collection Driver I	Sanitation-Garbage Collection	10	3	
5612	Refuse Collection Driver I	Sanitation-Garbage Collection	10	3	
5612	Refuse Collection Driver I	Sanitation-Garbage Collection	10	4	
5612	Refuse Collection Driver I	Sanitation-Garbage Collection	10	4	
5612	Refuse Collection Driver I	Sanitation-Garbage Collection	10	4	
5612	Refuse Collection Driver I	Sanitation-Garbage Collection	10	5	

Job Code	Title	Department	Range	Step	Salary
5613	Refuse Collection Driver II	Sanitation-Garbage Collection	11	0	
5613	Refuse Collection Driver II	Sanitation-Garbage Collection	11	0	
5613	Refuse Collection Driver II	Sanitation-Garbage Collection	11	0	
5613	Refuse Collection Driver II	Sanitation-Garbage Collection	11	0	
5613	Refuse Collection Driver II	Sanitation-Street Cleaning	11	0	
5613	Refuse Collection Driver II	Sanitation-Garbage Collection	11	1	
5613	Refuse Collection Driver II	Sanitation-Garbage Collection	11	1	
5613	Refuse Collection Driver II	Sanitation-Street Cleaning	11	1	
5613	Refuse Collection Driver II	Sanitation-Garbage Collection	11	2	
5613	Refuse Collection Driver II	Sanitation-Garbage Collection	11	2	
5613	Refuse Collection Driver II	Sanitation-Garbage Collection	11	2	
5613	Refuse Collection Driver II	Sanitation-Garbage Collection	11	2	
5613	Refuse Collection Driver II	Sanitation-Street Cleaning	11	2	
5613	Refuse Collection Driver II	Sanitation-Street Cleaning	11	2	
5613	Refuse Collection Driver II	Sanitation-Garbage Collection	11	3	
5613	Refuse Collection Driver II	Sanitation-Garbage Collection	11	3	
5613	Refuse Collection Driver II	Sanitation-Street Cleaning	11	4	
5614	Refuse Collection Driver III	Sanitation-Garbage Collection	13	2	
5614	Refuse Collection Driver III	Sanitation-Garbage Collection	13	3	
5614	Refuse Collection Driver III	Sanitation-Garbage Collection	13	3	
5614	Refuse Collection Driver III	Sanitation-Garbage Collection	13	3	
5614	Refuse Collection Driver III	Sanitation-Garbage Collection	13	3	
5614	Refuse Collection Driver III	Sanitation-Garbage Collection	13	3	
5614	Refuse Collection Driver III	Sanitation-Garbage Collection	13	3	
5714	Labor Supervisor I	Parks and Recreation	14	0	
5714	Labor Supervisor I	Parks and Recreation	14	0	
5714	Labor Supervisor I	Water-Sewer Distribution	14	2	
5714	Labor Supervisor I	Parks and Recreation	14	3	
5714	Labor Supervisor I	Streets	14	4	
5714	Labor Supervisor I	Parks and Recreation	14	5	
5715	Labor Supervisor II	Streets	16	3	
5715	Labor Supervisor II	Water-Sewer Distribution	16	3	
5715	Labor Supervisor II	Water-Sewer Distribution	16	3	
5716	Labor Supervisor III	Streets	17	3	
5716	Labor Supervisor III	Streets	17	4	
5716	Labor Supervisor III	Streets	17	4	
5716	Labor Supervisor III	Water-Sewer Distribution	17	5	
5725	General Maintenance Supervisor	Parks and Recreation	16	2	
5735	Custodial Supervisor	Parks and Recreation	14	2	
5755	Sanitation Supervisor	Sanitation-Garbage Collection	14	2	
5755	Sanitation Supervisor	Sanitation-Garbage Collection	14	5	
5755	Sanitation Supervisor	Sanitation-Street Cleaning	14	5	
5755	Sanitation Supervisor	Sanitation-Street Cleaning	14	5	
5758	Assistant Director of Sanitation	Sanitation-Garbage Collection	20	3	
5768	Street Superintendent	Streets	22	3	
5778	Water-Sewer Superintendent	Water Meters	27	0	
6114	Animal Services Officer	Animal Services	12	1	
6114	Animal Services Officer	Animal Services	12	2	
6118	Director of Animal Services	Animal Services	22	1	
6214	Animal Caretaker	Parks and Recreation	14	0	

Job Code	Title	Department	Range	Step	Salary
6214	Animal Caretaker	Parks and Recreation	14	2	
6312	Recreation Leader	Human Resources	8	0	
6312	Recreation Leader	Parks and Recreation	8	0	
6312	Recreation Leader	Parks and Recreation	8	0	
6312	Recreation Leader	Parks and Recreation	8	0	
6312	Recreation Leader	Parks and Recreation	8	0	
6312	Recreation Leader	Parks and Recreation	8	0	
6312	Recreation Leader	Parks and Recreation	8	1	
6312	Recreation Leader	Parks and Recreation	8	1	
6312	Recreation Leader	Parks and Recreation	8	2	
6312	Recreation Leader	Parks and Recreation	8	2	
6312	Recreation Leader	Parks and Recreation	8	2	
6313	Neighborhood Center Leader	Parks and Recreation	12	0	
6313	Neighborhood Center Leader	Parks and Recreation	12	0	
6313	Neighborhood Center Leader	Parks and Recreation	12	0	
6313	Neighborhood Center Leader	Parks and Recreation	12	1	
6313	Neighborhood Center Leader	Parks and Recreation	12	1	
6313	Neighborhood Center Leader	Parks and Recreation	12	1	
6313	Neighborhood Center Leader	Parks and Recreation	12	1	
6313	Neighborhood Center Leader	Parks and Recreation	12	4	
6315	Neighborhood Centers Supervisor	Parks and Recreation	14	3	
6316	Coordinator, Neighborhood Centers	Parks and Recreation	18	3	
6325	Assistant Community Center Director	Parks and Recreation	14	1	
6325	Assistant Community Center Director	Parks and Recreation	14	1	
6325	Assistant Community Center Director	Parks and Recreation	14	2	
6326	Community Center Director	Parks and Recreation	18	1	
6326	Community Center Director	Parks and Recreation	18	2	
6334	Assistant Sports Coordinator	Parks and Recreation	17	1	
6336	Sports Coordinator	Parks and Recreation	19	4	
6343	Dance Instructor	Parks and Recreation	16	4	
6345	Cultural Arts Supervisor	Parks and Recreation	16	1	
6345	Cultural Arts Supervisor	Parks and Recreation	16	1	
6346	Coordinator for Special Activities	Parks and Recreation	18	4	
6358	Superintendent of Recreation	Parks and Recreation	24	3	
6365	Assistant Park Manager	Parks and Recreation	16	0	
6366	Park Manager	Parks and Recreation	19	3	
6375	Maintenance Service Center Supervisor	Parks and Recreation	14	0	
6376	Coordinator for Grounds Development	Parks and Recreation	21	2	
6388	Superintendent of Parks	Parks and Recreation	24	2	
7100	Retired	General Administrative			240
7100	Retired	General Administrative			600
7100	Retired	General Administrative			120
7100	Retired	General Administrative			480
7100	Retired	General Administrative			600
7100	Retired	General Administrative			900
7100	Retired	General Administrative			600
7100	Retired	General Administrative			900
7100	Retired	General Administrative			600
7100	Retired	General Administrative			900
7100	Retired	General Administrative			900

Job Code	Title	Department	Range	Step	Salary
7100	Retired	General Administrative			360
7100	Retired	General Administrative			600
7100	Retired	General Administrative			720
7100	Retired	General Administrative			600
7100	Retired	General Administrative			480
7100	Retired	General Administrative			600
7100	Retired	General Administrative			600
7100	Retired	General Administrative			600
7100	Retired	General Administrative			900
7100	Retired	General Administrative			600
7100	Retired	General Administrative			600
8100	Council Member	Elective			6,000
8100	Council Member	Elective			6,000
8100	Council Member	Elective			6,000
8100	Council Member	Elective			6,000
8100	Council Member	Elective			6,000
8100	Council Member	Elective			6,000
8100	Council Member	Elective			6,000
8100	Council Member	Elective			6,000
8100	Council Member	Elective			6,000
8100	Council Member	Elective			6,000
8101	Mayor	Elective			24,000
9100	Recorder	Elective			14,500
9101	Personnel Board Member	Personnel			1,000
9101	Personnel Board Member	Personnel			1,000
9101	Personnel Board Member	Personnel			1,000
9101	Personnel Board Member	Personnel			1,000
9101	Personnel Board Member	Personnel			1,000
9102	Secretary	Clerk-Treasurer			7,994
9102	Secretary	Streets			21,000
9102	Secretary				14,076
9104	Administrative Assistant to the Mayor	Clerk-Treasurer			47,250
9105	City Attorney	Clerk-Treasurer			34,689
9106	City Clerk-Treasurer	Clerk-Treasurer			41,160
9107	City Engineer	Public Works			42,062
9108	City Marshal	City Marshal			37,080
9109	City Shop Manager	Service Garage			30,000
9112	Director of Personnel	Personnel			36,225
9113	Director, Computer Services	Computer and Data Processing			36,338
9114	Director of Community Development	Personnel			36,338
9115	Director of Human Resources	Human Resources			32,491
9116	Director, Parks and Recreation	Parks and Recreation			36,408
9118	Director of Sanitation	Sanitation-Garbage Collection			36,166
9119	Director, Permits and Inspection	Building Inspection			38,174
9120	Director, Planning Commission	Planning Commission			41,315
9121	Police Chief	Police			44,940
9122	Secretary to the Mayor	Clerk-Treasurer			20,459
9126	Fire Chief	Fire			40,136

Classification Index by Pay

This table lists position titles by pay range and salary. (Pay data corresponding with ranges and steps are found in the "40-Hour Personnel Pay Schedule" on pp. 146-49.)

Job Code	Title	Department	Range	Step	Salary
4121	School Crossing Guard	Police	6	2	
4121	School Crossing Guard	Police	6	2	
4121	School Crossing Guard	Police	6	2	
4121	School Crossing Guard	Police	6	2	
4121	School Crossing Guard	Police	6	2	
4121	School Crossing Guard	Police	6	2	
4121	School Crossing Guard	Police	6	2	
4121	School Crossing Guard	Police	6	2	
4121	School Crossing Guard	Police	6	2	
4121	School Crossing Guard	Police	6	2	
4121	School Crossing Guard	Police	6	2	
4121	School Crossing Guard	Police	6	2	
5211	Custodial Worker I	City Hall	7	3	
5211	Custodial Worker I	Parks and Recreation	7	3	
5211	Custodial Worker I	City Hall	7	5	
5212	Custodial Worker II	Parks and Recreation	8	0	
5212	Custodial Worker II	Parks and Recreation	8	0	
5212	Custodial Worker II	Parks and Recreation	8	0	
5212	Custodial Worker II	Parks and Recreation	8	2	
5212	Custodial Worker II	Water Filter Plant	8	2	
5111	Laborer I	Sanitation-Street Cleaning	8	0	
5111	Laborer I	Water-Sewer Distribution	8	0	
5111	Laborer I	Parks and Recreation	8	0	
5111	Laborer I	Police	8	0	
5111	Laborer I	Sanitation-Street Cleaning	8	0	
5111	Laborer I	Sanitation-Street Cleaning	8	0	
5111	Laborer I	Sanitation-Street Cleaning	8	0	
5111	Laborer I	Streets	8	0	
5111	Laborer I	Streets	8	0	
5111	Laborer I	Streets	8	0	
5111	Laborer I	Water-Sewer Distribution	8	0	
5111	Laborer I	Water-Sewer Distribution	8	0	
5111	Laborer I	Water-Sewer Distribution	8	0	
5111	Laborer I	Sanitation-Street Cleaning	8	1	
5111	Laborer I	Streets	8	1	
5111	Laborer I	Water-Sewer Distribution	8	1	
5111	Laborer I	Water-Sewer Distribution	8	1	
5111	Laborer I	Streets	8	2	
5111	Laborer I	Parks and Recreation	8	3	
5111	Laborer I	Sanitation-Street Cleaning	8	3	
4142	Neighborhood Service Officer	Police	8	0	
4142	Neighborhood Service Officer	Police	8	0	
4142	Neighborhood Service Officer	Police	8	1	
6312	Recreation Leader	Human Resources	8	0	
6312	Recreation Leader	Parks and Recreation	8	0	
6312	Recreation Leader	Parks and Recreation	8	0	

Job Code	Title	Department	Range	Step	Salary
6312	Recreation Leader	Parks and Recreation	8	0	
6312	Recreation Leader	Parks and Recreation	8	0	
6312	Recreation Leader	Parks and Recreation	8	0	
6312	Recreation Leader	Parks and Recreation	8	1	
6312	Recreation Leader	Parks and Recreation	8	1	
6312	Recreation Leader	Parks and Recreation	8	2	
6312	Recreation Leader	Parks and Recreation	8	2	
6312	Recreation Leader	Parks and Recreation	8	2	
5221	Security Guard	Sanitation-Garbage Collection	8	1	
5221	Security Guard	Sanitation-Garbage Collection	8	1	
5221	Security Guard	Sanitation-Garbage Collection	8	5	
5411	Automotive Servicer	Sanitation-Garbage Collection	9	3	
0121	Clerk Typist I	Police	9	0	
0121	Clerk Typist I	Parks and Recreation	9	1	
5611	Refuse Collector	Sanitation-Garbage Collection	9	0	
5611	Refuse Collector	Sanitation-Garbage Collection	9	0	
5611	Refuse Collector	Sanitation-Garbage Collection	9	0	
5611	Refuse Collector	Sanitation-Garbage Collection	9	0	
5611	Refuse Collector	Sanitation-Garbage Collection	9	0	
5611	Refuse Collector	Sanitation-Garbage Collection	9	0	
5611	Refuse Collector	Sanitation-Garbage Collection	9	1	
5611	Refuse Collector	Sanitation-Garbage Collection	9	1	
5611	Refuse Collector	Sanitation-Garbage Collection	9	1	
5611	Refuse Collector	Sanitation-Garbage Collection	9	2	
5611	Refuse Collector	Sanitation-Garbage Collection	9	2	
5611	Refuse Collector	Sanitation-Garbage Collection	9	3	
5611	Refuse Collector	Sanitation-Garbage Collection	9	3	
5611	Refuse Collector	Sanitation-Garbage Collection	9	3	
5611	Refuse Collector	Sanitation-Garbage Collection	9	5	
5611	Refuse Collector	Sanitation-Garbage Collection	9	5	
5611	Refuse Collector	Sanitation-Garbage Collection	9	5	
5412	Automotive Mechanic Helper	Service Garage	10	0	
5412	Automotive Mechanic Helper	Service Garage	10	1	
2211	Cartographer I	Planning Commission	10	0	
2211	Cartographer I	Planning Commission	10	0	
2111	Engineering Aide I	Streets	10	0	
3131	Laboratory Aide	Water Pollution Control Plant	10	1	
5112	Laborer II	Parks and Recreation	10	0	
5112	Laborer II	Parks and Recreation	10	0	
5112	Laborer II	Parks and Recreation	10	0	
5112	Laborer II	Streets	10	0	
5112	Laborer II	Streets	10	0	
5112	Laborer II	Streets	10	0	
5112	Laborer II	Parks and Recreation	10	2	
5112	Laborer II	Water-Sewer Distribution	10	2	
5112	Laborer II	Streets	10	3	
5112	Laborer II	Streets	10	3	
5112	Laborer II	Water Meters	10	3	
5112	Laborer II	Water-Sewer Distribution	10	3	
5112	Laborer II	Streets	10	4	

Job Code	Title	Department	Range	Step	Salary
5612	Refuse Collection Driver I	Sanitation-Garbage Collection	10	3	
5612	Refuse Collection Driver I	Sanitation-Garbage Collection	10	3	
5612	Refuse Collection Driver I	Sanitation-Garbage Collection	10	4	
5612	Refuse Collection Driver I	Sanitation-Garbage Collection	10	4	
5612	Refuse Collection Driver I	Sanitation-Garbage Collection	10	4	
5612	Refuse Collection Driver I	Sanitation-Garbage Collection	10	5	
0321	Cashier	Waterworks Commercial	11	2	
0112	Clerk II	Human Resources	11	0	
0112	Clerk II	Police	11	0	
0112	Clerk II	Police	11	1	
0112	Clerk II	Police	11	1	
0112	Clerk II	Water-Sewer Distribution	11	1	
0112	Clerk II	Personnel	11	2	
0112	Clerk II	Police	11	4	
0122	Clerk Typist II	Police	11	0	
5312	Equipment Operator I	Streets	11	0	
5312	Equipment Operator I	Streets	11	0	
5312	Equipment Operator I	Streets	11	0	
5312	Equipment Operator I	Streets	11	0	
5312	Equipment Operator I	Human Resources	11	0	
5312	Equipment Operator I	Parks and Recreation	11	0	
5312	Equipment Operator I	Parks and Recreation	11	1	
5312	Equipment Operator I	Parks and Recreation	11	1	
5312	Equipment Operator I	Streets	11	1	
5312	Equipment Operator I	Water-Sewer Distribution	11	1	
5312	Equipment Operator I	Streets	11	2	
5312	Equipment Operator I	Streets	11	2	
5312	Equipment Operator I	Streets	11	2	
5312	Equipment Operator I	Streets	11	2	
5312	Equipment Operator I	Streets	11	3	
5312	Equipment Operator I	Streets	11	3	
5312	Equipment Operator I	Streets	11	3	
5312	Equipment Operator I	Water-Sewer Distribution	11	3	
5312	Equipment Operator I	Water Pollution Control Plant	11	3	
5312	Equipment Operator I	Streets	11	4	
5613	Refuse Collection Driver II	Sanitation-Garbage Collection	11	0	
5613	Refuse Collection Driver II	Sanitation-Garbage Collection	11	0	
5613	Refuse Collection Driver II	Sanitation-Garbage Collection	11	0	
5613	Refuse Collection Driver II	Sanitation-Garbage Collection	11	0	
5613	Refuse Collection Driver II	Sanitation-Street Cleaning	11	0	
5613	Refuse Collection Driver II	Sanitation-Garbage Collection	11	1	
5613	Refuse Collection Driver II	Sanitation-Garbage Collection	11	1	
5613	Refuse Collection Driver II	Sanitation-Street Cleaning	11	1	
5613	Refuse Collection Driver II	Sanitation-Garbage Collection	11	2	
5613	Refuse Collection Driver II	Sanitation-Garbage Collection	11	2	
5613	Refuse Collection Driver II	Sanitation-Garbage Collection	11	2	
5613	Refuse Collection Driver II	Sanitation-Garbage Collection	11	2	
5613	Refuse Collection Driver II	Sanitation-Street Cleaning	11	2	
5613	Refuse Collection Driver II	Sanitation-Street Cleaning	11	2	
5613	Refuse Collection Driver II	Sanitation-Garbage Collection	11	3	

Job Code	Title	Department	Range	Step	Salary
5613	Refuse Collection Driver II	Sanitation-Garbage Collection	11	3	
5613	Refuse Collection Driver II	Sanitation-Street Cleaning	11	4	
0131	Secretary I	Parks and Recreation	11	0	
0131	Secretary I	Police	11	0	
0131	Secretary I	Parks and Recreation	11	1	
0131	Secretary I	Police	11	1	
0131	Secretary I	Personnel	11	3	
0131	Secretary I	Streets	11	3	
6114	Animal Services Officer	Animal Services	12	1	
6114	Animal Services Officer	Animal Services	12	2	
5113	Laborer III	Water-Sewer Distribution	12	0	
5113	Laborer III	Parks and Recreation	12	2	
5113	Laborer III	Streets	12	2	
5113	Laborer III	Streets	12	3	
5113	Laborer III	Water-Sewer Distribution	12	3	
0212	Meter Reader II	Waterworks Commercial	12	0	
0212	Meter Reader II	Waterworks Commercial	12	0	
0212	Meter Reader II	Waterworks Commercial	12	2	
0212	Meter Reader II	Waterworks Commercial	12	4	
0212	Meter Reader II	Waterworks Commercial	12	5	
6313	Neighborhood Center Leader	Parks and Recreation	12	0	
6313	Neighborhood Center Leader	Parks and Recreation	12	0	
6313	Neighborhood Center Leader	Parks and Recreation	12	0	
6313	Neighborhood Center Leader	Parks and Recreation	12	1	
6313	Neighborhood Center Leader	Parks and Recreation	12	1	
6313	Neighborhood Center Leader	Parks and Recreation	12	1	
6313	Neighborhood Center Leader	Parks and Recreation	12	1	
6313	Neighborhood Center Leader	Parks and Recreation	12	4	
3111	Wastewater Plant Operator Trainee	Water Pollution Control Plant	12	0	
3111	Wastewater Plant Operator Trainee	Water Pollution Control Plant	12	0	
3111	Wastewater Plant Operator Trainee	Water Pollution Control Plant	12	0	
5423	Water Meter Repairer	Water Meters	12	3	
3121	Water Plant Operator Trainee	Water Filter Plant	12	0	
3121	Water Plant Operator Trainee	Water Filter Plant	12	0	
3121	Water Plant Operator Trainee	Water Filter Plant	12	0	
3121	Water Plant Operator Trainee	Water Filter Plant	12	2	
0123	Clerk Typist III	Human Resources	13	2	
0123	Clerk Typist III	Human Resources	13	2	
0123	Clerk Typist III	Sanitation-Garbage Collection	13	4	
5313	Equipment Operator II	Parks and Recreation	13	2	
5313	Equipment Operator II	Parks and Recreation	13	2	
5313	Equipment Operator II	Sanitation-Street Cleaning	13	3	
5313	Equipment Operator II	Sanitation-Street Cleaning	13	3	
5313	Equipment Operator II	Streets	13	3	
5313	Equipment Operator II	Water-Sewer Distribution	13	3	
5313	Equipment Operator II	Water-Sewer Distribution	13	3	
3142	Maintenance Mechanic I WPC	Water Pollution Control Plant	13	0	
0312	Parking Meter Repairer	Police	13	5	
4122	Parking Violations Officer	Police	13	0	
4122	Parking Violations Officer	Police	13	3	

Job Code	Title	Department	Range	Step	Salary
4122	Parking Violations Officer	Police	13	3	
4122	Parking Violations Officer	Police	13	3	
4122	Parking Violations Officer	Police	13	3	
4122	Parking Violations Officer	Police	13	3	
5614	Refuse Collection Driver III	Sanitation-Garbage Collection	13	2	
5614	Refuse Collection Driver III	Sanitation-Garbage Collection	13	3	
5614	Refuse Collection Driver III	Sanitation-Garbage Collection	13	3	
5614	Refuse Collection Driver III	Sanitation-Garbage Collection	13	3	
5614	Refuse Collection Driver III	Sanitation-Garbage Collection	13	3	
5614	Refuse Collection Driver III	Sanitation-Garbage Collection	13	3	
5614	Refuse Collection Driver III	Sanitation-Garbage Collection	13	3	
6214	Animal Caretaker	Parks and Recreation	14	0	
6214	Animal Caretaker	Parks and Recreation	14	2	
6325	Assistant Community Center Director	Parks and Recreation	14	1	
6325	Assistant Community Center Director	Parks and Recreation	14	1	
6325	Assistant Community Center Director	Parks and Recreation	14	2	
5414	Automotive Mechanic	Service Garage	14	0	
5414	Automotive Mechanic	Service Garage	14	1	
5414	Automotive Mechanic	Sanitation-Garbage Collection	14	3	
5414	Automotive Mechanic	Service Garage	14	3	
2212	Cartographer II	Planning Commission	14	2	
0113	Clerk III	Police	14	0	
0113	Clerk III	Police	14	1	
0113	Clerk III	Police	14	2	
0113	Clerk III	Clerk-Treasurer	14	2	
0113	Clerk III	City Marshal	14	3	
0113	Clerk III	Service Garage	14	3	
0113	Clerk III	Police	14	5	
5735	Custodial Supervisor	Parks and Recreation	14	2	
5314	Equipment Operator III	Sanitation-Garbage Collection	14	0	
5314	Equipment Operator III	Water-Sewer Distribution	14	0	
5314	Equipment Operator III	Sanitation-Street Cleaning	14	2	
5314	Equipment Operator III	Sanitation-Street Cleaning	14	2	
5314	Equipment Operator III	Sanitation-Garbage Collection	14	3	
5314	Equipment Operator III	Water Meters	14	3	
5314	Equipment Operator III	Sanitation-Garbage Collection	14	5	
4111	Jailer	Stockade	14	0	
4111	Jailer	Stockade	14	0	
4111	Jailer	Stockade	14	0	
0412	Data Entry Operator II	Computer and Data Processing	14	3	
0412	Data Entry Operator II	Computer and Data Processing	14	5	
5714	Labor Supervisor I	Parks and Recreation	14	0	
5714	Labor Supervisor I	Parks and Recreation	14	0	
5714	Labor Supervisor I	Water Sewer Distribution	14	2	
5714	Labor Supervisor I	Parks and Recreation	14	3	
5714	Labor Supervisor I	Streets	14	4	
5714	Labor Supervisor I	Parks and Recreation	14	5	
3143	Maintenance Mechanic II	Water Pollution Control Plant	14	1	
6375	Maintenance Service Center Supervisor	Parks and Recreation	14	0	
6315	Neighborhood Centers Supervisor	Parks and Recreation	14	3	

Job Code	Title	Department	Range	Step	Salary
5755	Sanitation Supervisor	Sanitation-Garbage Collection	14	2	
5755	Sanitation Supervisor	Sanitation-Garbage Collection	14	5	
5755	Sanitation Supervisor	Sanitation-Street Cleaning	14	5	
5755	Sanitation Supervisor	Sanitation-Street Cleaning	14	5	
0132	Secretary II	Clerk-Treasurer	14	0	
0132	Secretary II	Personnel	14	1	
0132	Secretary II	Planning Commission	14	1	
0132	Secretary II	Police	14	2	
0132	Secretary II	Clerk-Treasurer	14	4	
0132	Secretary II	Building Inspection	14	5	
0132	Secretary II	Parks and Recreation	14	5	
3112	Wastewater Plant Operator	Water Pollution Control Plant	14	2	
3112	Wastewater Plant Operator	Water Pollution Control Plant	14	5	
3122	Water Plant Operator	Water Filter Plant	14	2	
3121	Water Plant Operator Trainee	Water Filter Plant	14	1	
3121	Water Plant Operator Trainee	Water Filter Plant	14	2	
0323	Accounting Clerk II	Waterworks Commercial	15	4	
0323	Accounting Clerk II	Clerk-Treasurer	15	5	
0334	Assistant to City Marshal	City Marshal	15	0	
0414	Computer Operator	Computer and Data Processing	15	0	
2112	Engineering Aide II	Streets	15	0	
4123	Police Radio Dispatcher	Police	15	0	
4123	Police Radio Dispatcher	Police	15	0	
4123	Police Radio Dispatcher	Police	15	0	
4123	Police Radio Dispatcher	Police	15	0	
4123	Police Radio Dispatcher	Police	15	0	
4123	Police Radio Dispatcher	Police	15	1	
4123	Police Radio Dispatcher	Police	15	1	
4123	Police Radio Dispatcher	Police	15	2	
6365	Assistant Park Manager	Parks and Recreation	16	0	
5415	Automotive Mechanic Technician	Service Garage	16	2	
6345	Cultural Arts Supervisor	Parks and Recreation	16	1	
6345	Cultural Arts Supervisor	Parks and Recreation	16	1	
6343	Dance Instructor	Parks and Recreation	16	4	
5513	Electrician's Assistant	Electrical	16	1	
5315	Equipment Operator IV	Streets	16	5	
5315	Equipment Operator IV	Streets	16	5	
5725	General Maintenance Supervisor	Parks and Recreation	16	2	
4115	Head Jailer	Stockade	16	2	
5715	Labor Supervisor II	Streets	16	3	
5715	Labor Supervisor II	Water-Sewer Distribution	16	3	
5715	Labor Supervisor II	Water-Sewer Distribution	16	3	
3134	Laboratory Technician	Water Pollution Control Plant	16	1	
3134	Laboratory Technician	Water Filter Plant	16	5	
3113	Senior Wastewater Plant Operator	Water Pollution Control Plant	16	2	
3123	Senior Water Filter Operator	Water Filter Plant	16	5	
3123	Senior Water Filter Operator	Water Filter Plant	16	5	
0324	Accounting Clerk III	Streets	17	4	
6334	Assistant Sports Coordinator	Parks and Recreation	17	1	
4213	Fire Dispatcher	Fire	17	4	

Job Code	Title	Department	Range	Step	Salary
4213	Fire Dispatcher	Fire	17	5	
4214	Firefighter	Fire	17	0	
4214	Firefighter	Fire	17	0	
4214	Firefighter	Fire	17	0	
4214	Firefighter	Fire	17	0	
4214	Firefighter	Fire	17	0	
4214	Firefighter	Fire	17	0	
4214	Firefighter	Fire Station, County	17	0	
4214	Firefighter	Fire Station, County	17	0	
4214	Firefighter	Fire Station, County	17	0	
4214	Firefighter	Fire Station, County	17	0	
4214	Firefighter	Fire Station, County	17	0	
4214	Firefighter	Fire	17	1	
4214	Firefighter	Fire	17	1	
4214	Firefighter	Fire	17	1	
4214	Firefighter	Fire	17	1	
4214	Firefighter	Fire	17	1	
4214	Firefighter	Fire	17	1	
4214	Firefighter	Fire	17	1	
4214	Firefighter	Fire	17	1	
4214	Firefighter	Fire	17	1	
4214	Firefighter	Fire	17	1	
4214	Firefighter	Fire Station, County	17	1	
4214	Firefighter	Fire Station, County	17	1	
4214	Firefighter	Fire	17	2	
4214	Firefighter	Fire	17	2	
4214	Firefighter	Fire	17	2	
4214	Firefighter	Fire	17	2	
4214	Firefighter	Fire	17	2	
4214	Firefighter	Fire	17	2	
4214	Firefighter	Fire	17	2	
4214	Firefighter	Fire	17	2	
4214	Firefighter	Fire Station, County	17	2	
4214	Firefighter	Fire	17	3	
4214	Firefighter	Fire	17	4	
1133	Information and Referral Specialist	Human Resources	17	0	
1133	Information and Referral Specialist	Human Resources	17	4	
1133	Information and Referral Specialist	Human Resources	17	4	
1133	Information and Referral Specialist	Human Resources	17	4	
5716	Labor Supervisor III	Streets	17	3	
5716	Labor Supervisor III	Streets	17	4	
5716	Labor Supervisor III	Streets	17	4	
5716	Labor Supervisor III	Water-Sewer Distribution	17	5	
0215	Meter Reader Supervisor	Waterworks Commercial	17	5	
0645	Personnel Technician	Personnel	17	4	
1144	Social Service Specialist	Human Resources	17	0	
0345	Supervisor, Tax Collection	Clerk-Treasurer	17	5	
5416	Automotive Technician II	Service Garage	18	0	
3124	Chief Maintenance Operator	Water Filter Plant	18	4	

Job Code	Title	Department	Range	Step	Salary
3114	Chief Maintenance Operator WPC	Water Pollution Control Plant	18	5	
3114	Chief Maintenance Operator WPC	Water Pollution Control Plant	18	5	
6326	Community Center Director	Parks and Recreation	18	1	
6326	Community Center Director	Parks and Recreation	18	2	
6346	Coordinator for Special Activities	Parks and Recreation	18	4	
6316	Coordinator, Neighborhood Centers	Parks and Recreation	18	3	
2113	Engineering Aide III	Streets	18	2	
4133	Police Officer	Police	18	0	
4133	Police Officer	Police	18	0	
4133	Police Officer	Police	18	0	
4133	Police Officer	Police	18	0	
4133	Police Officer	Police	18	1	
4133	Police Officer	Police	18	1	
4133	Police Officer	Police	18	1	
4133	Police Officer	Police	18	1	
4133	Police Officer	Police	18	1	
4133	Police Officer	Police	18	2	
4133	Police Officer	Police	18	2	
4133	Police Officer	Police	18	2	
4133	Police Officer	Police	18	2	
4133	Police Officer	Police	18	2	
4133	Police Officer	Police	18	2	
4133	Police Officer	Police	18	2	
4133	Police Officer	Police	18	2	
4133	Police Officer	Police	18	2	
4133	Police Officer	Police	18	2	
4133	Police Officer	Police	18	2	
4133	Police Officer	Police	18	2	
4133	Police Officer	Police	18	2	
4133	Police Officer	Police	18	3	
4133	Police Officer	Police	18	3	
4133	Police Officer	Police	18	3	
4133	Police Officer	Police	18	3	
4133	Police Officer	Police	18	3	
4133	Police Officer	Police	18	3	
4133	Police Officer	Police	18	3	
4133	Police Officer	Police	18	3	
4133	Police Officer	Police	18	3	
4133	Police Officer	Police	18	3	
4133	Police Officer	Police	18	3	
4133	Police Officer	Police	18	4	
4133	Police Officer	Police	18	4	
4133	Police Officer	Police	18	4	
4133	Police Officer	Police	18	4	
4133	Police Officer	Police	18	4	
4133	Police Officer	Police	18	4	
4133	Police Officer	Police	18	4	
4133	Police Officer	Police	18	5	
4133	Police Officer	Police	18	5	
4215	Fire Driver-Engineer	Fire	19	2	

Job Code	Title	Department	Range	Step	Salary
4215	Fire Driver-Engineer	Fire	19	2	
4215	Fire Driver-Engineer	Fire Station, County	19	2	
4215	Fire Driver-Engineer	Fire	19	3	
4215	Fire Driver-Engineer	Fire	19	3	
4215	Fire Driver-Engineer	Fire	19	3	
4215	Fire Driver-Engineer	Fire	19	3	
4215	Fire Driver-Engineer	Fire	19	3	
4215	Fire Driver-Engineer	Fire	19	3	
4215	Fire Driver-Engineer	Fire	19	3	
4215	Fire Driver-Engineer	Fire	19	3	
4215	Fire Driver-Engineer	Fire	19	3	
4215	Fire Driver-Engineer	Fire	19	3	
4215	Fire Driver-Engineer	Fire	19	3	
4215	Fire Driver-Engineer	Fire	19	3	
4215	Fire Driver-Engineer	Fire	19	3	
4215	Fire Driver-Engineer	Fire Station, County	19	3	
4215	Fire Driver-Engineer	Fire Station, County	19	3	
4215	Fire Driver-Engineer	Fire Station, County	19	3	
4215	Fire Driver-Engineer	Fire	19	4	
4235	Fire Prevention Officer	Fire Station, County	19	1	
4235	Fire Prevention Officer	Fire	19	2	
0515	Graphics and Printing Coordinator	Personnel	19	3	
6366	Park Manager	Parks and Recreation	19	3	
4134	Police Corporal	Police	19	4	
4134	Police Corporal	Police	19	4	
4134	Police Corporal	Police	19	4	
4134	Police Corporal	Police	19	5	
6336	Sports Coordinator	Parks and Recreation	19	4	
0225	Supervisor, Customer Service	Waterworks Commercial	19	4	
0325	Accountant	Clerk-Treasurer	20	0	
0325	Accountant	Human Resources	20	0	
0325	Accountant	Personnel	20	5	
2375	Administrator, Zoning and Subdivision	Planning Commission	20	3	
5758	Assistant Director, Sanitation	Sanitation-Garbage Collection	20	3	
3126	Chief Water Filter Operator	Water Filter Plant	20	3	
1145	Child-Care Coordinator	Human Resources	20	2	
0415	Computer Programmer	Computer and Data Processing	20	0	
0655	Deputy City Clerk	Clerk-Treasurer	20	4	
2114	Engineering Aide IV	Public Works	20	5	
4175	Police Detective	Police	20	2	
4175	Police Detective	Police	20	3	
4175	Police Detective	Police	20	3	
4175	Police Detective	Police	20	3	
4175	Police Detective	Police	20	4	
4175	Police Detective	Police	20	4	
4175	Police Detective	Police	20	4	
4175	Police Detective	Police	20	4	
4175	Police Detective	Police	20	5	
4175	Police Detective	Police	20	5	
3317	Assistant Superintendent, Water Filter Plant	Water Filter Plant	21	3	

Job Code	Title	Department	Range	Step	Salary
2345	Building Inspector	Building Inspection	21	3	
2345	Building Inspector	Building Inspection	21	5	
2345	Building Inspector	Fire	21	5	
6376	Coordinator for Grounds Development	Parks and Recreation	21	2	
4216	Fire Lieutenant	Fire Station, County	21	1	
4216	Fire Lieutenant	Fire	21	3	
4216	Fire Lieutenant	Fire	21	3	
4216	Fire Lieutenant	Fire	21	3	
4216	Fire Lieutenant	Fire	21	3	
4216	Fire Lieutenant	Fire	21	3	
4216	Fire Lieutenant	Fire	21	3	
4216	Fire Lieutenant	Fire	21	3	
4216	Fire Lieutenant	Fire	21	3	
4216	Fire Lieutenant	Fire	21	3	
4216	Fire Lieutenant	Fire	21	3	
4216	Fire Lieutenant	Fire	21	3	
4216	Fire Lieutenant	Fire	21	3	
4216	Fire Lieutenant	Fire	21	3	
4216	Fire Lieutenant	Fire Station, County	21	3	
2335	Heating and Air Conditioning Inspector	Building Inspection	21	2	
2315	Housing Inspector	Building Inspection	21	3	
4135	Police Sergeant	Police	21	3	
4135	Police Sergeant	Police	21	3	
4135	Police Sergeant	Police	21	5	
4135	Police Sergeant	Police	21	5	
4135	Police Sergeant	Police	21	5	
4135	Police Sergeant	Police	21	5	
4135	Police Sergeant	Police	21	5	
4135	Police Sergeant	Police	21	5	
4135	Police Sergeant	Police	21	5	
4135	Police Sergeant	Police	21	5	
4135	Police Sergeant	Police	21	5	
0635	Administrative Assistant	Clerk-Treasurer	22	0	
0635	Administrative Assistant	Public Works	22	5	
5518	City Electrician	Electrical	22	4	
6118	Director of Animal Services	Animal Services	22	1	
1135	Information and Referral Coordinator	Human Resources	22	5	
2325	Plumbing Inspector	Building Inspection	22	5	
5768	Street Superintendent	Streets	22	3	
4257	Fire Alarm Superintendent	Fire	23	2	
4217	Fire Captain	Fire	23	3	
4217	Fire Captain	Fire	23	3	
4217	Fire Captain	Fire	23	3	
4217	Fire Captain	Fire	23	3	
4217	Fire Captain	Fire	23	3	
4217	Fire Captain	Fire	23	3	
4217	Fire Captain	Fire	23	3	
4217	Fire Captain	Fire	23	3	
4217	Fire Captain	Fire Station, County	23	3	

Job Code	Title	Department	Range	Step	Salary
4217	Fire Captain	Fire Station, County	23	3	
4217	Fire Captain	Fire Station, County	23	3	
4217	Fire Captain	Fire	23	4	
4217	Fire Captain	Fire	23	4	
4217	Fire Captain	Fire	23	4	
4237	Fire Marshal	Fire	23	1	
4227	Fire Training Chief	Fire	23	3	
3318	Superintendent, Water Filter Plant	Water Filter Plant	23	5	
3218	Superintendent, Water Pollution Control	Water Pollution Control Plant	23	5	
1118	Assistant Director of Planning	Planning Commission	24	5	
1116	Environmental Planner	Planning Commission	24	5	
1128	Physical Program Specialist	Personnel	24	3	
4136	Police Lieutenant	Police	24	1	
4136	Police Lieutenant	Police	24	2	
4136	Police Lieutenant	Police	24	4	
4136	Police Lieutenant	Police	24	4	
4136	Police Lieutenant	Police	24	4	
4136	Police Lieutenant	Police	24	4	
4136	Police Lieutenant	Police	24	4	
4136	Police Lieutenant	Police	24	4	
4136	Police Lieutenant	Police	24	4	
4137	Police Shift Commander	Police	24	1	
4137	Police Shift Commander	Police	24	2	
6388	Superintendent of Parks	Parks and Recreation	24	2	
6358	Superintendent of Recreation	Parks and Recreation	24	3	
4125	Supervisor, Special Services	Police	24	3	
4138	Police Captain	Police	25	3	
4138	Police Captain	Police	25	5	
4268	Assistant Fire Chief	Fire	26	3	
4268	Assistant Fire Chief	Fire	26	3	
4268	Assistant Fire Chief	Fire	26	3	
0648	Assistant Personnel Director	Personnel	27	3	
1127	Physical Program Coordinator	Personnel	27	2	
4139	Police Major	Police	27	2	
4139	Police Major	Police	27	4	
4139	Police Major	Police	27	4	
2128	Special Projects Engineer	Public Works	27	0	
5778	Water-Sewer Superintendent	Water Meters	27	0	
4198	Assistant Police Chief	Police	28	5	
0656	Federal Aid Coordinator	Clerk-Treasurer	28	5	
2118	Assistant City Engineer	Public Works	29	3	
7100	Retired	General Administrative			240
7100	Retired	General Administrative			600
7100	Retired	General Administrative			120
7100	Retired	General Administrative			480
7100	Retired	General Administrative			600
7100	Retired	General Administrative			900
7100	Retired	General Administrative			600
7100	Retired	General Administrative			900
7100	Retired	General Administrative			600

Job Code	Title	Department	Range	Step	Salary
7100	Retired	General Administrative			900
7100	Retired	General Administrative			900
7100	Retired	General Administrative			360
7100	Retired	General Administrative			600
7100	Retired	General Administrative			720
7100	Retired	General Administrative			600
7100	Retired	General Administrative			480
7100	Retired	General Administrative			600
7100	Retired	General Administrative			600
7100	Retired	General Administrative			600
7100	Retired	General Administrative			900
7100	Retired	General Administrative			600
7100	Retired	General Administrative			600
8100	Council Member	Elective			6,000
8100	Council Member	Elective			6,000
8100	Council Member	Elective			6,000
8100	Council Member	Elective			6,000
8100	Council Member	Elective			6,000
8100	Council Member	Elective			6,000
8100	Council Member	Elective			6,000
8100	Council Member	Elective			6,000
8100	Council Member	Elective			6,000
8100	Council Member	Elective			6,000
8101	Mayor	Elective			24,000
9100	Recorder	Elective			14,500
9101	Personnel Board Member	Personnel			1,000
9101	Personnel Board Member	Personnel			1,000
9101	Personnel Board Member	Personnel			1,000
9101	Personnel Board Member	Personnel			1,000
9101	Personnel Board Member	Personnel			1,000
9102	Secretary	Clerk-Treasurer			7,994
9102	Secretary	Streets			21,000
9102	Secretary				14,076
9104	Administrative Assistant to the Mayor	Clerk-Treasurer			47,250
9105	City Attorney	Clerk-Treasurer			34,689
9106	City Clerk-Treasurer	Clerk-Treasurer			41,160
9107	City Engineer	Public Works			42,062
9108	City Marshal	City Marshal			37,080
9109	City Shop Manager	Service Garage			30,000
9112	Director of Personnel	Personnel			36,225
9113	Director, Computer Services	Computer and Data Processing			36,338
9114	Director of Community Development	Personnel			36,338
9115	Director of Human Resources	Human Resources			32,491
9116	Director, Parks and Recreation	Parks and Recreation			36,408
9118	Director of Sanitation	Sanitation-Garbage Collection			36,166
9119	Director, Permits and Inspection	Building Inspection			38,174
9120	Director, Planning Commission	Planning Commission			41,315
9121	Police Chief	Police			44,940
9122	Secretary to the Mayor	Clerk-Treasurer			20,459
9126	Fire Chief	Fire			40,136